IE Business Publishing

IE Business Publishing and Palgrave Macmillan have launched a collection of high-quality books in the areas of Business and Management, Economics and Finance. This important series is characterized by innovative ideas and theories, entrepreneurial perspectives, academic rigor and practical approaches which will make these books invaluable to the business professional, scholar and student alike. IE Business School is one of the world's leading institutions dedicated to educating business leaders. Palgrave Macmillan, part of Macmillan Group, has been serving the learning and professional sector for more than 160 years. The series, put together by these eminent international partners, will enable executives, students, management scholars and professionals worldwide to have access to the most valuable information and critical new arguments and theories in the fields of Business and Management, Economics and Finance from the leading experts at IE Business School.

More information about this series at
http://www.springer.com/series/14857

Santiago Iñiguez de Onzoño

Cosmopolitan Managers

Executive Development that Works

Preface by Nick H.M. van Dam
Global Chief Learning Offices
McKinsey & Company

Para Rafael

Con Cariño !

palgrave
macmillan

Santiago Iñiguez de Onzoño
Instituto de Empresa
Madrid, Spain

ISBN 978-1-137-54907-5   ISBN 978-1-137-54909-9   (eBook)
DOI 10.1057/978-1-137-54909-9

Library of Congress Control Number: 2016942632

Printed on acid-free paper

This Palgrave Macmillan imprint is published by Springer Nature
The registered company is Macmillan Publishers Ltd. London

To my parents, Jose Luis and Lourdes, an inestimable source of learning and inspiration

Foreword: The Future of Leadership Development

Corporations are facing unprecedented challenges in the twenty-first century, and this requires a different style of leadership. The demand arises from several new and disruptive realities:

- We live in a VUCA world of exponential change. This acronym developed by the US military to describe the changed nature of battle in the twenty-first century—**V**olatile, **U**ncertain, **C**omplex, and **A**mbiguous—applies to all organizations.
- With *disruptive technologies* emerging rapidly, businesses and their underlying business models change at a fast pace and deeply.
- The ongoing *automation of the workplace* creates a shift in the nature of work due to technology and automation.
- The lifespan of a Fortune 500 company was 90 years in 1935; by 1975 this was shortened to 30 years, and in 2011 it was 18 years. And the lifespan continues to dwindle (so does the tenure of the CEO and other top leaders).

Companies who want to survive in this VUCA world must continuously innovate and reinvent themselves. Executives need to play a critical role by leading positive change and building purposeful and sustainable organizations. But it isn't clear that they are prepared for success in this new and unpredictable environment.

CEOs identify the development of leadership talent equipped to meet these challenges as one of their most pressing concerns. As stated in an HBR article (June 2015), "People Before Strategy," "CEOs know that they depend on their companies' human resources to achieve success. Businesses don't create value—people do." McKinsey research verifies this perspective and finds that over 90% of CEOs are already planning to increase investment in leadership development because they see it as the single most important human–capital issue their organizations face.[1] Earlier McKinsey research indicated that this investment is spot on because good leadership is fundamental to organizational health, which is an important driver of shareholder returns.[2]

But serious questions arise:

(1) Are the current approaches to leadership development building the most needed leadership capabilities?
(2) What approaches best produce the new capabilities and foster successful transfer to the workplace?
(3) How can we leveraging all potential leadership earning opportunities and methods?
(4) Can we measure the return-on-investment of leadership development?

The Most Needed Leadership Capabilities for Our VUCA World

You cannot rely on what may have worked for leaders in the past. Today's world is different. The stakes are high and the challenges and issues changing at a rapid speed. Among researchers and thought leaders, there is some consensus that the most needed *characteristics and traits* for leaders today include: Authenticity, Inspiration, Passion, Flexibility, Comfort with Ambiguity, Collaboration, Optimism, Learning, Humility, and a Focus on Mental and Physical Health.

In an extensive survey of 189,000 people in 81 diverse organizations around the world,[3] McKinsey research has narrowed what is required to four essential leadership *behaviors* that matter most. These include:

- Solving problems effectively—which precedes decision-making. If not done well the outcomes of decisions will be compromised.
- Operating with a strong results orientation—following through on the promise of the vision to achieve results.
- Seeking diverse perspectives—watching internal and external trends, seeking input from others and differentiating the important from unimportant issues.
- Supporting the performance of others—building trust and helping colleagues overcome challenges.

There is another key to attaining and maintaining the new leader mindset. To keep up the demands of a rapid pace with clarity of mind and positive action, the leader cannot ignore the importance of exercise, reflection and mindfulness, good nutrition and enough sleep. Research has shown that sleep-deprived brains lose the ability to make accurate judgments. Neuroscientists know that although other brain areas can cope relatively well with too little sleep, the prefrontal cortex (seat of all the higher-order cognitive processes, such as problem solving, reasoning, organizing, planning, and executing plans) cannot.[4] This means that in order to be effective as a leader today and tomorrow, attention must be paid to building and preserving health.

Best Approaches to Produce the New Capabilities and Foster Successful Transfer to the Workplace

Given the vast and ever-evolving changes in the requirements of leaders, it is not possible to pursue traditional approaches and methods for development. Organizations recognize this. Only 7% of organizations think that their companies develop their global leaders effectively and only 34% of learning from development interventions is transferred into real behaviors back in the workplace. One-off face-to-face learning programs are not sufficient to overcome these issues. Therefore, it is critical that the next generation of leadership development programs are anchored upon key learning design principles.

Anchored in the Business Context and Reflects Reality

First, learnings must be focused on the practical day-to-day business context by linking to real world business leadership challenges. Secondly, the learning must be situated in the organizational and personal context of the people in the program, where they can work on real business problems and projects that are relevant to their job and apply acquired insights and skills back in the work environment. Third, leadership development must go beyond skill building—first, critical required behavior changes must be identified and defined and what is getting in the way revealed (e.g., underlying mindsets and root perspectives) to help people shift how they act at work.

Evidence-Based Learning Practices

Professional learning design has its roots in various disciplines including neuroscience, psychology, and pedagogy. Evidence-based approaches reveal that adults learn the best when they are motivated and in charge; are pushed to the edge of their comfort zone; are challenged by action and experience; are involved in a combination of formal and on-the-job training; learn from role models, experts, and their peers; and, are supported by effective just-in-time encouragement from coaches and mentors.[5]

Blended Learning

Most effective leadership learning combines a number of different learning interventions and solutions. For example, learning needs are assessed via stakeholder interviews and supplementary (online) diagnostics; participants are assigned meaningful pre-work; they learn tools and build skills in a classroom; use new skills to deliver on real world projects as part of field work; and employ (digital) tools to continuously reflect and track their progress. During this extended experience, participants engage regularly via a digital platform in courses at their own pace, experience coaching with faculty, and group work with their global cohorts.

Individualized Development Journeys

Every person has unique development needs and learning preferences. Most effective development programs can be customized by the leader to support his/her development. Elements of individualized learning journeys could include shadowing a leader, special job assignments, coaching, access to on-demand learning programs, on-the-job performance support, digital learning modules, leader as teacher, groupwork, in-person workshops, in addition to formal classroom programs.

Digital Learning

Digital learning solutions—such as videos, corporate MOOCs (Massive Open Online Course) (within an organization also-called SPOCs—Small Private Online Course), online assessments, online simulations and games, online performance support aids, e-coaching and mentoring, online communities, virtual classrooms, webinars—are key components of any leadership development program. They can be taken on demand at any time and any place and on different devices. Additionally, digital learning will support the knowledge transfer and application on the job.

Driven by the Organization

It is invaluable in any organization that company executives own and champion leadership development programs, engage meaningfully with the participants and recognize and reward new leadership behaviors.

Finally, many leaders tell us that not all learning can happen on the job. Leaders are simply incredibly busy during the day, much too busy to have time to focus on learning. Therefore, they value time away from the job which provides them with opportunities to connect with themselves, reflect on their actions, gain new insights, learn from others and practice new skills in a safe environment. As demonstrated above, one size no longer fits all: a leadership learning experience must be a rich tapestry of multiple approaches to leadership mastery.

Measuring Leadership Development ROI

To our final question, leadership development can have measurable returns:

- Organizations earn a substantial premium for great leadership—those performing in the top quartile on leadership outperform others by nearly 2× on EBITDA.[6]
- Organizations that invest in developing leaders during significant transformations are 2.4× more likely to hit their performance targets.[7]

The Importance of This Book

Personally, I found reading this book and gaining insights from it highly rewarding.

Santiago Iñiguez de Onzoño has provided a holistic view of the career he pursued and gives us the opportunity to enjoy his in-depth experiences as a global leader, Dean of IE Business School and the President of IE University. Enhanced by perspectives from the humanities, philosophy, history, and literature, his overview of stages in the development of leaders, description of the vibrant new collaborative partnerships with industries outside the academy, such as publishers, to design and deliver custom solutions for organizations, and the insights into the challenges and rewards of a progressive career, is brilliant.

He effectively paints a colorful canvas of leadership development for the twenty-first century and elevates the importance of what is reflected in the German philosophical word *Bildung* defined as personal, social, and cultural development. In preparing leaders for an unknown future, the most important skills include the ability to ask the right questions, to think, reflect, and decide. Leadership learning journeys benefit most from a broad spectrum of disciplines including philosophy, because leaders who study philosophy will leverage invaluable insights from the past which are extremely valuable in our world today and for the future.

This excellent book will significantly help people who are involved in leadership development to reflect on the cosmo leader, the importance of leadership development in today's world, gain insights into new learning and development practices, and explore the future expanding role of learning technologies.

Dr. Nick H.M. van Dam

Partner, Global Chief Learning Offices
McKinsey & Company, New York, NY, USA

Professor Corporate Learning & Development
Nyenrode Business Universteit,
Breukelen, The Netherlands

Founders & Chairman
The e-Learning for Kids Foundation,
Hilversum, The Netherlands

Preface

Continuous learning and executive development is a fascinating segment of higher education, and one that is expected to grow rapidly in the coming years. Since the publication in late 2011 of *The Learning Curve*, my appraisal of how business schools are reinventing education, the growing role of new technology, the entry of new players, and the impact of globalization are all driving the growth of executive development, shaping corporate training and business education in general into the most dynamic segments of higher education today.

With this in mind, I decided to write *Cosmopolitan Managers*, which aside from providing an analysis of the fast-changing executive education sector today, proposes successful strategies for companies to attract, develop, and retain their talent while promoting innovation and protecting their own competitive advantages: in short, how to grow cosmopolitan managers.

We live in times of pressing demand for new forms of leadership in all organizations, people I describe as cosmopolitan managers: highly competent professionals who are entrepreneurial, socially committed, competent cultivated and cross-culturally skilled.

The most valuable asset in the knowledge economy is human resources. In the future, companies will compete more and more intensely in the optimization of their human capital. The executive development, education, and training that business schools provide will play a key role in making that happen.

Demographic changes across the world, along with the extension of the age of retirement, mean that most of the customers of educational products in the future will be senior managers, not the so-called Millennial Generation. A major challenge in the future will be how to keep these older, experienced managers updated, competitive, and innovative.

This means business schools and executive education centers will need to make in-company educational programs genuinely transformational experiences. This has implications for at least three different areas: learning methodologies, the role of the professor or instructor, and the assessment systems used to measure not just the satisfaction of participants, but mostly the impact that learning has on the development of the individual as well as the organization at large.

Few people today would dispute the impact of ICT, MOOCs, and other related initiatives on the learning process. Surveys show that technology-supported learning is thriving, even inside corporate universities. Supported by new technologies, a plethora of methodologies is coming of age that can help business schools and companies in their task.

At the same time, executive training is being further impacted by globalization; very few companies have the resources, or the knowledge, to run their development and training activities on an international scale and all strategic fronts at the same time without establishing alliances with foreign institutions. A number of different strategies are available to cope with the challenges of globalization, ranging from traditional joint ventures to new multi-dimensional strategic alliances that are more open and indefinite in time, with competitors joining forces in collaborative initiatives. The evolution of international partnerships between companies and education suppliers has been impressive over the last five years.

Cosmopolitan Managers also addresses the changing demands within companies and from their stakeholders, mirroring not only the changing requirements of working environments, but also those of broader changes in society.

In short, my experience over the last five years is that companies and their senior managers expect a more holistic approach to executive development and training than ever before. An approach that also addresses the actual development needs of each organization involved.

Creating cosmopolitan managers is a work in progress; the days of taking an MBA after completing university in one's early twenties and then focusing solely on moving up the career ladder are long gone. As said, we will all be working later into life, something we probably didn't contemplate when we started our careers two or three decades ago. And throughout that working life, we will likely have a number of different employers, and may even be required to shift into another sector. This requires a commitment from all of us to continue learning throughout our careers. In turn, training will need to provide executives with a broader, more balanced outlook on the world, one that in my opinion needs to be founded in part on the humanities, such as art, history, and even philosophy.

Cosmopolitan Managers also looks at how companies have progressively assumed the role of educational hubs for their employees, and how knowledge management is directly linked to the development of talent at companies.

The purpose of this book is not only to describe the experience of in-company training departments, corporate universities, and business schools at large, but also to anticipate the shape of things to come—both in terms of executive development, but also business education and higher education in general. I share both my direct experiences as an education manager over the past three decades and also my vision of higher education and in-company training in the future.

The book is structured in two parts, with 13 chapters in total, along with an epilogue, all of which can be read independently. Part One, chapters one to seven, covers the current state of executive education, looking at the challenges and opportunities, as well as the emerging players in the sector. I specifically look at the impact of technology on teaching methodologies (Chap. 4), along with efforts to establish ways to assess the impact of learning (Chap. 5). I also look at the opportunities that managing diversity can provide companies with (Chap. 7). Part Two looks at the benefits from introducing the humanities into executive development, articulating the concept of the cosmopolitan manager, the core idea of the book. Much of the content here is developed from articles I have published over the last year on these two topics, some of them on LinkedIn

Pulse. There are multiple references to literature, philosophy, and the arts, following my belief in mixing business learning with the humanities and the liberal arts.

I hope the reader gets as much out of this book as I have from writing it, and is able to share the ideas outlined here with the people who really matter: managers.

Acknowledgments

Over the course of the last 25 years I have had the immense good fortune to combine the activity of teaching executives and entrepreneurs with that of academic management. The experience has left me in no doubt that few professions can match the satisfaction, both personal and professional, that a career in education provides.

Schools are unique institutions, requiring a particular approach to fulfilling their mission that makes the job both fascinating and challenging, while providing a lifelong learning experience along the way. In my own case, I have been lucky enough to work in the running of IE Business School and IE University, two exemplary institutions staffed by exceptionally talented people to whom I am indebted.

In particular, I would like to express my deepest gratitude for having been able to work alongside the founder and president of IE Business School, Diego del Alcázar Silvela, who I am privileged to count as both friend and mentor. He has taught me more than I can say with words, consistently seeking to bring out the best in me over the years. As well as being a born entrepreneur and possessed of a powerful intellect, Diego is committed to excellence, has always demonstrated strategic vision, and is an astute judge of human character. Throughout the process of writing this book I have discussed many ideas with Diego, and looking back, I do not believe it would be an overstatement to say he is its moral author.

I would also like to offer my heartfelt thanks for the steadfast collaboration provided by my colleagues on the board of IE Business School: Salvador Carmona, Rector of IE University and an inestimable fellow traveler and friend on our fascinating journey over the last quarter of a century; Diego del Alcázar Benjumea, Vice President of IE, who has inherited all his father's leadership qualities; Alfonso Martínez de Irujo, President of IE Executive Education; Juan José Güemes, Financial Vice President; Macarena Rosado, General Counsel; and Gonzalo Garland, Vice President of External Relations.

My team of close collaborators has been instrumental in the success of IE University, and I am also indebted to them for their input into making this book happen. My special thanks to: Martin Boehm, Dean of Programs; Arantza de Areilza, Dean of IE School of International Relations; Javier de Cendra, Dean of IE School of Law; Martha Thorne, Dean of IE School of Architecture and Design; Lee Newman, Dean of IE School of Human Science and Technology; Joaquín Garralda, Dean of Academic Affairs; and Antonio de Castro, Vice Rector of IE University. Allow me to thank also my other colleagues at the management board of IE: Nancy Cueto, Sonsoles Gil de Antuñano, Jorge Graña, Rafael Puyol, Miguel Sagüés, and Joaquin Uribarri.

At the forefront of my mind while writing this book has been the FT | IE Corporate Learning Alliance (CLA), one of the most exciting initiatives that IE Business School has undertaken in recent times, and a partnership that aims to establish itself as a global leader in the design and delivery of custom programs for companies. Among those involved, I would like to offer a special thanks to Tas Viglatzis, Chairman of CLA, with whom I held most negotiations for the constitution of our joint venture; Vandyck Silveira, CEO of FT | IE Corporate Learning Alliance, Antonio Montes, Chief Relationship Officer, Abbas Hassan, and Mark Thivessen; along with my colleagues on the board, Angela MacKay and James Lamont. In particular, John Ridding, CEO of the Financial Times Group, has played a key role in the creation of this joint venture between IE Business School and the *Financial Times*, and I would like to offer him my heartfelt thanks.

My participation in several business school networks has allowed me to further deepen my knowledge of executive education and developing managerial skills. In particular, being appointed Chair of AACSB was a unique moment in my life. For their support, ideas, and friendship, I would like to thank Linda Livingstone and Bill Glick, my two Co-Chairs, along with Tom Robinson, CEO of AACSB, John Martinez, past CEO, as well as Vice Presidents Dan Le Clair and Bob Reid. My thanks also to Christine Clements, Pat Moser, Neil Bosland, Kaya Jill, Julianne Iannarelli, Jennifer McIntosh, Tim Mescon, Al Renshaw, Debra Wise, Michael Wiemer, Tricia Bisoux, and Brandy Whited, along with the rest of the highly professional staff at AACSB.

At the same time, I would like to take this opportunity to thank all my friends at the EFMD for all that they have taught me over the course of my career. In particular, its Director General and CEO, Eric Cornuel, along with Helke Carvalho Hernandes and Matthew Wood. I would like to give a special mention to Gordon Shenton and Richard Straub for their invaluable insights that I have brought to this book.

My interviews with Della Bradshaw, John Byrne, Federico Castellanos, Laurent Choain, Stuart Crainer, Des Dearlove, Eiso Kant, Peter Lorange, Kai Peters, Nancy Petrillo, Dominique Turpin, and Dick Van Dam have been fundamental in acquiring key information and contrasting different points of view: a big thank you to all of them.

I am particularly grateful to Stephen Partridge, Publisher, Professional Business, at Palgrave Macmillan, for all his support in this, our latest project. I am also indebted to the members of the Communication team at IE, led by Jose Félix Valdivieso. They have supported me over the years in identifying and refining the ideas and messages conveyed in my public addresses. Many thanks to Maite Brualla, Igor Galo, Geoffroy Gerard, Kerry Parke, Yolanda Regodón, Juncal Sánchez Mendieta, and Verónica Urbiola, as well as to David Wells of CLA.

I would also like to thank Bryan O'Loughlin, Juan Ramón Zamorano, and Igone Jayo for their decisive help in the search for materials, arranging interviews, and ordering this manuscript.

And last, but not at all least, my special thanks to Nick Lyne, who over the last two years has helped edit my work. He is largely responsible for creating an entertaining and accessible tone in the pages that follow.

Contents

About the Author

Santiago Iñiguez de Onzoño is the Dean of IE Business School and the President of IE University. He holds a Degree in Law, a Ph.D. in Moral Philosophy and Jurisprudence (Complutense University, Spain) and an MBA from IE Business School. He is a Recognized Student at the University of Oxford, UK.

Iñiguez has worked as a management consultant and has played an active role in the field of quality control and development of business schools and higher education. He is Chairman of AACSB and also serves on the boards of Renmin University Business School (China), CENTRUM (Universidad Católica, Perú), Antai Business School (Jiao Tong University, China), Mazars University (France) the Russian Presidential Academy-RANEPA (Russia) and FGV-EASP Fundaçao Getulio Vargas (Brazil). He has been described by the *Financial Times* as "one of the most significant figures in promoting European business schools internationally."

Professor of Strategic Management at IE Business School, his previous book, *The Learning Curve: How Business Schools Are Reinventing Education*, also published by Palgrave Macmillan, focuses on the changes taking place in business education. A regular speaker at international conferences, Iñiguez is a LinkedIn Global Influencer and a regular contributor to journals and media on higher education and executive development.

Notes

1. *The State of Human Capital 2012—False Summit: Why the Human Capital Function Still Has Far to Go*, a joint report from The Conference Board and McKinsey, October 2012, on mckinsey.com.
2. See Aaron De Smet, Bill Schaninger, and Matthew Smith, "The Hidden Value of Organizational Health—And How to Capture It," *McKinsey Quarterly*, April 2014, on mckinsey.com.
3. Claudio Feser, Fernanda Mayol, and Ramesh Srinivasan, "Decoding Leadership: What Really Matters," *McKinsey Quarterly*, January 2015. The 81 organizations are diverse in geography (for instance, Asia, Europe, Latin America, and North America), industry (agriculture, consulting, energy, government, insurance, mining, and real estate), and size (from about 7,500 employees to 300,000), on mckinsey.com.
4. Nick van Dam and Els van der Helm, "The Organizational Cost of Insufficient Sleep," *McKinsey Quarterly*, January 2016 + Eileen Rogers and Nick van Dam, "YOU! The Positive Force in Change," LULU publishing, 2015.
5. Claus Benkert, Nick van Dam, "Experiential Learning: What's Missing in Most Change Programs," McKinsey Operations 2015, on mckinsey.com.
6. Organizational Health Index database (n = 60,000); ""Return on Leadership" report by Egon Zehnder Intl and McKinsey.
7. McKinsey Quarterly Transformational Change survey, January 2010; June 2009 McKinsey Global survey results.

List of Figures

Part I

In-Company Executive Education and Development

1

Human Resource Management and Leadership Development

1.1 Are Happy Days Here Again?

After years of stagnation, executive education and development is gaining momentum once more. During the financial crisis that started in 2007 firms were less willing to pay for their staff to attend executive training courses and degree programs, including the MBA. It is to be hoped that those days are done, though all stakeholders have learnt the lesson that, in times of crisis or in times of growth, people are the major source of competitive advantages. This has resulted in a steady demand for customized executive programs, which bring business schools closer to their natural constituency: the business world. Indeed, some business schools are struggling to keep up with the bevy of new business clients seeking courses on everything from leadership to big data. This growth is being driven by expansion into new territories. Outside Europe and the United States, which used to have the most revered schools and executive education providers, the grass looks increasingly greener. New frontiers are propelling the business of executive education to new heights. For example, many executive development centers are snapping up clients in Asia: India, Indonesia and Malaysia in particular are starting to ask

© The Author(s) 2016
S. Iñiguez de Onzoño, *Cosmopolitan Managers*,
DOI 10.1057/978-1-137-54909-9_1

for more executive courses. Asian companies are suffering from a dearth of management experience. Companies are willing to splash out on tailored programs from US and European schools that are flying flags in the region. The phenomenon is also prompting local players to develop their executive education units. Despite the fact that a lot of great talent is coming in, it's just not able to keep pace with all the opportunities that companies offer in Asia.[1]

Corporate training is a reliable barometer of economic activity: when companies slow down they often cut training spending, and then as business grows, they ramp back up to train new hires, sales people, and leaders. Last year the International Consortium for Executive Education (Unicon) released findings from its annual membership survey,[2] which includes nearly 100 educational institutions from around the world with executive education programs. The survey found that the industry has begun to rebound from a global slowdown, and that executive education providers around the world anticipate more growth. Of the survey's respondents, 82% experienced growth in 2011–12, with 49% of schools reporting revenue growth of more than 10%. Additionally, 94% of executive education providers expect their revenue to grow in 2012–13.

US spending on corporate training grew by 15% in 2014 (the highest growth rate in seven years) to over $70 billion in the US and over $130 billion worldwide. This tremendous increase follows two years of accelerated spending in this area (10% in 2011 and 12% in 2012), illustrating how companies see tremendous skills gaps as we recover from the recession.

On the other hand, business education and training, inside and outside companies, continue to be the most dynamic segment of higher education, and the MBA remains the most-demanded ticket among postgraduate offerings.

All these phenomena confirm a renaissance of human resources management and executive development.

Figure 1.1 represents the different layers of higher and continuous education in management, with some examples of the programs currently offered by business schools and other educational institutions.

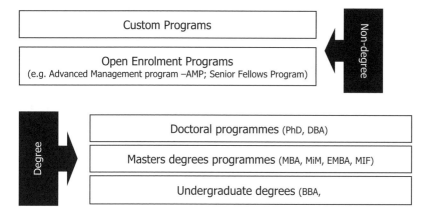

Fig. 1.1 Business education: layers of higher education and continuous learning

1.2   HR Management Will Become the Hottest Ticket in the C-Suite

Personnel, human resources, human capital, and talent: as management knowledge has developed over the decades, different terms have been used to describe the people that make up an organization. In the future we will probably use more sophisticated terms, given the decisive role people play in generating innovation and achieving results.

At the same time, the job title of those responsible for managing people in companies has evolved as well. They used to be called personnel managers, and then they were human resource managers, then human capital managers, then chief talent officers, or heads of corporate universities.

It's probably not going too far to say that human resources managers and their departments were historically the poor relation in many organizations. Their salaries were generally lower than those of other managers, their meetings with the CEO less frequent, and they usually had little to say when it came to making strategic decisions. What's more, as a rule, informing employees about good news, such as promotions, congratulations for a job well done, bonuses, and salary raises were usually the preserve of the department head concerned, probably to increase motivation or loyalty from employees.

Peter Capelli says critics accuse HR managers of focusing too much on "administration," and that they "lack vision and strategic insight" adding that their profile wanes or waxes according to the economic cycle: "When the economy is down and the labor market is slack, they see HR as a nuisance. But sentiments change when labor tightens up and HR practices become essential to companies' immediate success."[3]

The future of human resources, regardless of what it is next called, will be about developing the people who make up the organization, and this is a task directly related to training and education. Identifying talent, boosting strengths and inculcating the skills and virtues of management, evaluating progress and adjudicating salaries and other payments that take into account these factors: this will be what human resources heads will be focusing on in the coming years. And as Bob Audrey explains,[4] this will mean carrying out specific activities quite different to those they currently are responsible for, along with the appearance of new institutions specializing in management education.

Organizational management will be subject to a series of trends that will consolidate in the coming years:

- *Diversification of the activities related to the management of people and of the departments in question.* Many corporations have departments focused on managing personnel, developing talent, managing organizational knowledge, running corporate universities, or managing diversity, for example. How these departments and activities are integrated and coordinated will depend on each company's individual strategy. Periodically, companies centralize or decentralize these activities, either because they are going through a period of growth, diversification, or because they are consolidating and looking for synergies.

- *Recognition of the importance of human resource management* is growing, and it's clearly going to become a more important part of running a company. This can be seen, for example, in the fact that vice presidents of human resources are being seen more often in the C-suite, their professional profile is more sophisticated, and their salaries more in line with those of other senior executives. Concurrently, more time is spent on analysis and decisions about people-related questions at board meetings, boards of directors, and steering committees.

— *Connection of HR to corporate strategy*: The importance of the human factor in formulating, and especially in implementing strategies within companies will require human resources heads to actively participate in these processes, either with the CEO or the CFO, something that never used to happen during a time when the head of human resources was essentially there to do what the board decided.

— *The intensive use of ICT in managing HR and the many different processes related to people.* Most companies over a certain size use standard or applied platforms as part of the selection and evaluation process of people. Growing numbers of businesses are starting to use the social networks to locate new talent. Internal communities are being created to communicate and discuss the organization's knowledge or how to merge business units. At the same time, director development and training is increasingly being supported by online educational platforms. This coming together of technology and management processes is on the rise and in my opinion will lead to greater customization and humanization.

— *The rise of executive education programs and internal and external training*. Education is recognized as the most effective vehicle for updating knowledge, developing leadership skills, bringing groups closer together, and passing on the key aspects of the corporate culture. Management training programs are putting greater and greater emphasis on leadership, managing people and teams, and managing organizational change, as opposed to the traditional emphasis on hard skills such as supply chain management.

— *Managing diversity and inclusion are two corporate policies essential for driving innovation*. This will take on greater relevance in the future as directors and employees from different generations are incorporated into the workforce, particularly so-called senior talent, managers aged 55 and over.

- *The growing role of the CEO in all aspects of managing people.* From my own experience sitting on panels that award prizes to companies based on their ability to attract talent or their excellence in human resource management, one of the factors that carries the greatest weight is the amount of time and energy the CEO spends on talent management, which is perhaps the most relevant activity, along with formulating corporate strategy and acting as an interlocutor with key stakeholders. We can also expect to see more CEOs coming up through human resources.
- *Integrating technology and HR management.* A stronger human resources presence in organizations will also require updating knowledge in related areas that are subject to rapid technological change, for example, cognitive psychology, neuroscience, or behavioral economics. The success of human resource management in the future will depend in large measure on how elements of these disciplines can be incorporated into the company's activities.

Human resources is headed in an interesting direction, and it may well be one of the areas of management science that proves to be the most innovative in the coming years. As a result, it will increasingly attract entrepreneurial and innovative individuals from more varied backgrounds. The best is yet to come.

1.3   Successful Companies Embrace Change

Are companies and HR departments willing to embrace the transformation demanded by the new business environment?

In a much-quoted exchange from Giuseppe Lampedusa's *The Leopard*,[5] Tancredi tells his uncle, Don Fabrizio: "If we want things to stay as they are, everything will have to change," urging the older man to embrace Il *Risorgimento* (the unification of Italy led by Garibaldi in the late nineteenth century) if he wants to keep his patrimony and his political influence. Don Fabrizio is an old aristocrat of prominent Sicilian lineage, the Prince of Salina, and the epitome of melancholic adherence to traditions, of supreme but decadent style, and who sees the emergence of the new bourgeoisie with disdain and detachment. He even declines an offer to occupy a seat in the new Senate.

Tancredi, an aristocrat who lacks his uncle's wealth, is eager to climb the new social ladder and embraces the new establishment. He even breaks his engagement with Concetta, the Prince's daughter, to marry Angelica, an arresting young woman and the heir of the town's mayor, a parvenu who has accumulated a large fortune and leads local politics.

Tancredi's comment has been frequently cited to illustrate the changes that governments or managers, forced by the circumstances, may implement in order to preserve the status quo. In fact, "lampedusians" or "gattopards" are sometimes used in political science in relation to politicians who start apparent revolutions that result only in superficial changes.

The fact is that we humans are, in general, comfortable with customs and routines and are reluctant to change, particularly with age. As Mark Ghiasy said: "for some people, change is still associated with uncertainty, which brings about fear."[6] The same may be said of companies and their managers. As companies grow and become large corporations, they cement their vast presence through values and traditions that are embedded in their organization's culture, developing strong identities shared by both internal and external stakeholders that can prove hard to relinquish. As a consequence, major structural changes or deep transformations are often viewed with skepticism or diffidence.

That said, emerging industry players and their new competitive styles can force change within large corporations, making them dance to a new, more dynamic rhythm. Veteran thinker on change management Rosabeth Moss Kanter discussed this phenomenon lucidly in her 1989 book *When Giants Learn to Dance*[7]: "Today's corporate elephants must learn how to dance as nimbly and speedily as mice if they are to survive in our increasingly competitive and rapidly changing world." Her analysis focused on a number of corporations, such as IBM, that have championed their respective industries while handing over their global dominance to new players like Microsoft. But her metaphor about clumsy dancing elephants could be also applied to today's corporate giants who were once the innovators, disruptors, and category killers but that face new and more agile competitors. For example, Lenovo, China's leading producer of PCs and mobile devices, plans to overtake Apple and Samsung: "In several respects, Lenovo may already have leapfrogged some Western multinationals."[8]

There's no doubt that one of the main challenges facing large corporations is how to keep internal change flowing permanently and to stimulate innovation. The danger is to implement Lampedusian changes of the sort mentioned above, which are sometimes conveniently adopted by CEOs of large companies in order to produce the external impression of transformation and adjustment to new circumstances while avoiding true internal reinvention. Such changes may include, for example, new corporate logos or a corporate image, irrelevant reformulations of strategic missions and value statements, transitions to a new legal status, or updated organizational structures that retain previous distributions of functions and roles.

Sometimes Lampedusian changes occur when senior management is being restructured. Newly appointed CEOs frequently want to enhance a new management style and break the links with old corporate traditions. They are keen to adopt new slogans or mottos, remove veteran managers who symbolize the past, and to foster renovated strategies, launch new products and services, or open up new markets. Whether these are just Lampedusian changes or actual moves toward new directions can only be assessed over time. As widely agreed, the first 90 days of a new CEO are key to anticipating his or her management style and vision. However, true change, in companies as well as in society, is only fully felt over longer periods, normally years.

I am not against Lampedusian changes. Sometimes, opportunism and the production of quick visible effects with minor substantial impact are convenient at large corporations. In fact it is not always possible or desirable to implement total revolutions at big companies, which have to alternate times of change with times of consolidation and institutionalization. At the same time, experience also shows that in many cases it is more profitable in the long term to be a follower than a pioneer. Followers do not have to undergo the same trial and error and innovation costs as pioneers, among other things. Industries producing X-ray scanners, diet cola, digital cameras, or plain-paper copiers show that follower companies can garner a leading share of the market over time, even forcing the exit of the original leaders.[9]

When a company finds itself in turbulent times, I would say it is better to be a Tancredi than a Don Fabrizio. Reluctance to change is one of the worst attitudes that a manager can show. It is only admissible, and not always, for financial managers or legal advisors, since their function is to assess risk—remember that change brings uncertainty, which in turn means more risk.

Not that elephants can't learn to make their way round a ballroom, a process Louis Gerstner, former CEO of IBM, describes in his 2003 *Who Says Elephants Can't Dance?*, which charts his makeover of Big Blue from a hardware to services-oriented. Gerstner saved IBM from bankruptcy and his efforts saw its market capitalization rise from $29 billion to $168 billion in 2002 when he retired.[10]

1.4   The Emergence of a New Type of Leader: The Cosmopolitan Manager

Perhaps the best contribution corporate education can make to improve the world is to produce responsible, principled entrepreneurs and managers. As I like to tell my business graduates, the best antidote to bad international politics is good business.

The type of business leader I am proposing in this book is what I call the cosmopolitan manager, somebody we might define as responsible, cultivated, and competent.

That sense of business responsibility first comes into its own in the way a manager interacts with and relates to the people in the company he or she is managing. As with other areas of human activity, leaders know how to manage their teams and their people toward achieving objectives in the best way possible. But a manager has other responsibilities as well, mainly in relation to the owners of the company, as well as with other stakeholders. In so much as companies play a key role in our societies, when it comes to generating value, employment, and economic development, business leaders must also answer to society as a whole. And although this may not have legal ramifications, aside from obeying the law, business leaders are accountable not just to public opinion in their own country, but to how they and their company are seen in the countries they operate in.

The global reach of many companies, regardless of their size, requires business leaders to be cosmopolitan and to possess a vision and understanding of the world based on tolerance, an understanding of different cultures, respect for human diversity, and the many ways that civilization manifests itself: in a word, cosmopolitan managers must be cultivated and want to broaden and deepen their knowledge of other peoples, of the humanities, the arts, and the sciences over the course of their lives. It is sometimes thought that age brings with it sufficient culture and that once past a certain point, we need not spend as much time learning new things as we did when were younger. But we should remember that the truly wise have always been characterized by an insatiable curiosity to discover new things. This attitude of permanent openness to the humanities and the sciences can help to continue developing our entrepreneurial spirit into the mature stages of a director's life.

Finally, cosmopolitan managers are also competent and have a thoroughgoing understanding of their profession based on a continual process of updating the skills and knowledge they will need throughout their lives, both in their private and professional lives: let's not forget that we live in an ever-changing world. Lifelong learning, the search for new ways to innovate, for new business knowledge, is one of the core characteristics of the cosmopolitan manager.

1.5   The Qualities of Leadership

"The art of infusing his own spirit into others" was one of the distinctive features possessed by Lord Horatio Nelson, the legendary Vice-Admiral and one of England's favorite heroes, and a man who embodied the essence of leadership, influencing others decisively.

Terry Coleman, one of Nelson's modern biographers, identifies the qualities of the man, some shared by many other leaders: "strength of mind amounting to genius, often generosity (…) often uneasiness with his family and with superior officers, often ruthlessness, always fearlessness."[11] Through the account of Nelson's life, we also learn that he was ambitious, persevering, opportunistic, and strategically mindful, as evidenced in the innovative way he commanded the naval battles he won, notably at The Nile and at Trafalgar, where he finished off Napoleon's fleet. He also possessed an "intolerant impatience" in work matters. Indeed, a common feature among leaders, also in business, is the passion they show about their jobs and enterprises and the will to implement their ideas quickly.

However, as is the case for all mortals, Nelson also had clear and visible defects, a facet of the hero described mostly in modern biographies In this respect, few authorized biographies provide a complete account of their protagonists, dwelling not just on their brighter facets but also their darker sides, which is a pity, since we can learn as much from the errors and shortcomings of leaders as from their successes.

Returning to Nelson's weaknesses, he was vain and was constantly on the lookout for honors and recognition. He was also prompt to capitalize on the achievements of others and old-fashioned in his thoughts and views about the world and society. He could also be a merciless tyrant, as when he allied with the Neapolitan aristocrats to repress and kill the rebels that led the short-lived republic in southern Italy.

Nelson's time at the court of the Kingdom of the Two Sicilies in Naples is artfully recreated in Susan Sontag's historical novel *The Volcano's Lover*,[12] an account of the notorious relationship between Lord Hamilton, the British ambassador to Naples, Emma, his arresting wife, and Nelson, who became her lover until his death at Trafalgar. When Nelson arrived in Naples he was already crippled and blind in one eye. But he still possessed great charm and leadership qualities. He even learnt how to write with his left hand, allowing him to pen love letters to Emma.

Throughout his career, Nelson's personal leadership qualities were bolstered through the mentorship provided by his uncle, Captain Maurice Suckling, and later by Admiral Hyde Parker. Here, we may consider that companies that implement mentorship or coaching schemes are better at identifying and nurturing young talent, and consequently develop more leaders, than those lacking similar programs.

Like many successful leaders, Nelson also knew how to capitalize on luck. Good leaders let few opportunities pass and keep actively looking for chances, even if they're beyond their reach. This was also the case with Nelson. His impatience led him to ask persistently for new missions and commands of new ships. Apart from managing the entire British fleet during his later battles, he served on or mastered at least 23 different ships.

In his seminal 1990 article "What Leaders Really Do,"[13] John P. Kotter clarifies the recurrent distinction between leaders and managers.

Management is about coping with complexity, organizing and staffing, controlling, and planning. On the other hand, leadership is about coping with change, developing a vision, motivating and inspiring and, more fundamentally, aligning people toward a mission. Kotter insists that both management and leadership are complementary facets in organizations but are not easily found incarnated in a single person.

Even if management seems a more rational exercise than leadership, a sort of organizational engineering, leadership should not be perceived as a mystical or mysterious quality. "It has nothing to do with having 'charisma' or other exotic personality traits. It is not the province of a chosen few." It is, rather, a skill developed over time that comprises a set of characteristics, requiring intense communication with stakeholders—much more so than management. One of Nelson's contemporaries said of him: "there was something irresistibly pleasing in his address and conversation, and an enthusiasm when speaking on professional subjects."[14]

Leadership also relies on the ability to delegate throughout an organization. One of Nelson's key advantages when he went into battle was his men's superior training, coordination and alignment, allowing for more empowerment and autonomy to execute orders. "Engage the enemy more closely" was the last instruction given by Nelson to his fleet at Trafalgar, a generic request that required seasoned interpretation.

Management and leadership, as two different but complementary facets, may be well encapsulated in the title "Master and Commander" given to men such as Nelson[15]: masters because they were skillful organizers and planners, and commanders because they were effective leaders. Time and again, history provides us with invaluable management lessons.

1.6   Management Is About Leading People

One of my favorite quotes, which I frequently use in my addresses to students and executives, comes from Peter Drucker's memoires about attending a class given by John Maynard Keynes at Cambridge University in 1934. "I suddenly realized that Keynes and all the brilliant economics students in the room were interested in the behavior of commodities, while I was interested in the behavior of people."[16]

This quote comes to mind when I am asked about the essence of management, the core of leadership. Sometimes we read that management is about acquiring business knowledge, techniques and skills, about the importance of learning how to interpret macroeconomic trends, anticipate the evolution of a given industry, or how to read financial statements. However, I am very much attached to Drucker's view about the core importance of understanding people in relation to being a good manager: when all is said and done, management is about leading people.

Good managers generally know the basics of business, either because they learned about it at school or acquired such knowledge through experience. Yet if we aim at excelling in management we can do much better by learning more about people's behaviors, ideals, and aspirations. Tomorrow's successful business leaders need to cultivate the following areas:

- *Knowing their people in depth*—their concerns and worries, personal ambitions, and family circumstances—improves your management profile. How much time do you dedicate to them? Do you know about those aspects of their lives?
- *Identifying and retaining talent.*—business writer Claudio Fernández de Araoz frequently asks managers at his presentations how many of them have learnt the basics in selecting talent.[17] In most cases, the majority of them have not even read or studied the basics of selecting people. They play it by ear when they should be professionals.
- *Reading literature, philosophy, and history*—this can enhance our knowledge of human nature, which is fundamental for managing people and exercising leadership.

Management is irreducibly human: the more we know about the people we work with, the better managers we can become.

1.7   Is Executive Education Profitable? A Conversation with Kai Peters

When Kai Peters discusses business schools, he does so from the perspective of his 15 years' experience at the helm of Ashridge Management College, during which time he has faced the challenges affecting the executive education sector: increased competition, the arrival of major consultants, ever-tighter profit margins, and the demands posed by making executive development more applicable to the real world.

"In 1985, Ashridge's revenue from executive education open programs was £4 million. Thirty years on, the figure is the same. This illustrates the intensity of competition in this segment," says Peters, who believes that more and more business schools are entering the executive education sector because they think there is money to be made there. The problem, he says, is that they haven't thought through questions such as the need for more specialists, more expensive teaching staff, smaller classes, or greater use of the school's resources. "Larger undergraduate programs are more profitable and generate greater economies of scale," he adds, a view based on his experience with university systems during his time as dean of Rotterdam Business School.

Peters is emphatic about the importance of content when it comes to executive education. "During the early years at Ashridge, toward the end of the 1950s, executive education was about passing on knowledge, perhaps because so many executives lacked basic things like management skills, which today are taught as part of an MBA. People attending executive education courses have the basics, so our programs should focus more on questions to do with leadership, managing change or behavioral stuff."

Peters also believes that the best executive education teachers come from a markedly clinical background, as well as having had lengthy contact and experience with senior management. He is critical of the shift in the type of research business schools carry out, which he says has little to do with what executives and their businesses have to deal with each day in the real world. The results of some articles published in the journals are trivial, obvious, or just plain irrelevant to most stakeholders. Peters recalls a presentation by a researcher who announced that companies which generate profits tend to grow more quickly, and that the MBA curriculum should incorporate stochastic analysis methodology. He concluded that "It's pretty clear that the future of executive training isn't headed in this direction."

Nevertheless, the big advantage that business schools possess as academic centers in training directors—compared with the increasingly active strategic consultancies such as McKinsey or Deloitte, for example—is their ability to generate knowledge, to provide a learning environment and to be able to translate leadership into action.

At present, Ashridge has more than 36 open programs, along with its consultancy activities and an ever-bigger presence in executive coaching. In 2014, Ashridge merged with Hult Business School, creating an operation with 150 full-time teachers, more than 300 adjuncts, campuses in the United States, the United Kingdom, and China, along with some 4,000 undergraduates. The logic behind the move is to move toward management practice. As the *Financial Times* reported, this is probably the only fusion between business schools that has not resulted in cutbacks or downsizing, and in fact led to the opposite: it seems to have boosted the growth of both institutions and to have generated synergies.[18]

Notes

1. Data based on interviews held between the author and deans and program managers of different business schools and executive education centers.

   For further data used in this introduction, see the annual reports provided by UNICON ((Executive Education Consortium), comprising the leading business schools offering executive education programs, both open and custom. See also:

   Bersin by Deloitte, Corporate Education Factbook 2014, January 2014, and HR Factbook 2015: Benchmarks and Trends for U.S. HR Organizations, January 2015, http://www.bersin.com/Lib/Rs/ShowDocument.aspx?docid=18203.

   P. Cataldo, *Best Practices in Marketing Executive Education*, UNICON (Executive Education Consortium), November 2012.

   Bersin by Deloitte, "Global Human Capital Trends 2014: Engaging the 21st Century Workforce," Deloitte University Press, 2015.

2. M. Eiter, "Investigating Our Customer Clients' Evolving Needs," A Unicon Research Study, June 2009. https://Uniconexed.org/2009/research/Investigating-custom-client-needs-Eiter-2009.pdf.

3. P. Capelli, "Why We Love to Hate HR ... and What HR Can Do About It," *Harvard Business Review*, July–August 2015.

4. B. Audrey, "Why Tomorrow's HR Professionals Must Reinvent Their Role," *Global Focus*, EFMD, Vol. 9, Issue 3, 2015, pp. 28–31.
5. G. Di Lampedusa, *The Leopard* (translated by Guido Waldman) (New York: Random House, 2007).
6. M. Ghiasy, "The Only Constant is Change," *LinkedIn Pulse*, August 3, 2014.
7. R. Moss Kanter, *When Giants Learn to Dance* (New York: Simon & Schuster, 1989).
8. www.strategy-business.com—"Lenovo Goes Global," August 8, 2014.
9. D. Teece, *The Competitive Challenge: Strategies for Industrial Innovation and Renewal* (Cambridge, MA: Ballinger, 1987), pp. 186–188.
10. L. B. Gerstner, *Who Says Elephants Can't Dance? Leading a Great Enterprise Through Dramatic Change* (New York: Harper Collins, 2003).
11. T. Coleman, *Nelson: The Man and the Legend* (London: Bloomsbury, 2002), p. 31.
12. S. Sontag, *The Volcano Lover: A Romance* (London: Penguin Modern Classics, 2009).
13. J. P. Kotter, "What Leaders Really Do," in *Harvard Business Review on Leadership* (Boston: Harvard Business Review Press,1990), p. 38.
14. T. Coleman, *Nelson*, p. 68.
15. The title "master and commander" was created in the 18th century to call naval officers who managed ships of war too large to be commanded by a lieutenant but too small to require the assignment of a post captain.
16. P. F. Drucker, *The Ecological Vision* (Piscataway, NJ: Transaction Publishers, 1993), pp. 75–76.
17. C. Fernández de Araoz, *It's Not the How or the What but the Who: Succeed by Surrounding Yourself with the Best* (Boston, MA: Harvard Business Review Press, 2014), p. 23.
18. D. Bradshaw, "Ashridge and Hult International Announce Plans to Merge," *Financial Times*, July 4, 2014. http://www.ft.com/cms/s/2/7e199ea8-5251-11e5-8642-453585f2cfcd.html#axzz3rgDuWMVN.

2

Executive Education Examined

2.1 Executive Education Providers' Value Proposal

Training directors in the conventional areas of management, particularly leadership and strategy, has traditionally been the preserve of business schools focused on executive education. In the United States, for example, executive education is the bread and butter for such schools as Harvard Business School, Darden Business School, and Chicago Booth School of Business, which have had a major impact on the setting up of directorial leadership courses. A similar process has taken place in Europe through schools such as INSEAD and IMD, and in China with CEIBS.[1]

In recent years, there has been an increase in the type and number of development and training courses on offer, which include those from organizations outside of the traditional educational sphere, as well as from engineering and design schools, consultancies, and media and publishing companies. Della Bradshaw, the *Financial Times*' Business Education Editor, notes: "strategy consultancies such as Bain and Boston

© The Author(s) 2016
S. Iñiguez de Onzoño, *Cosmopolitan Managers*,
DOI 10.1057/978-1-137-54909-9_2

Consulting Group have long been executive education providers, but now publishing companies, technology start-ups and recruitment consultancies are circling in an attempt to land chunks of a global market worth in excess of $70bn a year."[2]

Needless to say, increased competition in executive education and the entry of new players into the sector is the result of a growth in demand coupled with increased investment in training by companies and individuals. A Deloitte by Bersin survey shows that executive education budgets have grown in the last three years by more than 25% in aggregate terms; leadership courses and programs represented 35% of the total budget.[3]

From a supply perspective, executive development programs have traditionally been open or custom. The first are available on the open market, and although in most cases a subscription is paid by the employer, participants are regarded as the clients, and it is they who are usually given a diploma or certificate.

In custom programs, it is the company that is the client, usually the human resource department or a corporate university, and content, methodology, and sequence are negotiated and adapted to the company's needs.

In recent years, big corporations have increasingly moved away from open programs to custom programs, because they allow for adaptation of objectives, contents, and evaluation, so as to better align them with the strategies and challenges of training people. Participants of open programs now tend to come from small and medium-sized enterprises (SMEs).

Institutions such as the Center for Creative Leadership, whose motto is "leadership is learned," and Duke Corporate Education (Duke CE) have developed design and delivery models for custom programs that have marked a turning point. A Unicon report explains: "clients today want programs that are focused in helping them execute their business strategies or solving business problems."[4]

The customized program segment can be characterized by a series of trends over recent years: (1) growing demand to demonstrate the impact of training on the development of participants and on the company's results; (2) demand for greater flexibility, shorter programs, and lower prices; and (3) request for applicable knowledge of a clinical nature that can be used in the company's operating environment.

In particular, as Andersen and Van Wijk explain, the platform model is increasingly being seen as the way forward, thanks to four key developments: (1) an explosion in the number of intellectual free agents who work outside or beyond the permeable organizational boundaries of academic institutions; (2) the increasing recognition of open collaboration as an engine of customization and innovation; (3) the pervasive spread of information and communication technologies that are enabling virtual teams to deliver integrated courses; and (4) the demand from clients that these courses should provide outcomes by matching intellectual resources with their needs, and not vice versa.[5]

Figure 2.1 contains what, in my opinion, are the main activities provided by business schools and consultancies to their corporate customers in the custom programs segment and identifies the players whose participation is more distinctive (Fig. 2.1).

What is the value proposal in executive education for businesses? Conger and Xin identify three main objectives:

1. To build awareness and support for strategic transitions
2. To facilitate the large-scale organizational change needed for a new strategic direction
3. To build depth of leadership talent[6]

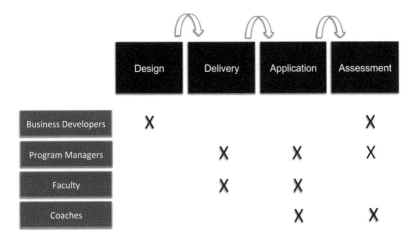

Fig. 2.1 Value chain of custom programs for corporations

These are broad and ambitious goals, and some stakeholders have questioned whether executive education providers are meeting them. Corporate customers' demands need to be carefully examined if effective responses are to be developed.

2.2   Do We Need a Copernican Revolution in Executive Education?

At this point, we might usefully ask how many business schools, particularly those offering executive education, are still living in what we might call the pre-Copernican age, with the view that academia is at the center of their universe instead of it orbiting around the business world?

I pose this question in the context of one of the biggest growth opportunities for business schools—regardless of whether they are active or not in executive education—and which is simultaneously one of the biggest challenges they face: how best to provide in-company training and tailored programs for organizations.

We can identify a number of factors driving growth in this particular sector of higher education:

- *Businesses need, more than ever, to attract, retain, and develop talent.* Research shows that an organization's commitment to in-house training and the concomitant opportunities for personal and professional development are among the most important factors for executives when deciding whether to join a company, particularly in the case of the so-called Millennial Generation.[7]
- *Modern aging.* In the not-too-distant future, businesses will be able to count on the most multi-generational workforce in history. For many countries, particularly in the developed world, the majority of their populations will soon be aged 50 or over. Longer life expectancy and delayed retirement will provide opportunities and challenges for companies. On the one hand, they will be able to draw on the experience of older directors and managers, their network of stakeholders, their reputation, and their knowledge of the sector. At the same time, a constantly changing environment will require periodic

retraining, maintaining older employees' capacity to innovate, and managing diversity between generations.

- *The need for businesses to convert knowledge management* into a differential competitive advantage directly linked to the development of talent internally. The question we need to ask ourselves is whether most business schools, and not just a few, are ready, willing, and able to meet the challenge of designing and delivering tailored programs for companies, in other words—to join the Copernican revolution. As things stand, at least based on what chief learning officers (CLOs) have to say, the answer is not yet.

- *Direct applicability.* CLOs say that educational content and teaching materials used in custom programs are not properly adapted to the development and training needs of businesses and call for less off-the-shelf, packaged, US-centric traditional MBA contents.[8] But the problem with developing adapted content for executive education is that research incentives at many business schools are not generally aligned with the needs of executive education.

- *Assessment of learning.* More than 50% of CLOs say they are unhappy with current learning measurement systems.[9] This is a growing problem for directors, who are increasingly required to justify the impact of any investment on the bottom line. As a recent survey shows, 85% of CLOs believe that measuring learning is an important or very important activity.[10] In the majority of cases, evaluation of the impact of in-company programs is currently focused mostly on how satisfied participants are with the program, and its outcome on how they carry out their assigned tasks.

- *Experienced professors.* Businesses are demanding faculties that are specialists in a wide range of subjects combined with particular skills that apply global knowledge locally. A global outlook, the quality of the faculty, and the expertise in executive development are now crucial factors when choosing an education supplier.[11] But, of course, not all business schools have teachers that are properly qualified to deliver executive education courses. A recent survey shows that the 50 top teachers taking part in custom programs belonged to just 29 business schools.[12]

- *Beyond education.* What's more, CLOs are demanding that business schools adopt an approach that integrates education with a thorough knowledge of their company's strategy and development needs. What companies are increasingly calling for might best be described as educational consulting and talent development, rather than training per se.
- *Increasing and varied competition.*' The preponderance of business schools in the in-company training sector has recently been challenged by the arrival of many new players. For example, engineering schools and departments of psychology and international relations are already offering tailor-made programs for companies, as are universities' continuous education and extension units. At the same time, consultancy firms see in-company training as part of their professional services portfolio, and are able to offer myriad synergies for their business units, as well as the possibility of implementing their programs in multinationals on every continent via their subsidiaries. Competition is further increasing thanks to the growing number of freelancers and coaches, whose services are available on an individual basis or as consociates.
- *Timing and pricing.* Finally, to further complicate matters, we are witnessing the emergence of just-in-time education, a response to companies demanding increasingly competitive prices and shorter design and execution times, while at the same time requiring programs to fit in with participants' schedules and locations, and expecting deliverers to scale up their offer for larger groups when needed.

In this increasingly demanding in-company training scenario, developing talent and managing knowledge has also sparked the growth of corporate universities with increasingly sophisticated processes and structures, including external quality accreditation systems such as the Corporate Learning Improvement Process (CLIP).

In response to all of the above, what initiatives can business schools come up with to take advantage of the growth of in-company training while meeting the demands of CLOs? Below are a few avenues that business schools could explore without substantially changing their mission, but that might allow them to take better advantage of the opportunities that present themselves in the custom programs sector, while at the same time building stronger relationships with their corporate clients.

(1) ***Teachsultants and Coachstructors***. Academics with relevant research experience in the business world, experience with companies, and contact with senior management are the best deliverers of in-company training. They combine a thorough technical knowledge of their disciplines with the necessary neutrality to be able to efficiently and independently advise companies on their training needs. To develop such profiles, business schools need to adapt their incentive systems to reward and recognize the involvement of their faculty in executive education.

Business schools need to bring in teachers with practical professional experience, people who are part of the academic community and who take part in research and teaching methodologies in schools. The type of educator businesses are demanding might be called *teachsultants*—a hybrid of teacher and consultant—or *coachstructors*—half coach, half instructor. These are people able to orchestrate learning, and who are capable of transcending traditional disciplines through understanding from within the decisive issues facing a company.

(2) ***Applied research***. Research needs to be transferred to teaching, while new ways to measure the impact of academic research on the real world are required. This means going beyond bibliometrics or article citation rates. As I have argued elsewhere,[13] this means designing systems to facilitate periodic analysis of schools' research and the extent of their use as management tools in the business world. Ideally, this would take the form of measuring systems reflecting a wide range of cultural and business practices, and thus the heterogeneity of the research.

(3) ***Blended programs***. The future belongs to programs best able to adapt to the needs of directors while at the same time integrating technology and teaching, and thus prolonging the learning momentum beyond the traditional face-to-face sessions that characterize classroom learning.

(4) ***Integrated learning platforms***. We need to develop new knowledge platforms managed jointly by business schools and their corporate cli-

ents. These would offer participants access to content adapted to their needs and environment while allowing them to interact with other directors in the company. Such platforms would also allow clients to use assessment schemes to measure personal or group learning progress.

(5) *Measuring the efficacy or impact of learning.* We have seen that many companies believe this need is not being met. I should say at this point that I do not believe it is possible to measure investment in education in terms of return on investment (ROI). In my opinion, this is akin to trying to measure the impact of implementing diversity measures and business ethics on the bottom line. That said, it is possible to develop methods that allow us to measure the impact of a program on the personal development of participants, and subsequently on how they carry out their tasks within the company. We are entering a fascinating period in the construction of tools based on technology that will allow us to better measure the effects of educational products on the development of directive skills and the behavior of participants.

(6) *Multiple partnerships.* Until now, business schools have been very cautious when providing information about their custom programs. This is slowly changing, and it now seems reasonable to hope we will see alliances between schools and consultancies, coaching networks, software, and technology and content platforms.

These proposals rest on a basic premise: business is the sun around which business schools orbit, and not the other way round. For this Copernican revolution to take place, our academic institutions must embrace a transformation in terms of their governance, mission, incentives, and portfolio of activities.

2.3   A New Species Is Born: FT | IE Corporate Learning Alliance

In response to the challenges identified in the previous section, in the fall of 2014, IE Business School created an alliance with the Financial Times Group: the FT | IE Corporate Learning Alliance, a joint venture whose mission is to combine academic muscle and direct knowledge of companies with a vocation for integrating technology and teaching. Its reach is global and it is open to collaboration with other business schools around the world. I believe that similar platforms will appear in the coming years. In fact, a few months after, Cornell University announced an agreement to run online learning programs with *Fortune* magazine and offer certificates to its participants.

One of IE Business School's most important competitive advantages has always been its system of governance, reinforced by it being a not-for-profit proprietary school forever in pursuit of academic and operating excellence.

The drive behind the school's strategic vision has come from its president and founder, Diego del Alcázar Silvela, a man committed to innovation, with a passion for change, and not afraid of disruption. IE's organizational structure involves a series of units in constant contact with each other, and subject to checks and balances that guarantee a clear orientation toward the needs of the market.

In turn, this structure rests on four pillars: (1) a strong academic institution, which provides new content and programs; (2) an executive training division with strong ties to the business world; (3) a commercial presence on every continent; and (4) a financial department with a remit to monitor long-term sustainability in every area of activity.

The entrepreneurial spirit of the school's founder continues to exercise a marked influence upon the daily running of the institution, and upon the teaching staff, many of whom have started and run their own businesses, and are empowered to identify and implement their own strategies. This creates a far quicker time to market than other academic institutions when it comes to launching new programs and revising teaching material, as well as when making changes to the organizational structure and reacting to changes in the world around us. At the same time, IE's international scope, wide range of programs, and teaching methods allow it to manage the risks of operating in a single area, and to effectively deal with any crises that might crop up in a particular region.

IE's vocation for innovation has been evident throughout its history. It was one of the first business schools in Europe to launch an executive MBA—criticized in some quarters for its lack of academic rigor. Since then, the Executive MBA has become of the most popular programs offered by business schools. Two other IE landmark initiatives were subject to similar critiques when they were launched.

The first was the school's decision to introduce functional master's programs in areas such as human resources and marketing, breaking with the generalist tradition of MBAs up to that time. Again, this kind of specialization in different sectors has become the norm in business teaching and is now recognized by accrediting bodies such as the Association of MBAs (AMBA).

The second was IE's entry into online and blended teaching in the late 1990s. This was an exciting time, with the appearance of many new e-learning offerings, such as UNext and Cardean University, although many fell by the wayside, as well as new players such as the Apollo Education Group and Laureate.

IE's decision to enter this burgeoning sector was considered bold at the time, and none of its peers among the top 10 European business schools followed suit. The key to the success of IE's online teaching strategy was to bring together all the possibilities the technologies of the time offered. The idea was to transform teaching by drawing on the advantages offered by combining online and classroom learning, which by its asynchronous nature could reach a much larger audience. Furthermore, the use of multimedia teaching materials and diverse forms of delivery such as forums and video conferences replicated and even improved on the traditional interaction that takes place in the classroom.

The idea was never to replace the teaching faculty with tutors or facilitators, which is what many online universities have done, but instead to employ academics in this new environment, and thereby further develop their online teaching skills. The advantage of IE's blended Executive MBA courses, which today top global rankings in this category, is not the technological platform that supports them, but the way in which they bring together faculty, program staff, and multimedia content while successfully replicating traditional learning experiences by keeping the same group of students together throughout the program, and accepting students based on demanding admission requirements, as opposed to the open access of many other online courses, whose flexibility paradoxically results in high drop-off rates. At IE, once students have been admitted, they stay the course.

Building on the success of IE's blended programs, in the spring of 2012, IE decided to explore a new area. They were already aware of the potential of applying their blended knowhow to business education via custom programs designed to meet the specific development needs of senior management and which are taught within the company. The needs of this segment have traditionally been met by a range of suppliers, from Europe's leading business schools to executive education centers, consultancies and corporate universities.

The thinking behind the initiative, which is just as valid today, was that the business education sector, and education in general, is converging globally, with multiple players at different levels, bringing together universities and business schools, along with publishing houses, the media, and even technology companies. There are multiple synergies resulting from the joint activity of companies operating in the sector, particularly as regards management education.

What IE had in mind was to provide development and education for businesses by using the latest learning technologies, delivered through blended programs that adapted to the time constraints and needs of directors. These communication technologies also allowed for content distribution and interaction through the social networks associated with the programs, while at the same time strengthening students' identification with the company. At the same time, it was possible to develop a near-encyclopedic content library drawn from the archives of global publishing houses specializing in management studies. What's more, IE were able to develop tools to evaluate the skills and knowledge acquisition of participants. Finally, the teaching staff combined theoretical rigor with practical ability and considerable experience in the world of senior management.

IE put together a business plan outlining in detail the project's mission and activities, and set about finding a business partner. They were clear from the start that they wanted to work with just one company so as to avoid lengthy and complex negotiations and to reach agreement quickly. They chose Pearson, a diversified multinational, which as well as being the largest educational company worldwide, is also the largest publishing company in the world. Pearson was the owner of the *Financial Times*, and had a 50% stake in *The Economist*. It also has a strong presence in the educational sector through acquisitions of a range of higher education academic institutions, among them the Wall Street Institute language teaching centers, which are now part of Pearson English.

IE approached Pearson because they believed the project offered a series of synergies identified in the company's 2011 annual report. On the one hand, the custom programs were an opportunity to broaden Pearson's customer base from mainly Business to Consumer (B2C) to include Business to Business (B2B), as well as the K-12 segment and Business to Government (B2G). Custom programs for businesses are more resilient in times of crisis than other education and training segments. When IE first contacted Pearson, many of Europe's economies had slowed down as a result of the financial crisis of 2007.

The possibility also existed to extend the use of educational platforms and applications developed by Pearson to executive education, taking advantage of the technology available in areas such as evaluation, content delivery, e-publishing, and online teaching. There was also the opportunity to diversify the corporation's geographic presence—60% of its sales are in the United States—to include emerging economies, notably in Latin America. Finally, the creation of a consortium of leading business schools, along with IE Business School, could help consolidate the Pearson brand in the business education sector, where until then it had virtually no presence.

Negotiating a deal with Pearson took longer than was foreseen. This was in large part due to the exit of Marjorie Scardino and her replacement as CEO by John Fallon. The change meant IE relocating from its International Higher Education division to the Financial Times Group, then called Pearson Professional, overseen by John Ridding, where all business related to business and professional education was previously located.

IE's negotiations with the FT allowed them to focus the project on custom programs, leaving aside open education offerings. In fact, it was the joint vision and shared objectives with the FT senior staff that prompted the agreement.

Negotiating a joint venture to set up a new business is complicated, particularly bearing in mind the diverse nature of the organizations involved in the project: an academic institution on the one hand, and a large corporation on the other, with a complex structure requiring dialogue at different levels. The process was completed successfully in part due to a shared strategic vision and the considerable empathy shared by both negotiating teams. As part of the IE team, I was fortunate to be able to count on the unwavering support and inspiration provided by Diego del Alcázar, as well as Antonio Montes' diplomatic skills, and Vandyck Silveira's vast knowledge of the executive education sector. Across the table from us we were privileged to be talking to professionals of the stature of Tas Viglatzis, while John Ridding was a permanent presence, whether behind the scenes or in person.

Arduous legal work was required by both teams to coordinate UK Common Law with Spain's Civil Law, and was overseen by IE's lawyer Macarena Rosado and Diego Alcazar Benjumea, Vice President of IE, while Juan José Güemes coordinated the financial aspects on IE's behalf. And so, in December 2014, the FT | IE Corporate Learning Alliance (FT | IE CLA) was born. This 50–50 joint venture created by IE Business School and the Financial Times Group, oriented toward developing in-company programs and custom education for businesses, already has an impressive client base in Europe, Latin America, and the Middle East.

The Corporate Learning Alliance (CLA) stands apart from other business schools, consultancies, and players in the custom education sector, and is built on the following value propositions:

- It combines IE's academic strength and the FT's clout in the global corporate environment, as well as both brands' prestige. This is an institution that brings together the university world and the rigor of academic investigation with professional experience and a long-standing presence in the business world.
- It couples the experience and leadership of IE's blended programs, which are generally considered to top their segment. The blended approach combines high-quality courses with classroom teaching. FT | IE CLA aims to develop a significant percentage of its programs using this blended methodology, which companies are increasingly turning to.
- It includes some of the world's leading business schools as academic partners in the design and teaching of programs, providing local

knowledge and links to stakeholders around the world, as well as facilitating the distribution of programs in several languages, among them English, Spanish, Mandarin, and Portuguese. Partner institutions include Yale School of Management, Brazil's Fundaçao Getulio Vargas, Mexico's Ted de Monterrey, the Jiao Tong University Business School and Renmin University Business School in China, and the Singapore Management University.

– We have put together a faculty with the kind of profile that companies require for in-company teaching made up of IE academics, associate lecturers to be contracted through the Joint Venture (JV), consultants specializing in management development, and high-profile FT opinion leaders. For example, the editors of several of the FT's sections have taken part in courses, and provide a rounded, unbiased overview of the main players in the fields they cover.

– We have also developed content in a range of formats, built on IE's highly successful multimedia material, the FT's editorial and archive resources, and content provided by other Pearson companies, such as Prentice Hall, Random House, and Penguin.

The FT | IE CLA is headquartered in London, one of the world's leading centers of executive and business education, and is due to open new campuses and affiliates that to further the offer of training and education services. At the same time, it has set up a subsidiary in Spain, to which all IE pre-existing in-company education has been transferred.

In July 2015, Pearson sold the FT to the Japanese based Nikkei Group, a leading global media company headquartered in Japan. The purchase marked a historical record in terms of the amount offered for the purchase of a newspaper. This will provide new opportunities for FT | IE CLA, opening up the Japanese executive education market. Additionally, the Nikkei Group is particularly interested in expanding its activities into executive education.

The creation of FT | IE CLA aroused considerable expectation in the academic and business worlds, and in its first months of operation has reached its growth objectives, consolidating its operating teams, while at the same time attracting a large number of teachers and instructors to the faculty. I believe that in the future we will see more alliances between educational institutions and consultancies, and within the media and professional services sectors, all driven by the need to exploit synergies in the creation and distribution of content, to create economies of scale, and to attain a truly global reach. Who will be next?

2.4 Organizational Knowledge: A Company's Most Valuable Asset

Ever since Peter Drucker coined the term "knowledge workers" to define the majority of modern employees, a good deal of research and consultancy has centered on the phenomenon of how companies generate, exploit, and share knowledge with society at large.

An initial conceptual clarification is necessary. Knowledge is not equivalent to aggregated information. Collecting information is necessary, but not sufficient, in growing organizational knowledge. A company may compile tons of data on its customers through customer relationship management (CRM) programs but if that information is not adequately processed and applicable for decision-making, then that CRM may be a waste of resources. Indeed, effective knowledge management requires the relevant operating processes and routines to be embedded in the organization's culture. A good example of effective knowledge management is the case of successful family businesses. There, the gathering, transfer, and use of relevant information is institutionalized and produces its desired effects as long as the members of the family maintain their bonds. Here, as in other management areas, large corporations can learn many lessons from family businesses.

A second clarification about knowledge management is also required. Systems that process information from multifarious sources (such as CRMs, supply-chain management frameworks, performance scorecards, and so on) have become integral to managerial activity and have expanded amazingly over the past decades, necessitating a core presence in business education, including MBA programs. The sheer volume of available information of all kinds, and from multiple sources, is unprecedented and growing exponentially, and has given birth to new phenomena such as Big Data. Many maintain that we are witnessing only the very beginning of the age of information society, including being at the advent of the Internet of Things.

However, as previously discussed, knowledge management goes beyond the accumulation of data and is intimately related to the exercise of leadership. While managers may be in charge of IT, creating original organizational knowledge is intrinsic to a company's culture and mission, and involves the CEO and the top leaders.

There are many fallacies about knowledge management—for example, that it is organizations that possess knowledge and not the persons belonging to them. The development of the social sciences, and of institutional theory in particular, has helped us to understand better the nature of organizations. The "personification" of organizations allows us to talk about their resilience, their subsistence independent of their managers, and about corporate responsibility, as though companies had a soul. We also refer to organizations as possessing knowledge, given that information and knowledge can be codified and used in systematic ways by all company members. This is plausible, but do not forget that knowledge is generated and applied by persons. In fact, in the hypothetical case that an entire commercial team leaves a company it is doubtful whether its remaining CRM will be enough to retain its clients.

There is also a widely held belief that the best way to capitalize knowledge is to cultivate secrecy. Different studies show that secrecy is one of the least trusted ways to protect innovations.[14] It is much more effective to exploit time-to-market and pioneering advantages. At the same time, maintaining secrecy is very difficult today, when intranets and social networks are closely intertwined and the latest news is virtually known worldwide in real time. We know that Steve Jobs was very eager to guard confidentiality about Apple's new products, particularly when their launch was approaching, but that was probably more linked to a marketing *mise-en-scène* than to a culture of secrecy per se.

I would also argue that it no longer makes sense to separate internal and external communication. A better approach may be to target different stakeholder groups, varying the content and extension of the information and knowledge.

Too many companies believe they cannot make decisions unless they have all the information. Even if proper knowledge management contributes to improved and sounder decision-making, we all know that very rarely, if ever, do we have complete certainty or full data prior to our decisions. Paradoxically, one of the challenges for business school educators, in a world where knowledge grows faster than ever, is to prepare leaders who are capable of managing under uncertainty and ambiguity.

Contrary to popular belief, innovation and new knowledge are not generated in R+D departments. New ideas, services, and products, and revitalized uses or applications, may emerge from many different places across companies and at all levels. Experience shows that, in particular, good sales teams that are close to customers and attentive to their feedback may be a key source of innovation.

Similarly, many people mistakenly believe knowledge management requires sophisticated, costly IT systems. However, we can see in the case of family businesses, for example, that knowledge is shared without major investments in technology. IT systems do not solve management or process problems by themselves. Managers need to understand the purpose and uses of IT applications, the expected result, and their advantages and shortcomings, and not leave those decisions only in the hands of the IT team.

Finally, there is the fallacy that knowledge management requires the appointment of Chief Knowledge Officers (CKOs). The appointment of a CKO may be understandable when organizations are in emerging stages as regards the codification and distribution of information and knowledge. However, in true knowledge organizations, knowledge is generated and flows freely, but in a coordinated way, among the various divisions and units. Again, the use of information technologies and social networks and communities may foster a knowledge culture in unexpected ways.

Notes

1. The *Financial Times* publishes annual rankings of business schools and executive education centers under two different categories: open programs and custom programs. They have become a commonly

used tool to identify the leading academic institutions offering executive education. However, the rankings do not include other important players in the sector, such as consultancies and other professional services firms.

2. D. Bradshaw, "New Market Entrants Create Competition for Business Schools," *Financial Times*, May 17, 2015. http://www.ft.com/intl/cms/s/2/896cfdc4-f016-11e4-ab73-00144feab7de.html#axzz3s9PyKSdR.
3. Bersin by Deloitte, Corporate Education Factbook 2014; January 2014, and HR Factbook 2015: Benchmarks and Trends for U.S. HR Organizations, January 2015. http://www.bersin.com/Lib/Rs/ShowDocument.aspx?docid=18203.
4. M. Eiter, "Investigating Our Custom Clients' Evolving Needs," A Unicon Research Study, June 2009, p. 2.
5. J. Anderson and G. J. Van Wijk, "Customized Executive Learning: A Business Model for the Twenty-first Century," *Journal of Management Development*, Vol. 29, No. 6, 2010, pp. 545–555.

   An interesting account of corporate customer's views can be found in B. Büchel and D. Antunes, "Reflections on Executive Education: The User and Providers Perspectives," *Academy of Management Learning & Education*, Vol. 6, No. 3, pp. 401–411.
6. J. A. Conger and K. Xin, "Executive Education in the 21st Century," *Journal of Management Education*, Vol. 24, No. 1 (February 2000), pp. 73–101.
7. Over 90% of millennials strongly agree that an employer should provide on-the-job training and opportunities for continuing education, according to a survey authored by L. Stiller Rikleen, "Creating Tomorrow's Leaders: The Expanding Roles of Millennials in the Workplace" (Boston College, Center for Work and Family). http://www.bc.edu/content/dam/files/centers/cwf/pdf/BCCWFpercent20EBS-Millennialspercent20FINAL.pdf.
8. F. R. Lloyd and D. Newirk, "University Based Executive Education Markets and Trends," A Unicon Study (Consortium of Executive Education), 2011.
9. "Chief Learning Officer Business Intelligence Board," 2013. http://clomedia.com/articles/view/slowly-steadily-measuring-impact/2.

10. The Parthenon Group, "Learning and Development in 2011" (parthenon.ey.com). Duke CE, "Preparing Leaders for Todays Challenges," 2012 (dukece.com).
11. Henley Business School, "Henley Corporate Learning Survey," 2014 (henley.ac.uk).
12. A. Carter, "World's 50 Business Schools Professors," *Poets & Quants,* 2012 (poetsandquants.com).
13. S. Iñiguez de Onzoño, *The Learning Curve* (London: Palgrave Macmillan, 2011), Chap. 10.
14. For example, R. Grant, *Contemporary Strategy Analysis* (New York; Wiley & Sons, 2013); 9th edition, Chap. 7.

3

The Managerial Lifecycle

3.1 The Millennial Spirit

Most people joining companies nowadays belong to the so-called Millennial Generation (or millennials), born in the late 1980s and 1990s. Myriad surveys have tried to identify the defining characteristics of this group, but ultimately, the main preoccupation of HR managers is to attract and retain talent, and what interests them is whether millennials respond to certain types of incentives and whether they share the values of previous generations. Another important consideration for HR managers is how to integrate diverse generations so as to produce synergies from them.

One of the more apparent characteristics of the millennials is their familiarity with technology and their capacity to relate with each other through the social networks. A PwC survey draws the conclusion that millennials are attracted by working environments that are flexible and that they are far from convinced that the demands of work should mean sacrifices in their personal lives, or at least most of the time.[1] They value

© The Author(s) 2016   **39**
S. Iñiguez de Onzoño, *Cosmopolitan Managers*,
DOI 10.1057/978-1-137-54909-9_3

a strong, cohesive team-oriented culture in the workplace and require more frequent feedback than their older counterparts. The report warns against what it calls the stereotypes associated with millennials, for example that they are not as hardworking as previous generations. In contrast to their forebears, who were, and are still, prepared to spend long hours at the office, millennials focus instead on productivity, on getting the job done, and this can often be achieved, for example, by working from home.

Another survey notes that when choosing an employer, millennials look for companies that offer them opportunities for personal and professional development, and that they are attracted by businesses with a clear commitment to social responsibility policies.[2] The survey adds that 91% of millennial respondents wanted fast-track promotion, that 52% would like to pursue their career abroad, and that 71% believe their employers should be upfront and clear about bonuses and promotion opportunities.

Each generation has its own defining characteristics, but surely the point is that a manager's career should adapt to the life cycle, taking into account our personal development, biology, professional experience, relationships, networks, and reputation. In this chapter I look at the different stages of a manager's career, seen from the perspective of both the individual as well as the company.

Figure 3.1 reproduces the different phases of a typical manager's life cycle, as is discussed in this chapter, with a sample of educational programs targeted to professionals at each of this phases.

3.2   The Early Stages of a Career

By the time they graduate, many young people are already clear in their minds about what they want to do in life. Some have known since childhood or simply decide to follow in their parents' professional footsteps. The braver among them may decide to open their own businesses—arguably the most interesting option and one that, while it requires sacrifice to begin with, in the long term can garner the greatest rewards, financially as well as professionally.

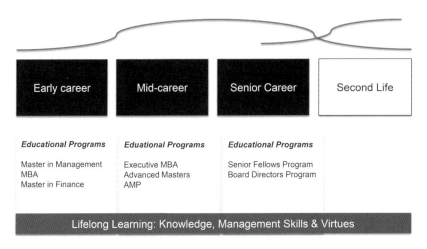

Fig. 3.1   The manager's lifecycle

Nevertheless, there are still a lot of people in their early twenties, fresh out of university, who are still undecided about what they want to do or which company to join, if any.

In the first place, and using a much-employed but appropriate analogy, a career is a long-distance race, and one that is subject to constant change and filled with uncertainty. There are three phases: what we might call the early years, followed by the mid-career, and finally, the senior career. But careers are rarely linear. Instead, they are prone to luck, good and bad, along with disruptive opportunities, and will require the help of mentors. I would say it is more appropriate to characterize a career as a series of different lives related to each other and that become a whole only when seen from the vantage point of later life. In short, most people live blended lives.

Amber Wigmore, Executive Manager of the Careers Department at IE Business School, likens the career path to an ice-skating rink: "Employers require agile individuals who proactively embrace challenges and continuous learning, including communication and interpersonal skills encompassing integrity, drive and cross-cultural sensitivity," says the former professional athlete, adding: "A career strategy starts with stretching in order to grow and maintaining balance and stability while gliding back and forth. Strategic lateral moves are often a faster way to the top, especially when they allow one to advance in a new direction, gain competencies or increase visibility in an organization or community. While recent graduates should not be afraid of taking a risk early in their careers, it is important to develop a career strategy for the short, medium and long-term. This is all a part of conducting a realistic self-assessment, of understanding strengths and limitations, in order to be assertive at just the right time, while ensuring they're prepared to succeed at the next level."[3]

It is important at the beginning of a career to avoid shortcuts, putting money first, and risking one's professional or private reputation. I'm not talking about making mistakes, which happens to everybody, but behaving ethically, and not putting too much emphasis on money early on. My experience has been that the best and the brightest are not overly concerned about their salary in the early stages of their career.

The two questions anybody who isn't going to work for oneself faces are which position to fill and which company to work for. In addressing the first question, candidates need to know their strengths and weaknesses, which can take time to become apparent. It is also natural to focus on the profession that most appeals, regardless of family pressures. From an employer's perspective, there are a few key questions worth asking that should give us an idea of who the person sitting in front of is. Are they an analyst, a back office person, or are they a front-of-house person comfortable with interpersonal relations? Are their analytical skills better than their colleagues' or are soft skills their forte? Are they a team player or a loner?

Do they like to think things through or bolt into action? Over the course of a career people improve their skills or acquire new ones, particularly if they continue studying. But initially, they should associate their strengths and preferences with the responsibilities of the post, so as to carry it out as well as possible, while increasing their chances of promotion. Some graduates have rather mystical ideas about consultancy or financial analysis, and apply for jobs in these areas without knowing what the work really consists of or without having the necessary skills. The best way to think about which job might suit best is to identify those areas of study where somebody might have excelled or that they particularly enjoyed. In any event, the first jobs people take do not determine how successful they will be in later years.

One piece of advice I often give to people looking for their first job is to remember that while it's important to read surveys and guides about careers and tendencies, they shouldn't be too influenced by data. Statistics shouldn't determine somebody's career: at most they should be an incentive to be the exception to the rule. There are successful CEOs with degrees in English Literature, or who have spent much of their career working in human resources rather than finance or sales.

The second big decision is which company to work for. There is a widespread misunderstanding that large multinationals are preferable. But don't forget that in smaller companies, candidates will likely take on more responsibilities and have a more direct relationship with senior management while developing a more global view of what the company does and how it does it.

That said, large corporations do offer candidates the chance to link their career with well-known brands. A line in a CV with the name of a Fortune 500 company or one of the big four from any global sector can be a deciding factor in future selection processes. For example, in the area of business schools, reputation is the first factor taken into account when teaching staff apply for new positions. In my opinion, aside from reputation, another fundamental decisive factor in deciding which company to join is the existence of internal training programs for young people who have recently joined.

Other criteria that somebody starting out on their career should take into account are whether the company has mentorship programs, along with diversity and inclusiveness policies. A recent study by Bain & Company,[4] revealed that while 43% of women aspire to reach top management positions at the beginning of their careers (compared to 34% of men); this percentage drops sharply within just two years to 16%, while for men the figure doesn't change. The main reasons, cites the survey, are the lack of support by bosses and supervisors, and a lack of role models: "The majority of leaders celebrated in a corporate newsletter or an off-site meeting tend to consist of men hailed for pulling all-nighters or for networking their way through the golf course to land the big account."[5] Increasingly, diversity and inclusivity programs are managing to counter these types of situations. Before choosing a company, candidates might want to know how many women there are at middle management level, how many in the C-suite, and how many sit on the board.

Another important decision that needs to be addressed is whether or not to go for a job that will mean an international posting. In the early stages of a career, before starting a family or when children are still young, working abroad is relatively easy, and a candidate with a few international miles on their CV is going to stand out.

Finally, and bearing in mind the drive that characterizes young professionals, they should not be overly concerned with immediate success. Generally speaking, success comes after lengthy effort—after one's prestige has been consolidated by working with a wide range of stakeholders, rather than through a lucky break.

In terms of considerations for recruiters, a quality to look out for in candidates is whether they have executive presence. As Wigmore notes: "It's never too early to focus on executive presence and on incorporating elements of personal branding and employability, even for recent graduates. In my workshops with pre-experience candidates, I set the stage by underlining the importance of non-verbal communication, emphasizing the fact that only 7% of our communication happens through the spoken word, while the rest is our facial expressions, gestures, posture and tone of voice."

Although patience is particularly necessary in the early stages of a career, it is important to monitor one's professional and personal progress, and to make sure that one's merits and efforts are being recognized. In general, for those who haven't been promoted within four years, despite working hard, or if other people with similar profiles have moved up or been given pay increases, it may be time to ask for a transfer to another department or even to think about moving to another company or sector.

Each generation tends to think it faces unique problems, which in some ways is true, but it is also the case that some questions about what we are to do with our lives are sempiternal. One of the best pieces of advice about choosing one's career can be found in George Eliot's masterpiece *Middlemarch*, which provides a vivid portrait of life in early nineteenth century England, a time when the country was changing rapidly. Fred Vincy's family wants him to join the clergy, but he feels no calling.

He asks his future father-in-law what he should do, and is told: "You must love your work, and not be always looking over the edge of it, wanting your play to begin. And the other is, you must not be ashamed of your work, and think it would be more honorable to you to be doing something else. You must have a pride in your own work and in learning to do it well, and not be always saying, There's this and there's that—if I had this or that to do, I might make something of it."[6]

3.3   Mid-Career: Crisis Time?

As the name suggests, the mid-career crisis is a fairly common event among executives between the ages of 40 and 55, affecting the married, divorced, those with children, and regardless of whether they have enjoyed professional success, how much money they have made, or their nationality.

Studies show that between these ages, many people's happiness experiences a U-shaped curve: they enter a crisis that seems to show no sign of bottoming out; but eventually it does, and they start to feel better, typically emerging from the crisis in their mid-fifties.[7]

It is no secret that mid-career is often associated with crisis, rupture, and change. Mid-career employees are more likely to question the meaning of their work, the value of their company's mission, their job autonomy, their contributions, and their relationships. Companies need to be aware of the warning signs. "Leaders mistakenly tend to leave mid-career personnel alone to work as they normally do," writes Australian educationalist Athena Vongalis-Macrow.[8]

Contrary to what most people making their way through a mid-career crisis think, the reasons for their predicament are not necessarily to do with their job, but are instead often the result of unavoidable biological factors. In fact, studies show that even our cousins the primates go through a similar phase. That said, we shouldn't rule out the impact of the stress generated by factors such as family responsibilities, the death of parents, the feeling that professional expectations haven't been met, the suspicion that their peers are doing better than them, or simply the big existential question as to whether "this" was what they really wanted.

These are issues that will sound familiar to many readers. It's important to remind people going through a mid-career crisis that they shouldn't feel guilty, harbor regrets, or be resentful toward others. Given that the mid-career crisis will eventually bottom out and then dissipate, we should remind people going through it to keep their spirits up—they will come out of this crisis, and in all likelihood, when they do, they'll see things from a different perspective, even taking into account the new realities and challenges associated with entering old age.

During the downward part of this U-shaped journey, a lot of people come to believe they need to make big changes in their lives, either professionally or personally, and begin looking for tantalizing paradises that really only exist in their minds. Because the truth of the matter is that mid-career is awash with opportunities that can take executives and entrepreneurs to a new level, if they know how to take advantage of them. This is the time when they secure their professional reputation, when their network of contacts is at its most extensive, when their leadership skills are at their height, and when they consolidate their management knowledge.

Monika Hamori, a professor at IE Business School, identifies three fallacies associated with the mid-career period.[9] The first is that changing company every four or five years creates more opportunity for promotion. But what Hamori's research shows is that on average, US and European CEOs have only worked for three companies over their career, and that a quarter of them have been with the same company all their working lives. Behind these statistics is the logic that the people who are valuable to a company acquire more knowledge about the business and the sector, as well as having an internal network that further helps them to develop. Loyalty has its rewards.

The second fallacy is that all professional moves should be in one direction: upward. But the truth is that around 40% of promotions are sideways, something that Hamori says provides executives with the big picture of their company and allows them to develop complementary skills. Lateral moves, together with traditional promotions, can be a way of assuring a route to the top positions.

Finally, there are two deep-rooted beliefs that aren't justified by the data: moving to another sector damages one's chances of promotion, and the only way to the top is by signing up to a big multinational. In reality, the truth is that around half of CEOs have experience in more than one sector, while a significant percentage of executives that move from a mid-sized company to a large corporation do so to a lower position, while moving to a smaller company tends to be to occupy a more senior post.

Generally speaking, mid-career promotions depend on leadership abilities and performance. Some specialists, such as engineers, exhaust the opportunities their technical profile offers and need to complement their expert knowledge and skills with a more general understanding of management, while developing their soft skills and boosting their directorial abilities. As a result, people in this situation frequently take an Executive MBA or Advanced Management Program, or will attend director development courses offered by their companies in-house.

For executives with families, and particularly women, mid-career is when we have to face up to the challenge of balancing our professional and personal lives. Fortunately, more and more companies are implementing special programs to try to halt the number of women who abandon the fast track to focus more on their families. By reducing the working week, and introducing flexible working hours and programs to help them return to work, among them online programs, organizations are able to keep female staff in the loop. Companies that adopt these kinds of policy obviously have a stronger chance of attracting and retaining women who have demonstrated potential early on in their careers.

From an employer's perspective, mid-career executives are one of the most important talent sources. They have had their learning curves and in general are more productive than their younger colleagues, while also having built up a solid core of knowledge and a large network that can make a major contribution to the business. At the same time, their salaries are higher than new signings, and promoting them can be held back by bottlenecks. Little wonder that the majority of downsizing measures in companies hit mid-career execs hardest.

To retain mid-career executives, as well as to further develop their talent, many experts recommend that human resource departments act on three fronts: (1) by offering competition remuneration packages that meet the circumstances and status of senior management, including pension plans offering long-term financial stability; (2) through flexible working hours that allow for a better work–life balance; and (3) by motivating executives to increase their productivity and by helping them identify with the company's strategy and objectives.[10]

Every year, I ask my Executive MBA students how many mergers and acquisitions they have lived through. Their answers provide food for thought: more than half have been through at least two, and more than a quarter through three or more. Mergers and acquisitions always bring the potential for downsizing. What does an executive do when he or she suddenly finds himself or herself out on the street in what they thought was the middle of their career?

By this stage in the game they should have built up a solid network of contacts, as well as accruing a good reputation in their sector. In such situations, aside from actively looking for work, directly or through head-hunters, their compensation package should provide some alternatives: signing up for an MBA program to boost their employability and bring them up to speed in management areas they're lagging behind in. Other former executives rebrand themselves as freelancers, giving them the chance to use their experience to create a professional services company they can dedicate the rest of their careers to.

Mid-career is also associated with overseas appointments. It is worth bearing in mind three things in regard to such opportunities. In the first place, is the impact on the family and the possible conflicts this might create with partners who are also working, and in which the better-paid side tends to win out, or with children, who may be at an important point in their education. Secondly, whether this is a genuine promotion or being parked in a side lot, meaning they'll miss out on development opportunities at the main office. Finally, it's important to bear in mind that the trend is for overseas positions to be occupied by local staff that are familiar with stakeholders and who understand the working culture better; companies are keen to avoid practices that could be interpreted as imperialist. In short, an offer to work abroad needs careful consideration of the pros and cons, along with much more detailed career and family planning than with other types of offers.

3.4   Planning the Second Half of a Career

Speaking at a conference in June 2015 on the future of finance organized by his Singularity University, Salim Ismail highlighted the impact of greater longevity on society at all levels. "We're adding three months to life per calendar year," he said, adding: "In a decade or two, or three, there will be a class of people taking treatments who can live for a long time, and that affects employment planning, retirement planning … Society will never have seen that before."[11] In other words, many of us around the age of 50 will probably live to beyond 100, which will mean giving careful thought to planning for the second half, or perhaps even the remaining two-thirds, of our lives, particularly bearing in mind that retirement age is being pushed back steadily by our governments, delaying access to a state pension.

Twelve years ago, when I was appointed Dean of IE Business School at the age of 42, I spoke with a friend and coach about further developing my potential and whether it would be a good idea to come up with a plan to continue progressing my career, particularly if things took didn't work out. He asked me the following question: Have you ever planned your career? "No," I answered. "Then why start now?" he said. I have to admit his advice made me feel better, and I stopped speculating about my professional future. What's more, one of the advantages of working in academia is that if you tire of management you can always return to teaching and research.

That said, given our extended life expectancy, it would be foolish not to have a plan B for one's working life after the age of 45 until whatever time we retire. This is when we are reaching the peak of our maturity, a time when we tend to be more emotionally stable, when perhaps we have attained a certain reputation in our work and among our colleagues, when we can benefit from our experiences in life, and can trust our judgment. In this senior age we are perhaps less motivated by financial reward and inclined to look for other satisfactions from our work; at the same time, we will have established strong ties with the organization that employs us that go beyond dependence on the boss or CEO.

In short, it is important for executives to maintain the initiative and to keep thinking about goals: "It's up to you to keep yourself engaged and productive during a work life that may span some 50 years," says Peter Drucker, the father of modern management, in an article that should be read by everybody.[12] He advises his readers not to leave this to the state or the company they may have worked for.

As we are living longer than ever before, which is surely something to celebrate, more than ever, executives need to think about a number of issues related to managing the future of their careers. In the first place, they need to be optimistic and see this later stage in life as the best of all of them, the one in which they can put to use everything they've learned so far. By now, they should have taken the Ancient Greeks' advice to know thyself, and acquired a little self-knowledge. But as Drucker explains, few people have any idea about their strengths and weaknesses. Introspection, the search for feedback from colleagues or coaches, the advice of friends, and taking into consideration the opinions of others are a good idea. In my experience, the passage of time generates two types of attitude among successful people: they are either arrogant and distant, or modest, open, and accessible.

Drucker lays out a series of questions aimed at helping those in the second half of their careers know themselves a little better, and thus get an idea of the management tasks they need to carry out. He asks his readers to think about how they learn best, whether we're readers or listeners, whether we work well with other people or are loners, and whether we are decision-makers or advisers. These are all relevant questions, because even if we've developed abilities that allow us to lead, even when we're outside our comfort zones, it is always best to build on our strengths rather than to try to correct our weaknesses. This advice is particularly relevant in the second half of our life, given that it is harder to correct long-established behavior patterns, not that it cannot be achieved through systematic practice.

You can't teach an old dog new tricks, as the saying goes. Which is perhaps why it stills comes as a surprise when older people show an interest in listening to what younger people have to say, and are open to new ideas and experiences. It's possible, in fact I would say necessary, to cultivate this attitude of openness to change as the years roll on, particularly if people are going to be staying in their jobs longer into the future. This requires humility, particularly with younger people—so much can be learned from them. Little wonder that a growing number of companies are implementing inverse mentoring programs wherein younger employees can open the eyes of their older colleagues to new trends, and explain technology and what the younger generation is concerned about.

Lifelong learning means just that: we need to continue acquiring new skills into old age. There is an increasing number of studies showing that using our memory and analytical skills helps generate new brain cells. And if executives can meet younger people when studying, then their education will be a much more enlightening experience. Study is a great leveler, and classrooms composed of students of all ages mean that younger members become older, so to speak, while the older participants are rejuvenated. Lifelong learning is one of the best treatments to combat old age.

The second half of a career, says Peter Drucker, can be an opportunity to change direction and start a new career, for example starting a company, becoming a social entrepreneur, or working for a not-for-profit organization. The professional experience accrued over the years, the network of contacts, and in some cases money saved up provide a head start.

The chance to begin a second career is particularly recommended for people who have had to take early retirement in their mid-fifties, or if the board of directors is changed, the CEO leaves, or the company is acquired or merged. The same might also apply to members of the armed forces passed up for promotion and assigned to the reserve.

Business schools are waking up to the opportunities this older student segment represents and are increasingly creating programs for professionals with a couple of decades of useful working life that want to change direction, start their own company, work with not-for-profit organizations, or put their experience to use as coaches or mentors.[13]

Mid-career also provides an opportunity to put a career in perspective, consolidating the arc of success in our earlier life. Frank Sinatra summed this up perfectly when he once said: "I'm flying high kid. I've planned my career. From the first minute I walked on a stage I determined to get exactly where I am."[14]

Maturity is also a time when the personal values that have guided us over the years stand out more, take on greater meaning, and can form part of a narrative to be passed on to younger generations. Among the opportunities available to older professionals is serving as a non-executive director. Highlighting the increased responsibilities of board directors, demands for greater compliance, the need to spend more time preparing or reading reports, as well as keeping up to date on developments in their sectors, Eugene H. Fram has suggested appointing people with more than 20 years' experience at director level to take care of these responsibilities. This is already the case for retired senior partners in accounting firms, who are highly sought after for their insight, assuming there is no conflict of interest.[15]

I have always believed that a knowledge and appreciation of the humanities and the arts deeply enriches the work of a director; after all, the true meaning of philosophy really only comes to us later in life. At the same time, cultivating the humanities allows us to see our endeavors in the context of other civilizations and other times.

If there is one thing we should have learned as we enter our fifties, it's that luck will have played a bigger part than we thought in our careers. A growing number of economists are now recognizing how unpredictable events can play a decisive role at certain moments. In his *Diamond Model*, Michael Porter, an expert in strategic management at Harvard Business School, puts luck alongside other factors such as government policy in establishing a nation's competitive strengths.[16]

The poet T. S. Eliot once said: "The years between fifty and seventy are the hardest. You are always being asked to do more, and you are not yet decrepit enough to turn them down."[17] Perhaps we are entering an age when the most productive and motivated generations will be those past fifty, and perhaps the best poetry and novels will be written not by people in their thirties, but by those in their seventies.

Notes

1. PWC, University of Southern California and London Business School, "PWC's Next Gen: A Global Generational Study: Evolving Talent Strategy to Match the New Workforce Study," London 2013.

http://www.pwc.com/us/en/people-management/publications/assets/pwc-nextgen-summary-of-findings.pdf.

2. Robert Walters Whitepaper, Attracting and retaining millennial professionals   http://www.robertwalters.com.au/wwwmedialibrary/WWW2/country/australia/content/whitepapers/millennial_white-paper.pdf.

3. Interview held on July 23, 2015.

4. J. Colman and B. Neuenfeldt, "Everyday Moments of Truth: Frontline Managers are Key to Women's Career Aspirations," Bain Report, June 17, 2014.

5. O. Badiesh and J. Coffman, "Companies Drain Women's Ambition After Only 2 Years," *Harvard Business Review*, May 18, 2015.

6. G. Eliot, *Middlemarch* (London: Penguin Classics, 2010).

7. A. Clark, A. Oswald and P. Wars, "Is Job Satisfaction U-shaped in Age?," *Journal of Occupational and Organizational Psychology*, Vol. 69, Issue 1, March 1996; pp. 57–81.

8. A. Vongalis-Macrow, "Stopping the Mid-Career Crisis," *Harvard Business Review*, September 7, 2011.

9. M. Hamori, "Job-Hopping to the Top and Other Career Fallacies," *Harvard Business Review*, July–August 2010.

10. K. Dychtwald, T. J. Erickson and R. Morison, *Workforce Crisis: How to Beat the Coming Shortage of Skills and Talent* (Boston, MA: Harvard Business Press, 2006.

11. Quote from Salim Ismail taken from exponential.singularityu.org.

12. P. Drucker, *Managing Oneself*, Harvard Business Review, January 2005.

13. E.g., the Senior Fellow Program at IE Business School or at Harvard Business School.

14. http://www.nybooks.com/articles/archives/2011/feb/10/portrait-artist-young-man/.

15. E. H. Fram, "Are Professional Board Directors the Solution?," *MIT Sloan Management Review*, Vol. 46, No. 7, Winter 2005.

16. M. Porter; *The Competitive Advantage of Nations* (Cambridge, MA: Harvard Business School Press, 1990).

17. *Time*, October 23, 1950.

4

Blending Technology and Learning

4.1   A Paradigm Shift

Technology, in parallel with developments in cognitive psychology and the education sciences, is producing a formidable paradigm shift in the learning process and the mission of educators. Traditionally, the objective of education has been to teach students the three Rs, prepare for a particular job, and to develop the skills required for them to take their place in society.

That said, the future of the learning process is increasingly being seen as an opportunity to develop and strengthen our individual qualities. This is where the real change lies. In the future, thanks to technology, education will not just be about acquiring the knowledge needed to do a particular job, but will allow us to help develop students' personalities, focusing particularly on their strengths, and adapting the amount of time spent studying to their needs and capacity, while measuring the results of the learning process and which teaching methods can best help with personal and professional development.

© The Author(s) 2016   **55**
S. Iñiguez de Onzoño, *Cosmopolitan Managers*,
DOI 10.1057/978-1-137-54909-9_4

This is where technology can contribute to the humanization of the learning process. We sometimes seem to think that technology is an obstacle to personalization, proximity, sociability, or humanity, but this is a fallacy rooted in ideas that technology is a threat to mankind—for example, the destruction of jobs through automation, and in short, that robots will end up taking over the world.

Integrating technology and teaching can help humanize, as never before, the learning process. Aside from adapting to students' circumstances, it brings teachers closer to their pupils, and pupils closer to each other. It also helps teachers, particularly with repetitive tasks such as assessing academic performance, passing on basic information, and answering frequently asked questions. In doing all this, technology can free up teachers' time, allowing them to focus on activities with greater added value for the faculty and the alumni alike.

Flexible, adaptable, intensive, user-friendly, even entertaining: these are the hallmarks of blended learning, combining online learning with a classroom-based approach. The advantage of online learning is that it can keep the learning momentum going by adapting to the circumstances of the learner. It also allows for greater interactivity with other participants.

Blended teaching methods, both in university education and in corporate learning, are here to stay. That said, there are still some analysts who play down the importance of the impact of online learning, or who argue that nothing can replace face-to-face teaching.[1] At this point, though, it is important to highlight that I am talking here about blended programs of the highest quality, with online modules delivered by the same academics as those giving classroom sessions, and to small groups of highly motivated students. There is a tendency to assume that online teaching automatically means the cheaper option of open entry, open access, as well as mass open online courses (MOOCs).

It is also widely believed that senior management is averse to online in-company training. This is largely true, but we need to ask ourselves whether this is a generational problem and whether the upcoming generation of CEOs, who will be much more familiar with the online environment and communication via mobile platforms, will be more receptive to these methodologies. We need only think back to the paneled boardrooms of a century ago, with their ornate furniture, coal fires, and other luxuries and compare with their twenty-first century counterparts, which rely on digital platforms, video conferencing, and other technologies that allow directors to communicate globally, round the clock.

Lindsay Redpath says that despite research showing that online learning can be at least as effective as classroom sessions, there is still a widespread bias against it among educators, HR managers, and executives.[2] Interestingly enough, some 80% of teachers with no experience of online teaching say it is less effective than face-to-face teaching, while the majority of educators with online experience say the results are as good, if not better. We should also add that many academics believe that online teaching will ultimately lead to layoffs.

This bias against online teaching also extends to many other professionals, particularly senior managers, who have been educated along traditional lines and tend to associate quality education with face-to-face teaching. But as Redpath argues, what really determines the quality of a program is its teaching and learning methods, not the means by which they are delivered: "While concerns about the quality of some providers may be valid, the method of delivery should not be confounded with the quality of an institution, its programs, or its teaching and learning effectiveness."[3]

Whatever the arguments, the simple truth is that educational institutions that offer blended courses, combining quality online training with traditional classroom teaching, are growing rapidly. For example, the 2015 report *Grade Level: Tracking Online Education in the United States* shows that 70.8% of chief academic leaders believe online education is a critical component of their long-term strategies (up from the 48.8% who believed this back in 2002).[4] At the same time, 77% believe that online training produces the same or better results than traditional face-to-face teaching. Just 28% admit that their teaching staff accept the value and legitimacy of online teaching.

A survey of corporate learning by Roland Berger estimated that in 2014, 77% of US companies used e-learning for their professional development programs, while in Europe more than 3,000 companies used these types of teaching methods. The same survey estimated that 90% of companies would be using e-learning platforms by 2017.[5]

It is clear, then, that blended learning is going to play an increasingly bigger role in executive education in cases where participants are unable to attend classroom sessions. The question is thus not whether blended learning is the future, or whether classroom teaching is more effective than online teaching, but, as Redpath asks: "What is the optimal mode or blend for a given learning situation?"

Obviously, achieving the right blend of online with classroom teaching will depend on the program's objectives, the profile of participants, the content being delivered, the abilities and skills being developed, and even costs, infrastructure, and the ability of the instructors and the faculty to teach online.

4.2   The Comparative Advantages of Blended Learning

In 1999 a significant number of universities, business schools, start-ups focused on education, and new for-profit entrants joined the e-learning educational sector. This seemed a promising new environment, attracting old and new players who saw the advantages that learning offered, aside from the possibilities of scaling up some educational activities, while at the same time reducing costs.

Some institutions rushed to invest large sums of money into developing e-learning platforms. One notable case was UNext, created by several business schools and individual investors, and conceived as a B2B company focused on developing and distributing online courses for businesses. UNext is believed to have invested several tens of millions of dollars to develop a platform that would be of use both in distributing educational content as well as in imparting online sessions. The project failed, perhaps because it was a decade ahead of the needs of corporate clients, and perhaps because it failed to see what is the basis for competitive advantage in this sector.

In *The Learning Curve*,[6] I looked at the UNext story in the context of the first wave of e-learning companies in an attempt to identify where it had gone wrong and what it had got right. One of my conclusions, based on my own experience at IE Business School, was that competitive advantage doesn't lie in developing an educational platform or in the technology that supports it. Educational institutions' advantage in entering the e-learning segment was based on the extent to which they where able to get their faculty and program managers involved in the online experience, helping them become innovators in all aspects of the learning process, and in being able to replicate and improve teaching through the traditional and face-to-face methods in the new virtual environment. The competitive advantage, in my opinion, was not about developing and exploiting an educational platform.

In the specific case of IE Business School, their competitive advantage, confirmed by their leading position in several rankings of online and blended programs,[7] was the construction of organizational routines, as well as of consolidated processes that included teaching staff, program directors, support teams, multimedia teaching content, and the pupils themselves, as well as how we replicated traditional teaching in this virtual environment.

IE's characteristic blended methodology combines face-to-face teaching at the beginning and end of the program, marking a counterpoint to the personal relationship between participants and the teacher. The online sessions are made up of synchronized sessions delivered through video conferencing, and there are also discussions using forums and chat rooms. This variety in teaching methods lends itself to the needs and availability of participants, helping with interaction, both in the classroom and the school. This learning circle is completed through the use of multimedia teaching methods, along with interactive cases studies and simulations that can be accessed from mobile platforms.

The development of digital platforms or learning management systems (LMSs) for online teaching is not necessarily an activity that can use the same assets or competitive advantages as in education. What's more, it is difficult to capitalize on the investment required to develop such platforms unless they are used by large numbers of students or institutions. That said, universities are usually unwilling to use platforms developed by competing institutions, particularly if they have to part with money to do so.

In fact, the majority of educational platforms or LMSs in use at the moment do not belong to traditional educational institutions. Among the most popular is Blackboard, with a 34.2% market share, followed by Moodle (22.8%), Brightspace D2L (10.5%), and Canvas (9.2%).[8]

There are also a growing number of software suppliers, technological solutions, and all kinds of educational applications. Given the growth in the educational sector and its importance in many developed countries' economies, it is no wonder that this sector will grow and will become more sophisticated. The big players with a presence in all sectors of education (from K-12 to higher education and lifelong learning), do not seem to be consolidating their position or showing themselves as able to offer a wide range of educational solutions. Pearson, which describes itself as "the world's largest education company,"[9] is probably the corporation that has tried hardest in this regard. In short, this is a sector that for the moment has resisted excessive concentration, although there is a growing trend for convergence, and in general, the different technological standards used by different providers are largely compatible.

4.3   Is Content Still King?

How should educational institutions consolidate their competitive advantages in offering significant development and innovation opportunities within this relatively fragmented context? Will the educational experience in itself, associated with a particular brand, continue to provide the main competitive advantage? Given that access to information these days is virtually limitless, with a lot of educational content distributed via openware, will content be king, and the companies able to create content, the winners? Or is it possible that an LMS platform will emerge as emperor? Perhaps some educational institution will combine their presence on all these fronts.

As things stand, it is hard to see how things will evolve; there is a lot of uncertainty and lack of knowledge about the effectiveness and viability of ICT in education. In my view, some analysts have overreacted, predicting a tsunami in the educational sector. Given the heavy regulation it is subject to, the existence of a powerful public sector, and the general inertia and conservatism of the main stakeholders, I don't think this is very likely. MOOC platforms are possibly the most representative players, with some aspiring to become content distributors and deliverers of programs offered by the traditional educational institutions. I will look in greater detail at the MOOC phenomenon and how they have disrupted education. Here, I assess the likelihood of MOOCs becoming dominant competitors and that of players being able to capture a significant amount of the added value generated by educational activity.

In my opinion, the two MOOC providers with the best long-term outlook are EdX and Coursera. EdX, set up by Harvard University and MIT, is a not-for-profit project that offers educational institutions providing free education the use of its platform, and it could well emerge as the benchmark in this segment. Partners that use EdX's platform for MOOCs or for their own programs receive a percentage of the earnings from programs of between 40% and 60%. More than 90 institutions in the educational and corporate learning sectors are currently using EdX's platform.

Coursera has more than 150 partners in the education sector and invests in creating MOOCs, with its partners receiving up to 50% of the earnings, although not when partners use its programs for internal use.

Will the biggest players in the education sector rush to join these MOOC platforms for fear of missing out? If this happens, then the leading MOOC players will likely develop into providers of content, LMS educational platforms, online meetings, and conferencing applications. Obviously, the competitive advantage of the universities and corporate learning units taking part in these huge consortia will be based on the differentiation provided by their academics, program managers, and by the characteristics inherent in the learning process.

Another interesting development is the growing use of the social networks as learning platforms and content distributors, particularly LinkedIn, which in 2015 bought Linda, an online training company focused on business, technology, and creative skills, in a move that was a clear attempt to create synergies with the executive development and education sector: "Our mission is to connect the world's professionals to make them more productive and successful."[10] As LinkedIn grows, while at the same time building a more complete picture of its members' activities, both personal and professional, it could soon be in a position to come up with courses to enable them to reach their goals.

4.4   The Teacher's Role Will Remain Key

The race has already begun, and educational institutions and businesses' corporate learning units will need to be open to innovation in the revived e-learning environment. In the past, developing educational platforms was the preserve of external providers. But the rules have changed, and EdX and Coursera will emerge as leaders in this sector, garnering an important part of the added value created by blended education.

In this context of growing integration between technology and teaching, the role of the teacher will become decisive, moving from that of the conductor of the learning process to managing online modules. This new breed of teacher will not only require a deep understanding of the area of study, but also be skilled in online teaching methodologies, the use of educational platforms, and in managing information and multimedia materials.

Attracting teachers to this new environment will not be easy, partly because so many academic institutions' collegial governments require substantial quorums to approve major curriculum changes. This collegial approach, which has deep roots in academia, could hinder a transformation process that requires a rapid response to the changes taking place, or be slow to adapt the role of academics to the new needs of education.

The other institution that could delay the adoption of new teaching methods and the integration of technology and teaching is tenure, which gives senior academic staff a lifetime position, regardless of how they perform or their commitment to innovation. Only those with a true academic vocation and a firm commitment to teaching will be motivated to operate change.

These two institutions, collegiality and tenure, are driving some institutions to try to bring about change by creating independent businesses such as Duke CE, or contracting teaching staff from outside the system, as has happened on Cornell University's New York campus.

In order to carry out the transformation that the new teaching environment requires, as well as to win the support of the most important group of stakeholders, I would suggest the following lines of action, based on the formula created by Tricia Bisoux and based on her survey of specialists operating in the sector.[11]

- *Economic and other incentives to encourage faculty to embrace new teaching methods.* As a rule, blended methodologies require more time and effort for teaching staff than face-to-face sessions. This could be compensated for by tallying blended sessions as equivalent to two or more traditional sessions.
- *Preparation, training, and use of MOOCs.* Involving teachers in preparing and delivering MOOCs and small network online courses (SNOCs) will help them better understand and appreciate online methods, as well as familiarizing them with the technologies involved.
- *Encourage flipping.* Face-to-face and online sessions can be turned into interactive experiences with the capacity to reach far beyond traditional teaching formats. This process will elicit better evaluations from participants, thus boosting teachers' reputations, which in turn will likely be matched by better salaries.
- *Enhance the role of academics as teacher*s. In general, teaching has been undervalued in recent years in favor of research. I have always said that the two aspects must go together. With this in mind, it might be worth reviewing the current system of incentives within universities, while recognizing and valuing the increase in teaching activity, particularly in the new online context. This is something that might best be addressed at origin—for example, during the PhD programs studied by future business academics with the aim of raising awareness and providing them with the skills they need to be good teachers.
- *Support.* It is also necessary to invest in the resources needed to develop the teaching skills required by teachers in the new online environment. This is where technology companies can play a fundamental role by investing in training, something that will be in their own interests, given that they will win over an important ally in the process.

Blending technology and pedagogy continues to provide new approaches in improving the learning experience. Much research has been conducted on the benefits and drawbacks of online courses, and more is needed if we are to increase our understanding of the transfer process from technology integration learning to the classroom.

4.5   The Robots Are Coming

Robots, replicants, androids, cyborgs, automata… call them what you will; we humans have been fascinated by the idea of creating beings to do our bidding since the beginnings of civilization. In *The Illiad*, Homer tells how Hephaestus, the blacksmith of the gods, created two golden maidens in his forge to keep him company, endowing them each with the powers of speech and reason. Ovid's *Metamorphosis* has Pygmalion carving a statue that he falls in love with, and which eventually comes to life. The tale was reprised in the early twentieth century by George Bernard Shaw, in which diction expert Henry Higgins believes he can teach Cockney flower seller Eliza Doolittle to pass herself off as a high-born lady, and of course he too ends up enamored by his creation.

And a 100 years later, motion pictures and television continue to reflect our fascination with robotics, highlighting the dangers they present to humans, which are as often sentimental as they are existential. Ridley Scott's seminal *Blade Runner* portrays a dystopian future where the dirty work is done by replicants—genetically engineered beings, with many human qualities, programmed to live for four years. The job of the film's hero is to liquidate rogue replicants, but of course, echoing Pygmalion, he falls in love, eventually fleeing with her, unsure if he can program her to live longer, and so coming to terms with our other obsession, mortality. In fairness, perhaps love really is the acid test of our relationship with automatons: if we can accept the idea of affection flowering between us and them, then surely it is just a short step to establishing other kinds of emotional ties such as friendship or the unique bond that can develop between a teacher and a pupil.

By 1968, when Arthur C. Clarke wrote *2001: A Space Odyssey*, which was adapted that same year into a movie by Stanley Kubrick, computers were already being used in some areas of business and were at the heart of our project to conquer space. In the film, a computer called Hal (Heuristically Algorithmic Computer) is partly responsible for running a spaceship on an interplanetary mission. In many ways, he is just another member of the crew, interacting with his human colleagues and is, for example, able to express humor. But Hal soon starts taking his own decisions, dispatching his human colleagues one by one, until the captain manages to disable him. In his final, pathos-filled moments, as he winds down, Hal intones an old music hall tune he was taught by his human creator. The story highlights our lurking fear about robots: that they cannot really be trusted, and that one day they will try to take over the world.

According to Martin Ford, author of the sinisterly titled *The Rise of the Robots: Technology and the Threat of a Jobless Future*,[12] computers are not so much taking over the world, as our jobs, which, thinking about it, may amount to the same thing. In part, the blame for this shift lies with globalization, says Ford, which has seen companies relocate to areas of the planet where wages are cheaper, a process aided by the decline of the unions. The result is growing inequality and an ever-widening wage gap. All this has created the perfect storm, with diminishing job creation, economic recoveries that take longer to generate employment, and soaring long-term unemployment that means lower wages and underemployment among recent graduates. This picture not only applies to the United States, but also to Europe.

Technology initially impacts most on sectors susceptible to scaling up, such as agriculture or industry, but over time it ends up affecting many other business areas. As we have seen over the last century, repetitive and routine jobs are the most vulnerable to the impact of technology. Automation is set to transform the logistics and transport sector in the coming years with the arrival of driverless vehicles, which are already being road tested in the United States and some European countries. At the same time, more creative activities, and those with greater added value, will also be hit. For example, the development of sophisticated software and the evolution of algorithms make it easier than ever for companies to manage big data.

High value added professions, such as financial analysis, are increasingly susceptible to automation, with complex applications that can follow the markets in real time, relieving analysts of part of their traditional workload. That said, a final risk evaluation of a financial operation is still an activity that, due in large part to a range of subjective factors, cannot easily be determined by algorithms.

The Rise of the Robots cites a recent study predicting that over the next two decades half of the jobs in the United States currently carried out by humans will be automated. Ford even goes so far as to suggest that this prediction is overly conservative: "A great many college-educated, white collar workers are going to discover that their jobs, too, are squarely in the sights as software automation and predictive algorithms advance rapidly in capability."[13]

As Ford points out, machines have already been developed that are able to beat humans at many intellectual tasks or at abstract thinking, among them IBM's *Watson*, which has scored better than many contestants on the popular US quiz show *Jeopardy*. Google Translate, while still far from perfect, is now widely used around the planet for basic communication, while a company called Narrative Sciences is developing ever-more sophisticated software capable of writing syntactically and grammatically correct reports, drawing on a wide range of sources and at speeds flesh and blood consultants cannot imagine competing with.

Narrative Sciences' software can write articles and highly detailed analyses synthesizing the vast amount of information available on the cloud or that is held by businesses and other organizations, formulating reports that can be used to make decisions. Furthermore, the software can be used to produce news items, literary reviews, and even opinion articles, and may well put many journalists out of a job or enable enterprising editors to set up new online publications with just a few key staff.[14] In fact, Ford notes that several respected major publications already use such software. With an eye on the future, the CIA has invested in Narrative Sciences, presumably hoping to make better use of the huge amounts of data it produces.

But other scholars have described Ford's vision of a robot-run world in our lifetime as exaggerated. Thomas Davenport, for example, Distinguished Professor in Information Technology and Management at Babson College, argues that even in the most automated sectors, traditional jobs will remain.[15] Automation will take time to implement, he says, and in the meantime, new types of jobs will appear. What's more: "there are cultural, legal, and financial barriers to widespread automation in a variety of industries (and) these obstacles won't ultimately prevent automation-based job loss, but they will certainly slow it down." Even Martin Ford has to admit that some sectors are relatively protected from the rise of the robots and, along with other academics, identifies healthcare, management, engineering services, and notably education as relatively resistant to automation.[16]

There are perhaps two main reasons why education is holding its own: greater government control and regulation, and the way in which most academic institutions are run, which tends to slow down decision-making processes.

Ford discusses the disruptive phenomenon of MOOCs, but concludes that for the moment, they have not had the devastating impact on formal education that so many people predicted. Our ivory towers will not protect us forever against the rise of the robots, and so we in academia are obliged to think about the educational tasks, specifically teaching, that could be substituted or complemented by technology. In short, will we really see classrooms led by a robot teacher?

Perhaps not, but there are any number of routine activities related to teaching that could easily be assisted or replaced by software—for example, marking papers, examinations, and assessing performance. At present, software applications are largely limited to marking multiple-choice tests or simple exams, but we can easily imagine how the programs Narrative Sciences is working on could be used to mark essays. That said, surely a student's final assessment, even taking into account the benefits with which technology can provide us in terms of performance, would require a more complex analysis that only a teacher could satisfactorily provide.

But as Ford notes, even when it comes to using computers to lighten their workload, relieving them of tedious tasks such as marking exam papers, many academics suspect the worst. In 2013 academics throughout the United States signed a petition against the introduction of automated essay scoring (AES) called Professionals Against Machine Scoring Student Essays in High Stakes Assessment. The organizers, from some of the United States' most prestigious academic institutions, dismissed AES as, "simplistic, inaccurate, arbitrary and discriminatory," citing research to back up their opposition, but without providing specific examples of where students' work had been mismarked. At the same time, we should remember that similar programs are used when processing applications to the same universities where many of these academics work.

When it comes to assisting with one-on-one activities such as tutorials, coaching, and mentorship, the software currently available is still not sufficiently developed, and progress is unlikely in the medium term, with the exception of activities focused on transmitting information and testing knowledge, and self-help activities to strengthen the learning process. The benefits of a motivation session with a coach cannot be likened to the limited replies currently offered by recent artificial intelligence projects such as EMOSpark, which can analyze 90 different facial expressions, thus supposedly enabling it to work out its owner's feelings and emit a corresponding message of greeting, encouragement, and support, for example.[17]

It is easy to see how lectures, where it is no longer necessary to attend in person, will soon be replaced by MOOCs, video conferencing, recordings in a range of formats, and other solutions. This is already evident in the phenomenon of the "flipped classroom," a blended approach where teaching is often delivered online, moving activities such as homework into the classroom, and thereby creating a more engaging and deeper learning experience. For this approach to work, the teacher must be able to innovate and take a more creative role, something that is still outside the remit of algorithms.

The flipped classroom extends the learning momentum, creating a continuum between classroom teaching and individual work, and aiding the understanding and application of ideas and concepts. To a large degree, learning is about repetition, as well as about finding ways for students to assimilate knowledge, and this is one approach that can help.

Similarly, interactive sessions such as case studies require a teacher to coordinate debate—again, a role unlikely to be given to a robot. But teachers can use computer programs to help them in the classroom, setting time limits, monitoring who is taking part, and aiding them in assessing students' contributions to the discussion.

Once again, artificial intelligence machines are more likely to be able to manage classrooms when it comes to activities related to facts, data, and information, which are easier for them to recognize. But at present, most such machines would not be able to deal with contributions that include abstract thinking, concepts, and more original thinking, all things that identify the brightest and best students.

Applications also exist that can measure the extent to which students are following and understanding topics by using rapid confirmation tests, and that over time will doubtless be perfected. We can also imagine more sophisticated solutions that adapt teaching to the habits and tastes of individual students, as well as to their distinctive forms of intelligence. For example, for a student with artistic inclinations, math could be explained in the context of painting or architecture, while more action-oriented pupils could be taught through the use of sports examples. The benefits of using specialist technologies in teaching certain groups who have difficulty integrating, such as autistic children, have already been shown.[18]

Technology also makes it possible to convert a classroom session into an event where content, information, and opinions can all be accessed in real time, while permitting the virtual participation of any guest, regardless of their location. Similarly, students scattered all over the world can interact, making for greater diversity, with the corresponding learning benefits. Many universities offer classes or seminars in which their own students connect via streaming with those from other places of learning. SNOCs such as those developed by schools that are part of the Global Network for Advanced Management use this type of methodology, allowing students from member business schools around the world to take part in classes.

Taking everything into account, my feeling is that technology isn't a zero-sum game. There is no point in thinking about the relationship between teachers and technology, or robots and software, in terms of one or the other; instead, they should be seen as complementary, the goal of which is to improve students' teaching and learning experience, and ultimately, education overall. In reality, teaching technology should be an extension of the teacher, which may mean at some point in the future that we see biotechnological integration. Bill Gates is one of the biggest investors in introducing technology into education, and asked the question in his *The Road Ahead* whether teachers should or could be replaced by technology—answering with an emphatic no.[19]

The creativity, originality, and sincerity of the best educators are not qualities that will ever be replicated in robots or programmed into artificial intelligence machines. Anybody who doubts this need only remember their school or university days and those unique moments when suddenly something makes sense, thanks to the patience and empathy of a skilled teacher. Do we really believe that a machine or an algorithm could ever help shape our character or inspire us to pursue a particular profession?

In Woody Allen's 1973 classic comedy *Sleeper*, the inhabitants of a future world have a machine, the *Orgasmatron*, a capsule big enough for two people that produces a near-instantaneous orgasm, seemingly without the need for any physical contact. As a result, we learn that the members of this civilization have become impotent, and that traditional forms of sex have been abandoned.

Let's imagine for a moment that we could invent a similar machine, but this time with didactic properties, called the *Educatron*, a capsule in which students could, in a few minutes, learn an entire university degree course, or acquire the contents of an encyclopedia, or learn any number of new languages. The problem with such an approach to education, as with the Orgasmatron's towards sex, is that we would miss out on the learning experience, on the effort and demands it puts on us, as well as the benefits of making choices and thinking things through. Learning from a teacher is not just about the end result, whether that applies to learning a theory or a language, but the road traveled and the means used to take us to our destination, which should be enjoyable, satisfying, and as valuable in terms of our personal development as in the knowledge accrued. And it is for this reason that those who see technology as a shortcut, as a replacement for the learning process, are wrong; there is as much value in what we learn as how we learn. Education can be seen as a voyage that lasts a lifetime, where knowledge of the destinations we reach is just as important as the experience lived along the way.

4.6   Taking MOOCs Seriously

A passionate debate has taken place in higher education between defenders and detractors of MOOCs. The former predict that MOOCs will sweep higher education like a tsunami;[20] the latter retort that MOOCs are just blowing a light breeze over education. Let me outline my own position here. I believe that MOOCs are here to stay and that they can complement traditional education in multiple ways, though their full impact will probably be only incremental and visible in the long run.

At the time of the emergence of MOOC platforms, three years ago, education analysts pondered about the disruptive impact of these new education offerings in at least three ways:

– *MOOCS would provide free and universal access to education*
   This proposition has not become reality (at least not yet). Despite the fact that many MOOCs are offered for free on the Internet, broadband, which is required to access these courses, is still very restricted or costly in many countries. The noble dream of reaching the entire world population, regardless of location or wealth, although possible in the future, remains a dream to be fulfilled, and it is not only in the hands of educators. Additionally, as of now, the statistics show that a large proportion of students attending MOOCs are graduate or even postgraduate students, and thus have a comparatively high purchasing power.
– *MOOCs would replace or substitute formal education*
   This has not happened and it is questionable whether it will happen in the future. Currently, few accredited universities validate MOOCs for academic credits and there are no formal degrees available consisting just of an aggregation of MOOCs. It is very likely that universities will proceed very slowly as regards the formal recognition of MOOCs unless there is clear potential for additional income flows (which is not the case), with the provision that all aspects regarding the quality of the learning process, for example admissions and assessment, are covered. Moreover, and perhaps the major challenge, employers just do not seem to recognize MOOCs as an equivalent preparation to traditional degrees at universities. Even business school students' awareness of them is in doubt.[21]

But the fundamental issue here is that formal education at universities comprise many different facets beyond the transmission of knowledge. The rich experiential dimension of studying at university, with all the surrounding learning services and the interaction of all the education stakeholders, cannot be replicated by MOOCs in their current format. This is also reflected in the high drop-off rate of MOOC participants—on average around 85% of the total enrolled—which has no comparison to that of formal education programs.

- *MOOCs would decrease the costs of higher education*
  This has yet to be seen. The production and delivery costs of MOOCs are potentially high, ranging from USD $3,000, for very basic courses, up to $250,000. Given that MOOCs do not replace traditional degrees, as discussed, the costs for universities running MOOCs have to be added to those for implementing existing regular programs.

In parallel, a question remains: what should be the business model of MOOC operators and how can they generate the necessary returns to at least cover the high investments related to production and delivery? I propose that there may be three alternative ways in developing a sustainable MOOC platform:

(1) Publicity or cross-selling services, analogous to the practices followed by some digital media.
(2) Charging fees for some courses, or progressively as participants get further services, such as mentorship, certificates or professional advice. This misses the original motto of MOOCs: *free for all*, a claim that most of its users take literally, who, (speaking from our experience at IE), rise vehemently at the mere hypothetical proposition of whether they would pay for it.
(3) Fund-raising or support from public institutions, a method chosen by some European portals that aggregate public-universities MOOCs, but this is not applicable to major MOOC companies since they operate for-profit.

Since MOOCs do not represent a frontal, nor devastating, threat for universities, how can we benefit from them? I list here some of the potential uses in our educational activities:

(1) *Complementing regular courses*: Given the pressures on the duration of programs, particularly among business executives, MOOCs may provide further depth on matters not covered in class or in areas beyond the core of the curriculum. Also, they may permit flip-learning where students can revise the content before class and spend class-time teasing out the finer points.

(2) *Delivering knowledge.* MOOCs are well suited for pre-program modules that may standardize participants' knowledge level, or they may provide introductions to most management disciplines.

(3) *Improving and enhancing institutional reputation and global visibility.* The high numbers of MOOC participants and the limitless geographical reach brings a unique opportunity to expand international brand reputation, particularly in those regions where your university may have less presence.

(4) *Exploring marketing initiatives and access to potential candidates.* MOOC distribution channels may provide traditional programs, admission possibilities for future students. What remains to be seen is if those channels are more effective than other ways of marketing your programs.

(5) *Exposing faculty to new methodologies.* Faculty members, associates and teaching assistants can all learn from the singular integration of pedagogy and technology provided by MOOCs, as well as the experience of handling large-scale student groups.

I am very confident that the impact of MOOCs will be very beneficial for most universities, as well as for business schools, at all levels of education, from undergraduate programs to executive-education non-degree offerings. MOOCs are another confirmation of one of my firm beliefs: the future of education is blended.[22]

Notes

1. P. Hunter, "Why MOOCs and Executives Don't Mix," *Management Issues*, 28 (April 2015). http://www.management-issues.com/opinion/7051/why-moocs-and-executives-dont-mix/.

2. L. Redpath, "Confronting the Bias Against On-Line Learning in Management Education," *Academy of Management Learning & Education*, Vol 11, No. 1, 2012, pp. 125–140.

3. Redpath, "Confronting the Bias," p. 27.

4. I. E. Allen and J. Seaman, "Grade Level: Tracking Online Education in the United States," February 2015. http://www.onlinelearningsurvey.com/reports/gradelevel.pdf.

5. Roland Berger, "Corporate Learning Goes Digital: How Companies Can Benefit from Online Education," May 2014. https://www.rolandberger.com/media/pdf/Roland_Berger_TAB_Corporate_Learning_E_20140602.pdf.

6. S. Iñiguez de Onzoño, *The Learning Curve: How Business Schools Are Reinventing Education* (London: Palgrave Macmillan, 2011), pp. 75–79.

7. *The Economist*, Executive MBA Rankings 2015, http://www.economist.com/whichmba/executive-mba-ranking/2015. *Financial Times*, Online MBA Ranking 2015, http://rankings.ft.com/businessschool-rankings/online-mba-ranking-2015.

8. ELearning Industry, "Choosing An Online Learning Platform: Which Makes Sense?". http://listedtech.com/lms-market-share/.

9. www.pearson.com.

10. Mission statement of LinkedIn, as formulated by Jeff Weiner (www.linkedIn.com).

11. T. Bisoux, "The Blended Campus," BizEd, July–August 2014, pp. 17–22.

12. M. Ford, *The Rise of the Robots: Technology and the Threat of a Jobless Future* (New York: Basic Books, 2015). References to this book here are made to the Kindle version.

13. Ford, *The Rise of the Robots*, location 147.

14. An article in *Wired* mentions this software. See S. Levy, "Can an Algorithm Write a Better News Story Than a Human Reporter?", *Wired* April 24, 2012. http://www.wired.com/2012/04/can-an-algorithm-write-a-better-news-story-than-a-human-reporter/.

15. T. H. Davenport, "Just How Serious Is The Automation Problem?", *The Wall Street Journal*, May 20, 2015. https://www.linkedin.com/pulse/article/just-how-serious-automation-problem-tom-davenport.

16. C. Benedikt Frey and M. A. Osborne, "The Future of Employment: How Susceptible are Jobs to Computerization?", 17 September 2013, Department of Engineering Science, University of Oxford, Oxford, UK. http://www.oxfordmartin.ox.ac.uk/downloads/academic/The_Future_of_Employment.pdf.

17. S. Adee, "Say Hello to Machines that Read your Emotions to Make you Happy," *New Scientist*, May 14, 2015. http://www.newscientist.com/article/mg22630212.900-say-hello-to-machines-that-read-your-emotions-to-make-you-happy.html.

18. T. R. Goldsmith and L. A. LeBlanc, "Use of Technology in Interventions for Children with Autism," *JEIBI*, Vol. 1, Issue 2, 2014. http://files.eric.ed.gov/fulltext/EJ848688.pdf.

19. B. Gates, *The Road Ahead* (Spanish edition: *Camino al Futuro*) (Madrid: McGraw Hill, 1995), p. 182.

20. www.nytimes.com/2012/05/04/opinion/brooks-the-campus-tsunami.html.

21. www.ziprecruiter.com/blog/2014/06/09/do-employers-take-massive-open-online-courses-seriously.

22. Della Bradshaw, "What Moocs Mean for Executive Education," *Financial Times*, May 11, 2014.

5

Measuring the Impact of Executive Learning

5.1 Looking for an ROI from Executive Education

Intuition, experience, and myriad surveys show that developing talent is directly related to the investment companies make in training their managers and directors. Yet conclusively demonstrating that a specific investment in a training program has produced measurable results in terms of a company's performance is another matter.[1]

A survey carried out by Ashridge Business School for Unicon showed that 88% of HR heads it talked to agreed that "HR professionals will have to get better at improving the worth of executive education in the future," along the same lines as other departments have shown that other intangible resources can be measured in some way.[2] The survey also showed that 43% of HR professionals think that in most cases it is not possible to objectively calculate the ROI of executive education initiatives, and concluded that finding a way to do so was akin to the search for the Holy Grail.

© The Author(s) 2016
S. Iñiguez de Onzoño, *Cosmopolitan Managers*,
DOI 10.1057/978-1-137-54909-9_5

CLOs have long sought for ways on how best to measure the impact of their companies' investment in training and development programs for executives, and whether they increase profitability. Sadly, the results of their efforts have not always been entirely satisfactory. Perhaps there is simply no model as yet that establishes a cause and effect between better-trained executives and a bigger number on the bottom line. It's pretty much the same story with corporate social responsibility (CSR): are companies more profitable because they have invested in CSR, or do they invest in CSR because they are already more profitable than those that don't? The fact that there is a relationship between one and another doesn't mean that there is necessarily causality. It's basically a chicken and egg situation.

I understand the pressure CLOs are under to justify training in terms of ROI. As with any other aspect to do with assigning resources in companies, an economic explanation that goes beyond the qualitative arguments about education boosting talent is required. CLOs like to keep things simple and talk in the same language as CFOs.

Nevertheless, the search for the magic formula that connects investment in training with the bottom line continues without success. Until new methods are found that can establish that connection in the future, perhaps in tandem with analytical accounting that links the quantitative with the qualitative, the only hope for the moment is to try to connect an investment with the individual development of the executives involved, by measuring how education can bring about a transformation in terms of his or her knowledge or directorial skills.

In this chapter, I discuss assessing the impact of training on a business's performance and value creation, both from the individual and the corporate perspectives. As regards the individual, I will look at the most commonly used methods for measuring how successfully the objectives of training have been met. From the corporate point of view, I will examine the best-known systems used to accredit or validate in-company training, as well as the overall structure dedicated to developing talent in a business, as is the case with corporate universities. As discussed earlier, this is essentially a qualitative analysis, although its impact on the company's results is hard to question.

Evaluating the impact of training can be done in two main ways. The first focuses on the improvement experienced by the individual or participant, measuring his or her progress in terms of knowledge acquisition or the development of new directorial or interpersonal skills. The second is based on evaluating the quality of the activities of the HR department or the corporate university by carrying out an assessment as to whether they are aligned with the company's strategy, its contribution to growth, and in general, to its dynamism as a corporate learning organization.

5.2   Assessing the Impact of Education on an Individual

Traditionally, the paradigm used to measure the impact of training on the individual is the Four-Level Evaluation Model, created by Donald Kirkpatrick.[3] The four levels, or different evaluation areas, measurement the effectiveness of a program, and are ordered on the basis of their complexity, ease, and even whether it can be implemented.

5.2.1   Level One

This measures participants' response and satisfaction. Normally, the effectiveness of this level is measured through surveys after the session or course, registering the opinion of participants about the teacher's abilities (e.g., communication, knowledge, attention paid to participants), and how interesting or useful the material was. This is the most commonly used approach, and possibly the one most valued by CLOs, who are under pressure to offer courses that capture participants' attention.

Perhaps the biggest risk in giving such importance to evaluation surveys is that it may overrate the performance of professors: "star academics" and gurus tend to deliver very entertaining and interesting courses, even if there is little evidence of any improved learning experience in relation to effort or the development of certain skills. But the simple truth is that satisfaction surveys are necessary; participants on executive training programs must score at least 4.5 out of five, or 8.5 out of 10. We should remember that directors attend these types of programs while continuing to work, sometimes giving up their own leisure or family time, meaning that CLOs expect them to be both entertaining and informative. Poor results in satisfaction surveys do not just affect teachers of the institutions delivering the program, but also directly the credibility of the CLO.

5.2.2 Level Two

This focuses on what participants have learned on a course and looks at two main areas: knowledge and skills. In relation to knowledge, this tends to divide into concepts, models, and ideas, which can be measured through role-playing exercises, exams, quizzes, or tests, as well as the application of this knowledge in practice, for example through participation in projects or problem-solving.

The second area of learning, related to skill acquisition, is harder to measure, particularly in the case of abilities related to our personalities, such as leadership. That said, there are abilities that improve over time and can be measured, for example, spoken and written communication, leading groups, time management, delegating, and so on.

5.2.3 Level Three

The third level of evaluation assesses the impact of training on participants' behavior. The first difficulty with this approach is that changes to behavior only manifest over time, whereas CLOs and other department heads are under pressure to obtain results in the short term.

As we'll see elsewhere in this chapter 6 companies are under pressure to shorten the length of in-company training programs, which makes it harder for them to impact positively on participants' behavior, given that this depends on repeated exercises and messages, interiorizing, and comparing with alternative situations, before and after. One way of prolonging the educational moment to bring about changes in behavior is by tracing the continuum between training and work, for example by running sessions or modules periodically over a period of, say, a year after a course.

5.2.4 Level Four

This last level refers to the combined results of a training program, which is to say on both the individual and the collective. These results tend to be of a qualitative nature, for example, improved morale, a better understanding of the company's mission and values, and a greater willingness to focus on the clients' or stakeholders' needs. The effectiveness of training programs can also be measured through increased sales in a department where the workforce have attended a program, or through the launch of a new business unit discussed or conceived during a program.

One thing is clear: there is no sense in expecting any immediate results from training or development programs. I remember the case of a middle-sized medical products company, a leader in its region, that commissioned my business school to come up with a year-long management skills program for directors considered to have potential, many of them in sales. The CLO was expecting an increase in sales within a few months of the program starting, but this wasn't going to happen, in large part due to the participants' dedication to the program and its intensity. Nevertheless, the year after the program ended, sales rose by 25% on the previous year. Added to which, more of those directors with potential stayed on, they identified with the company's aims, and morale rose. Logically, given that this was only a medium-sized company, with less than 500 directors—although it had a growth and diversification plan—it was recommended that it repeat the program every two years, so as to avoid any incompatibility between dedication to the program and the sales increase that could impact on its results.

There are other ways to measure the impact of a training program on participants and companies. For example, a multinational that develops software measured the success of a program delivered by two well-known business schools on the basis of the number of participants that were promoted to vice president.[4] But this approach raises a number of doubts: was the program competing with others of a similar nature offered by other business schools? Such an approach would allow for measurement of several programs at the same time. On the other hand, were participants selected a priori for their potential to occupy vice presidential posts?

If so, then the program could be a good platform for testing their abilities and leadership, and even to boost them.

That said, converting the program into a selection process for a limited number of people could distort the learning process, increase competitiveness, and undervalue the results of those who weren't promoted but who could possibly continue to make a valuable contribution to the company.

As mentioned previously, it is possible to create relatively sophisticated mechanisms within Kirkpatrick's evaluation method. It is easier to assess the impact of training in levels one and two, as well as in relation to some of the results at the individual or collective stage in level four. Then there is the question of whether there is a direct causal link between the collective objectives that are reached and a specific training program. That said, level three, which assesses the impact on behavior, seems to raise the most problems: either programs need to be of significant duration or participants need to be monitored for several years after they have completed the course. Longer programs need to include mentorship that supports candidates with the best potential for senior positions.

A credible evaluation also requires the inclusion of other stakeholders in the design of a program, particularly senior management. This means clearly establishing the objectives of the program, how they fit with the company's strategy, what the desired learning outcomes are, which methodologies to use, and of course implementing monitoring mechanisms that analyze the impact of training over time, and not just in the immediate aftermath of delivery.

Although Kirkpatrick's model made a good start in trying to measure the cost-effectiveness of training, and is still widely used, its limitations have also become clear. The main criticism is that it doesn't answer such key questions as: "Are we doing the right thing, and are we doing it well?"[5] It's a simple enough model to use and is one that provides a systematic tool to demonstrate the rest of the firm's business units. Furthermore, Level Four, which helps measure whether the company is achieving its objectives, is attractive to HR directors because it links their initiatives directly to the company's bottom line.

Perhaps Kirkpatrick's main contribution was to pave the way for other evaluation systems that delved deeper into each of the four levels, along with other approaches to measuring the impact of training, both on the individual and the company. A McKinsey survey carried out among HR managers on measuring the impact of training showed that this question is of considerable importance when deciding on which supplier to go with. That said, only 25% of those surveyed said that their programs were effective at measurably improving performance. On the other hand, 8% of those questioned said they already had methods for analyzing the ROI in training. The survey concluded that for a program to have any real impact on the company's activities, the curriculum should reflect its key business performance metrics.[6]

5.3   From Individual Assessment to Corporate Results

A survey commissioned by Unicon,[7] the executive education consortium of business schools, reveals a number of different practices adopted by some of its members in developing custom programs, showing that the adoption of diverse and complementary systems in the design phase, and in accordance with the agreed objectives of HR directors, is the trend. Measurement systems are no longer solely focused on the number of participants and the cost associated with each, or on satisfaction, widely known as smile sheets, and instead take into account more qualitative and sophisticated topics such as the ideas discussed during a course that were subsequently put into practice, or which management models were later applied by the company when making key decisions.

Fred Reicheld of Bairn Consulting has come up with another measurement model known as the Net Promoter Score (NPS), which focuses more on participants' satisfaction levels, based on the answers to questions such as: "How likely is it that you would recommend this program to a colleague?" Responses are collated between promoters (those that answer between nine and ten), passives (between seven and eight), and detractors (between zero and six). The NPS is calculated by subtracting detractors and passives from promoters. The system is clear and allows HR directors to base their decisions on the majority opinion.

However, as discussed, such an approach can favor gurus and star teachers who are excellent communicators, but whose sessions may not have much to do directly with the company's strategic needs nor reflect its organizational singularity. The system doesn't necessarily penalize those courses where the work load is heavy, but does require participants to make more effort, assuming the tasks assigned are directly related to the challenges of their own day-to-day tasks or those they will take up in the near future. Similarly, my own experience is that tasks that require additional work outside the classroom, such as extra reading, can have a negative impact on participants' satisfaction levels because they may not be aware of the return in terms of individual progress.

The Unicon survey also examines the approach taken by three business schools. Wharton continues evaluating its programs after they are finished. Participants identify three specific things they intend to implement in the following six to nine months, and each month are contacted by the school to chart their progress. The information is then sent to their employers, but without naming them.

Duke Corporate Education (Duke CE) works with its clients to identify their objectives from a given program and calls this Design to Outcome. In five successive stages, Duke CE's representatives sit down with its clients to see how they can generate the results they want from a program. The teaching staff, coaches, and presenters that have taken part in the course know these objectives and try to align their input to achieve them. It also establishes mechanisms to measure how successful they have been in achieving these objectives and in which time frame.

In general, we can see that these measuring systems are being adapted to the needs of companies, to their strategies, and to the demands of HR directors, while at the same time compared to existing evaluation methods. However, this increasingly customized approach has been questioned by some. Dominique Turpin, the dean of IMD, argues that it is better for companies to select a standard assessment model of senior management's skills, taking advantage of the accumulated experience in applying them, and that allows for comparison with other companies in the same sector, for example.[8] Where Turpin does see space for the development of customized measurement tools, once the standard assessment has been carried out, is in creating models to measure leadership development or organizational skills, and that is in line with the strategies and objectives of the company.

Benchmarking practices of human resource management can be a win-win experience for the companies taking part. For example, IE Business School's human resources department has set up a club made up of Spain's leading companies that provides them with a report detailing the most important aspects of performance, along with a personalized, benchmarked report about each company which includes a wide range of human resource indicators.

5.4 Assessing the Performance of Corporate Learning Units

The growth of Corporate Learning Units (CLUs) over the last three decades has been significant, particularly within large companies, and it would seem that they will play a bigger role in the future. As we have seen, in some cases these CLUs are run along corporate university lines, with their own identity, a campus, specific programs, and even their own teaching staff, even if lecturers will be affiliated principally with other institutions.

The growth in CLUs has seen the development of accreditation and quality control systems in parallel. At the same time, some corporate universities are now looking for growth beyond training their own teams, and are trying to attract external participants. This expansion of activities and external projection has raised the need for acquiring formal recognition, for the same kind of accreditation that traditional universities are given, so as to be able to compete on a level playing field to attract students and teachers, and to be able to access research funding, for example.

Some commentators have even suggested that corporate universities could become direct competitors of traditional universities. Writing 15 years ago, Gordon Thompson describes the "rapid expansion in the 1970s and 1980s of accredited degree-granting institutions created and sustained by corporate sponsors prompted speculation that many more corporate colleges would be created and could pose a significant competitive challenge to established universities and colleges."[9]

This argument is backed by the decision of the American Council on Education's Program on Noncollegiate Sponsored Instruction (ACE/PONSI) to accredit courses run by some 250 different organizations, among them McDonald's, Ford, and Bell Telephone, recommending that these course be given university-equivalent credits.[10]

More such initiatives are underway to formally recognize learning programs delivered in-house, and for the credits garnered for attending them to have the same value as those attained on a university course. A number of accreditation agencies are also widening their areas of activity, for example the European Foundation for Management Development (EFMD) with its Corporate Learning Improvement Process (CLIP) system, or Germany's FIBAA, which accredits business schools—both now accredit CLUs.[11]

Another trend worth highlighting is the recognition of credits, equivalent to those obtained on a university course, for working as an intern at a company or for other informal learning processes. There is a consistent strand of research which suggests that managers learn as much, and potentially more, from their day-to-day work, from colleagues, from observing managers, and from other life experiences as they do from management training programs.[12]

Richard Dealtry notes: "Accreditation has moved away from highly structured notions of formal 'campus based credit based qualifications' to new forms of learning based accreditation using 'organic learning experiences in real time events'."[13]

5.5   Corporate Learning Meets Accreditation: CLIP

One of the most interesting recent developments in assessing corporate learning is the EFMD's CLIP system, which so far has accredited CLUs of 18 multinationals, the majority of them based in Europe, although it is set to grow in Asia and other regions. CLIP's accreditation process focuses on CLU activities and the extent to which they align with a company's strategy. Being a peer review system, the final decision is taken by an accreditation body made up of four corporate representatives.

The CLIP accreditation system has 35 quality standards structured in eight chapters that look at the CLU's mission in relation to the company's overall strategy, its programs and their resources, management of external suppliers, which is to say the educational institutions that are subcontracted to provide programs, inclination toward innovation, and global reach. The accreditation program includes a self-assessment report by each candidate company, along with an on-site visit by a team of auditors made up of peer companies and academics specializing in executive education. CLIP is the result of a joint initiative by HR directors and EFMD members, inspired by EQUIS, the business school accreditation system.

Gordon Shenton, one of the founders of CLIP, told me the idea came as a result of companies asking the EFMD for an accreditation system to recognize their courses; they wanted more than just consulting or benchmarking.[14] "A representative from a well-known company said to me: 'It's important for us to have external recognition'," Shenton says. Unlike university accreditation systems, which are looking for external approval to raise their profile and use it to market themselves, businesses were interested in CLIP because they wanted other organizations to recognize their training programs, particularly those for senior management. The idea principally was to legitimate their human resource policies.

One of the most debated issues right from the start was how to design an accreditation system that preserved the already existing diversity between companies in different sectors, countries, and strategies. "You can't put learning organizations into a mold: there is no one single solution that fits all," says Shenton. This is particularly true of the corporate world, where each company has a very different culture, structure, and activities. As with other accreditation systems, the challenge is to design a system that recognizes best practices, isn't overly regulatory, and leaves space for diversity, innovation, and even disruption.

CLIP's standards have even been used by some corporations to design their own corporate universities. One of the founding principles of the CLIP accreditation system is effectiveness: to what extent CLUs are meeting their objectives in parallel with the company's strategy. CLIP also assesses the structure of the CLU: which departments, and whether they have sufficient resources, financial and human. It also looks at whether its activities translate into a portfolio of programs and services. For example, corporate universities tend to offer more than just programs; they also take on the role of consultants, as well as tutoring and coaching their executives, while distributing the organization's knowledge and culture. CLIP effectively articulates a value chain of training and development services within a company.

Other areas that the CLIP accreditation system looks at are the objectives of training and development programs and just what it is that is delivered in the end. If, for example, the objective is focused on leadership development, this requires a different approach than that taken if the objective is middle-management skills. CLIP also looks in detail at the interface and the relationship between the different human resources processes.

CLIP is governed by an accreditation committee made up of four elected members who are renewed periodically. It decides on which CLUs are eligible for evaluation, as well as validating the recommendations of peer review teams, and decides on the final accreditation.

Shenton says his experience of CLIP is very satisfactory, and predicts a bigger role for HR departments. But he adds: "You don't find many companies that are not even close to perfection." He explains that CLIP's mission is not to compare corporate universities with traditional universities, although it does look at the connections that might exist between the two, for example in developing research projects. Neither has it considered accrediting consultancies focused on training or so-called executive education centers. Its remit is strictly the CLUs of large corporations.

During the first years of the system, the Achilles' heel of many organizations has been the institutionalization and continuity of training and development activities. Due to the frequent changes that take place in companies and the resulting instability of HR [Human Resources] initiatives, Shenton adds: "Changes at the top, for example the CEO, may result in dramatic changes in the HR management and CU [Corporate University]. In the university world there is much more inertia, historical, and institutional continuity This might be the downside of corporate universities." The upside of this is how effective many corporate universities are in diffusing corporate culture or spreading the company's strategy, particularly in cases of mergers and acquisitions.

Shenton says the future of in-company learning will in large part depend on the increasing digitalization of many services related to leadership development and talent management, along with the impact of technology on many processes managed by CLUs. What's more, the search will be on for a balance between individual development and organizational learning (individual vs. company), along with that between formal learning, through corporate learning programs and activities, and informal learning, task implementation, and what our colleagues at work teach us. "There is no denying that we will lose part of the spontaneity associated with informal learning along the way. At the same time, informal learning can be dysfunctional if it is not aligned with the interests and objectives of the company."

Shenton also says CLIP can be applied to any CLU, anywhere in the world, but adds that this doesn't mean it is automatically appropriate for any company. He also points out that each company will organize its training needs as it sees fit, suggesting that over time we will likely see greater decentralization, with individual business units managing their requirements. He adds that it is important to be aware of sensibilities when training takes place across different departments. In some companies there is overlap between the head of HR and the director of the corporate university, which makes perfect sense if the asset we're talking about is people. The challenge is integrating these responsibilities.

5.6   The Future of Open Programs: Dominique Turpin, Dean of IMD

One of the world's most respected executive education centers is IMD, based in Lausanne. Dominique Turpin, the school's director, has been pursuing an expansion strategy in Asia, while at the same time consolidating a portfolio of open programs that have been acclaimed for their innovativeness.[15] Asked about the most significant trends in the open programs segment, Turpin identifies four.

In the first place, competition between the different players is intense and growing. For example, in the second half of 2015, Turpin and his team identified 120 new programs in Asia. As a result of this competence, says Turpin, it isn't clear whether all these business schools will survive.

Secondly, it's not always clear how programs really differ, and there is a certain degree of commoditization. On the other hand, even though innovative proposals do percolate from time to time, some competitors are able to replicate them quickly, meaning that there's not much advantage to be had from being a pioneer.

Thirdly, a growing number of companies are cutting back spending on open programs for their executives in favor of in-company programs, which are shorter and focused on achieving specific company goals.

Reduced spending by companies on open programs means it is down to individuals to decide, which in turn has important marketing consequences. The appeal of open programs for executives is that they allow them to spend more time at their workplace, rather than having to attend purely classroom-based teaching. Turpin says that executives need some coaching from time to time to make the most of online programs, and that it is a good idea to blend them with classroom teaching, especially in the early stages. In the final analysis, Turpin believes that nothing can replace face-to-face teaching in a classroom, which allows students to discuss the issues with their peers—particularly in the case of senior management. In his opinion, there is a bigger market for online programs aimed at middle managers, but that it is a highly competitive segment.

Although in recent years consultancies have also entered the executive education segment, Turpin believes that business schools have the advantage of being seen as more impartial, as well as having better teachers and program facilitators. In cases where clients have asked for a mix of academics and consultants, there is evidence showing that business school teachers outperform. "Consultants tend to provide solutions, while teachers show you how to find the solution," says Turpin, adding that he doesn't believe the consultancies' hearts are in teaching, given that it is not one of their core businesses and neither does it generate the margins their other divisions do. He believes that at most they will end up creating specialist training programs aligned with their other products and services.

As regards assessing the impact of programs, Turpin's experience is that a particularly effective evaluation can be made on the basis of the individual projects participants created during the program and which they subsequently implemented in their business schools. What's more, IMD's program management team is in touch with HR heads who give them feedback about their executives' development when they have finished a program. Another way to measure impact, says Turpin, is to see which participants go on to be promoted.

IMD has worked closely with corporate universities and corporate learning units since its beginnings, for example, with Nestlé, one of its founders. Turpin believes that corporate universities have upped their game in recent years and are developing more internal programs. There is an opportunity for business schools to work with corporate universities, assisting them in the design and implementation of their programs. IMD has assigned a senior member of staff to work with corporate universities.

One of the biggest challenges business schools will continue to face is how to attract and retain the best teachers. IMD doesn't divide its teachers into different categories, says Turpin: "This avoids having first and second category faculty: those who research and are assigned to certain programs, and those whose job is to attract companies and that are closer to senior management." Turpin insists on the importance of recognizing the contribution made by teachers who work with corporate clients.

Notes

1. See: M. Buckingham and A. Goodhall, "Reinventing Performance Management", *Harvard Business Review*, April 2015; M. Eiter, J. Pulcrano, J. Stine and T. Wolf, "Same Solar Planet, Different Orbits: Opportunities and Challenges in Executive Education and Corporate University Partnerships," UNICO (Executive Education Consortium), 2014; Bersin by Deloitte, "Global Human Capital Trends 2014: Engaging the 21st Century Workforce," Deloitte University Press, 2015.
2. K. Charlton, "Executive Education: Evaluating the Return on Investment. Bringing the Client Voice Into the Debate," Ashridge Business School and Unicon, 2005.
3. D. Kirkpatrick, *Evaluating Training Programs. The Four Levels* (San Francisco, CA: Berrett-Koehler Publishers Inc.), 3rd edition, 2006.

4. http://www.ft.com/intl/cms/s/2/896cfdc4-f016-11e4-ab73-00144feab7de.html#axzz3sP9uUpKg.

5. R. Bats, "A Critical Analysis of Evaluation Practice: The Kirkpatrick Model and the Principle of Beneficence," *Evaluation and Program Planning*, 27 (2004), pp. 341–347.

6. J. Cermak and M. McGurk, "Putting a Value in Training," *McKinsey Quarterly*, July 2010. http://www.mckinsey.com/business-functions/organization/our-insights/putting-a-value-on-training.

7. M. Eiter and R. Halperin, "Investigating Emerging Practices in Executive Program Evaluation," A Unicon Research Study, September 2010.

8. D. Turpin, "How to Measure and Develop Great Leaders," LinkedIn Pulse, October 12, 2015.

9. G. Thompson, "Unfulfilled Prophecy: The Evolution of Corporate Colleges," *The Journal of Higher Education*, Vol. 71, No. 3 (2000) p. 322–324.

10. D. R. Hearn, "Education in the Workplace: An Examination of Corporate University Models," *Organizational Theory*. http://www.newfoundations.com/OrgTheory/Hearn721.html.

11. https://www.efmd.org/accreditation-main/clip.

12. C. Prince, "University Accreditation and the Corporate Learning Agenda," *The Journal of Management Development*, Vol. 23, No. 3/4 (2004), pp. 256–269.

13. R. Dealtry, "Issues Relating to Learning Accreditation in Corporate University Management," *Journal of Workplace Learning*, Vol. 15 No. 2 (2003), pp. 80–86.

14. Comments taken from a conversation with Gordon Shenton, October 2015.

15. Comments gathered from a conversation with Dominique Turpin, November 2015.

6

Attracting, Developing, and Retaining Talent

6.1   The Online Recruitment Revolution

"Hillary Clinton joins LinkedIn because 'she's looking for a new job'" ran a Fortune headline in mid-2015.[1] The piece explains that the candidate for the US presidency does what everybody else who is looking for work does: sign up to LinkedIn or another of the social networks that put professionals in touch with employers.

These online platforms are revolutionizing the way firms identify and attract talent, one of the biggest concerns of human resource departments, as well as CEOs, who are all too aware that supply and demand in the labor market is not being met properly. A recent survey by multinational human resource consultancy Manpower shows that 36% of global employers cannot find the professionals they need.[2] Another survey estimates that 58% of companies have difficulty in identifying and attracting digital talent.[3] At the same time, unemployment and short-term contracts affect millions of people around the world, hitting the under-30s particularly hard, especially in southern Europe, where many highly qualified

© The Author(s) 2016   **93**
S. Iñiguez de Onzoño, *Cosmopolitan Managers*,
DOI 10.1057/978-1-137-54909-9_6

young people are not fulfilling their potential; yet another survey shows that 37% of employees feel they are overqualified for their positions.[4] In which case, what can social networks do to improve the efficiency of the global labor market?

A report by McKinsey from June 2015 predicts that online talent platforms will be worth an aggregated value of $2.7 trillion,[5] equivalent to 2% of global GDP by 2025, and will have created 72 million jobs in the process. To reach the critical mass that could generate these results, says McKinsey, a few things need to happen, such as much greater access to broadband, freer cross-border movement of people, along with new ways of paying people, and all backed up by stronger data and privacy protection legislation.

McKinsey identifies three types of online talent platforms, based on what they do, their use of data, and their functionality:

— **Individual profile aggregators** match people with job offers. These platforms host CVs and job profiles, providing search engines for suitable candidates and matching job offers with the skills and experience of users. Among the best known are Careerbuilder, Glassdoor, Indeed, LinkedIn, Monster, Vault, Viadeo, and Xing.
— **Digital marketplaces for services** connect people offering freelance services with temporary job offers, providing information about the abilities of candidates via ratings or through customer feedback. Among the most popular are Amazon Home Services, Angie's List, TaskRabbit, Uber, and Upwork.
— **Talent platforms** offer users, companies, and individuals applications and programs to assess the abilities and skills of candidates, examine their technical and professional knowledge, and provide courses to improve their training. This is a broad category, and also includes educational institutions, consultancies, and specialist providers.

There are many advantages of online recruitment over traditional hiring procedures, in terms of efficiency both in the search and hiring phase and in identifying talent. From the potential employee's perspective online recruitment platforms provide access to a much wider range of job options, reducing the amount of time spent unemployed, and speeding up entry to posts or projects. Furthermore, they increase mobility to new areas and sectors, while at the same time identifying opportunities that offer more flexible working conditions.

From an employer's point of view, the advantages of online recruiting include access to an enormous global talent base, the possibility of a better match between job offers and individual profiles through the use of big data, and a reduction in the transaction costs and time spent looking at candidates.

Not only do online talent platforms make it easier to find and hire talent, they are particularly good for finding candidates with international management experience and digital skills. Since they are interacting on the social networks. Equally importantly, they are a way of sourcing passive candidates: people who are not actively looking for work, but that may be overqualified or unhappy in their current position. Increasingly, we are seeing that professional platforms are putting headhunters out of a job by allowing companies to make selective searches for candidates without having to depend exclusively on the replies they receive for a particular job offer.

Yet the experts warn that these platforms are not the solution to all recruiting problems, and shouldn't be seen as a replacement for the personalized approach that has characterized recruitment until now. Andy Headworth, a recruitment specialist, says in his excellent book *Social Media Recruitment: How to Successfully Integrate Social Media into Recruitment Strategy* that human resources departments are still wary of the social networks, even though marketing and sales departments are using them more and more.[6] One reason might be that recruiters using online platforms need to be "great communicators; better listeners; relationship builders; sales people; marketers, copywriters; socially media savvy; curious; project managers; resourcers; researchers; negotiators; bold; and professional." In other words, far from making their lives easier—or worse, making them redundant—the new digital environment boosts the role of human resources heads, but demands of them more skills than ever before.

Headworth adds that companies need to design their own online recruitment strategy, and be clear on what it is that they want from an online platform. This will mean setting up procedures to monitor and evaluate the use of social networks, rather than simply taking a reactive, "me too" approach. Depending on a company's talent management strategy, the choice of social network can vary. Headworth admits that LinkedIn is the most popular and offers the best possibilities, particularly for management posts, but says that Facebook, Google+, Twitter, and even Spotify can be used in tandem or on their own to help identify the right candidates.

Jeff Weiner, LinkedIn's CEO, explained in a 2014 interview that his company's goal was to be "the definitive professional publishing platform."[7] His strategy is to bring together on the site the global professional workforce, all the companies these people work for, and the posts on offer, along with universities and education centers where users have studied. At present, LinkedIn has more than 354 million users from every country on earth, and offers its services in 24 languages. Among LinkedIn's standout services are its Groups, which bring professionals from the same sectors together to network, as well as LinkedIn Recruiter, a page that is only visible to companies that pay to use LinkedIn as a candidate sourcing and hiring tool. It was described in a 2013 *Wired* article as "a bit like a two-way mirror where companies and recruiters can see all of your profile information, without you knowing they're checking you out. For example, recruiters can search for people with specific skill sets, flag them and add a dossier to their profile — all without that person knowing."[8]

Looking ahead, online talent platforms will set new trends within the labor market, the most important of which will likely be the continued rise of freelancers across all sectors. In 1995 in the United States, 93% of workers were employed full- or part-time by companies. Today, freelancers are estimated to make up around 15% of companies' workforces, and by 2020, that figure will likely have grown to 20%.[9] The phenomenon, which parallels the rise of the so-called sharing economy, will spread to other countries and businesses of all kinds and sizes, while at the same time raising questions about performance evaluation, ethics, and taxes. But what's going to hold back the more widespread use of online talent platforms more than anything is the time it will take for companies to adopt talent management systems internally that take full advantage of what technology offers, along with the concomitant cultural and organizational changes required. A report by Deloitte from 2015 shows that although 75% of businesses recognize the importance of people analytics, particularly when it comes to finding, attracting, and holding on to talent, only 8% consider it a strength.[10] Bearing in mind that more and more people are using smartphones to look for work, it is also worth highlighting another survey showing that only 150 Fortune 500 companies have mobile-friendly career sites, and of these, 108 do not redirect mobile users to the mobile page.[11] Nevertheless, given that most large companies probably already have in-house recruitment departments, we can assume they will probably develop their own apps internally to find candidates.

Headhunters have been hit hard by the crisis, and will likely see some of their business eaten away as online recruitment becomes more popular. But they will probably continue to be the go-to people when it comes to filling the very top positions, where confidentiality, exclusivity, and corporate secrecy come into play. In 2014 headhunter agencies grew by around 11% after a lengthy period of adjustment. In response to the changing panorama, Korn Ferry, Spencer Stuart, Heidrick & Struggles, Egon Zehnder, and Russell Reynolds, the big five, are diversifying their activities toward talent development, which is complementary to search and selection.[12]

In the coming years we can expect to see more strategic alliances between online talent platforms, recruitment agencies, part-time agencies, educational bodies, and even governments. They are all part of the same value system, one that could be described loosely as the development and selection of talent. The joint objective would be to train and develop professionals from a wide range of sectors, and put their talents to the best use possible.

As a result, many universities are setting up careers and professional orientation initiatives for their graduates to actively look for work opportunities online. It's worth pointing out that while the social networks are now an integral part of mainstream education, and the digital environment is the natural place to share knowledge and learning processes, that doesn't rule out the need for business schools and universities to provide their students with training on how to use LinkedIn and other interactive platforms.

In short, we have before us a new way of matching jobseekers with talent hunters: more transparent, user-friendlier, and more efficient. The best is yet to come.

6.2   What a Candidate's *World of Warcraft* Skills Says About Their Suitability for a Position

Who would hire a senior management team on the basis of their members' *World of Warcraft* skills? Writing in the *Harvard Business Review* back in 2008, three academics recommended giving the idea some serious thought, noting suggestively that: "Leadership in online games offers a sneak preview of tomorrow's business world."[13] The trio argues that Massively Multiplayer Online Games, known in the trade as MMOG, can help to identify the skills required by tomorrow's directors by recreating the decentralized and interactive scenarios increasingly found in the new global environments, places where leadership is a collective effort carried out via a chain of people each assigned responsibility for key tasks.

Gamification, the use of games in teaching and learning, is enjoying something of a boom, fueled in part by business schools that find it clicks with a Millennial Generation raised on video games. Proponents say it enriches the learning experience and can be pretty much applied to any context or educational content. At the same time, they say, games provide a good learning environment, as well as offering participants instant feedback. There are even those who argue that it can help change personal behavior, and perhaps most appealingly, that it has a positive impact on the bottom line.[14]

I recently asked the CEO of a large professional services and auditing company what he thought about requiring job applicants to carry out an assault on Blackwing Lair or to take on the Dark Horde; joking aside, he said that the most interesting aspect of online games is the way they reflect the transparency and full disclosure increasingly demanded of companies, particularly in an area such as auditing. Which is all well and good, but with the proviso that he wouldn't hire somebody solely on the basis of their gaming skills: "Games can help create the conditions for interaction between participants, motivating them and getting them to work together, but games players are always aware that they are playing a game, and that this isn't real life, and nor does it reflect teaching methods. Furthermore, there are subtleties involved in leading people that only emerge after lengthy and deep analysis."

Using video games to teach isn't such a radical departure from traditional methods: it is really just an extension of practices that have been around for years and are now widely accepted, such as action learning, role playing, and simulations, although its methodology, objectives, and content are obviously different. Karl M. Kapp[15] of Bloomsburg University identifies a number of useful elements to help in the use of video games in education:

- *Games are models* or abstractions taken from real events, in which a story is constructed using characters, plot, and an ending.
- *Goals*: this is the fundamental difference between gaming and playing. Educational games should have specific objectives that are clear and unequivocal. When a player reaches one of these objectives, for example, winning a race, freeing hostages, or conquering a territory, the game ends.
- *Rules*: there can be no game without rules, which are not only about explaining the way the game is played, but which can also affect whether people decide to play, as well as, of course, resolving any conflict that might arise over the moves players make.
- *Time*: games usually begin and end within a reasonable time frame. This puts players under some pressure to perform, making it possible to monitor skill related to reflexes, decision-making, dealing with other people, and searching for solutions to problems.
- *Rewards and prizes*: badges and points, generally of a symbolic rather than monetary nature, are essential parts of gaming. Furthermore, games can provide participants with feedback about their performance in comparison with that of other players. Prizes and feedback are two important ways of leveraging inspiration and motivation in contestants.

At the same time, gamification has its limits: games simplify reality, while managers and directors move in a much more complex world. They also establish clear and unequivocal links between cause and effect, which, while useful in understanding the meaning of a particular concept or model, again are not a faithful reflection of the realities involved in running a company, where the use of models and systems is limited. At this point, it is useful to remember Albert Einstein's advice that, "everything should be made as simple as possible, but not simpler." The skills a director develops over time require the use of experience and intuition, and cannot be reduced to a model.

In games, the rules are clear and not up for discussion. But in reality rules are open to interpretation, and depending on the circumstances, can even seem contradictory. Established ways of doing things, often enshrined in law, can be brought into question by the appearance of innovative or disruptive businesses. At the same time, business practices are subject not just to rules and regulations of a particular sector, but also to ethical guidelines, as well as consideration of their role in society. For example, the generally accepted rule of looking to make the maximum profit has to be balanced by respect for human rights or sustainability. How do you factor that rule into a game? Kapp accepts that players are bound by implicit rules governing acceptable behavior, thereby creating a kind of social contract. Nevertheless, as he admits, these are more about protocol than ethics.

Another key difference between games and the real world is the way in which we identify objectives. This becomes more marked as we move up the management chain, where new goals are constantly being set and changing according to the environment, sometimes radically so. What sets good directors apart from their peers is their ability to think on their feet, and to change their objectives as they receive and process new information. In real life, we work on an ongoing basis, targets are moving and shifting all the time, and so we need to be constantly recalibrating. In short, the unavoidable uncertainty that characterizes real life is largely absent in most games, although it must be said that some designers have recognized this and tried to incorporate random factors that can suddenly change situations, requiring players to establish new objectives. And then, of course, there is the question of the immediate rewards games offer, a practice that we can safely say tends not to happen in real life, and that in my opinion is largely how it should be. We do not want directors to be constantly looking for rewards simply for doing their job; this creates false expectations, and could even discourage people if they don't get what they see as their deserved recognition. Executives are not performing seals, to be thrown fish when they get something right. Directors must develop the self-resilience that will allow them to carry out long-term missions that will likely only yield criticism and problems along the way.

But our war gaming trio's article in the *Harvard Business Review* insists that we can learn from the incentives and prizes proffered by the gaming world, and what's more, we might want to think about dropping practices such as annual performance reviews, bonuses, and salary increases, and instead start rewarding directors immediately.[16]

Finally, the other unavoidable reality setting games and real life apart is time. Games begin and end, but a director's work is never really done; it is an ongoing process, even when a position or project has a limited mandate. Players would take a very different approach to games if they knew there was no end or there were any number of outcomes. In games where there is no real time frame, players soon realize that collaboration rather than competition is the way to survive. The same thing happens in companies, where stakeholders, even competitors, will work together if they want to sustain a given situation.

In *Politics*, Aristotle writes: "Obviously, youths are not to be instructed with a view to their amusement, for learning is no amusement, but is accompanied with pain."[17] The philosopher's comment is an attempt to justify teaching music to children, not on the grounds of any utility, in order to practice a profession—except in the case of musicians—but for its contribution to the development of their character and to enable them to enjoy their free time so much the better.

Surely what Aristotle is saying here is that all learning requires effort, particularly in the early stages of a discipline or career, rather than that the learning process itself should be made deliberately painful. The so-called learning curve illustrates this perfectly: when we begin studying, say, a new language, we need to put a huge amount of time and effort into the process, but as time passes and we acquire greater knowledge and skill, the amount of effort required diminishes, until the next stage begins and once again progress becomes difficult and very time consuming. We have all experienced difficulties when starting a new course, until such time as we begin to feel comfortable with the concepts being used. At that moment we feel enormous intellectual satisfaction, a healthy sense of contentment at the knowledge acquired.

Similarly, games and sports require a period of adaptation until the rules are fully understood, and the necessary skills and ability have been acquired enabling us to compete and cooperate with the other players.

Whatever their limitations, we're going to see a lot more of gaming in business education in the coming years. IE Business School's José Esteves has carried out research among 21 companies that have used gamification in their development programs, noting: "the approach has moved from simply promoting competition using rewards and monetary compensation to a much more sophisticated and subtle tool able to influence and change employee behavior."[18] His work includes examples of the SAP computer network, used by some 2.5 million professionals, and the implementation of platforms such as Jive or Salesforce Rypple, which encourage employee participation and allow their performance to be recognized.

A final point: some critics of gamification in training and education have highlighted the possible dangers of addiction. We should never forget that what we are doing here is playing; gambling, as in real life, is quite another thing. At worst, the former is simply about entertainment; the latter, as we know, can have far more serious consequences. Nevertheless, it can sometimes be a fine line between the two, as Charles Lamb once noted: "Man is a gaming animal. He must always be trying to get the better in something or other."[19]

6.3   The Fine Art of Delivering Negative Feedback

Few of us relish the prospect of delivering bad news. But while these days the recipient of our negative feedback is unlikely to have us put to death on the spot, they will very likely simply ignore what we have to say. At least that's what a good friend of mine who teaches Leadership and Organizational Behavior believes. "In more than 90% of cases, giving negative feedback is counterproductive," he told me recently, adding: "My experience tells me that few people know how to accept criticism and use it for personal improvement. Most people react badly and turn against you, even if they know you're right. Frankly, negative feedback should only be given in exceptional cases."

Hard though it may be sometimes, the truth is that we shouldn't shy away from telling it like it is when we need to, be it at work, in the family, or with friends. After all, the negative and positive feedback we're given from an early age helps us to get on with others, achieve our goals, develop good habits, and limit or control what we might call our defects or weaknesses later in life.

As professionals, making tough decisions goes with the territory, and we know that the business world is no flower-arranging competition and that oftentimes it's necessary to act quickly and decisively to clear up misunderstandings or to correct situations that are in danger of spiraling out of control. One of the fundamental tasks of a leader is to attract and develop management talent, which means finding a way to combine positive and negative feedback along with motivational constructive criticism.

In addressing this challenge, I find it helpful to first distinguish between two types of negative feedback. The first is what I call feedback on perceptions and outcomes, which is aimed at avoiding a factual error, resolving a lack of alignment between an employee's vision and the objectives of the company, or evaluating poor results. This type of feedback tends to be given face-to-face or in group meetings, and reflects the lively and productive dynamic characteristic of innovative companies. For example, discussions over a particular department's cost overshoot, or disagreement about the launch of a new product that doesn't fit with the company's strategy. It is worth remembering what Steve Jobs used to say all too often to the design team at Apple when he felt a product didn't meet the company's expectations: "It's a piece of shit," no less.

When providing feedback on perceptions and outcomes, the message should not include any value judgments about the person, but focus exclusively on the events and opinions in question. Furthermore, this sort of feedback is best given quickly, even in group meetings, so that everybody is clear about the vision, values, and objectives of the company. Feedback on perceptions and outcomes are an important contribution to the organization's culture, particularly in the early stages of a department's or business's life, or when strategy is being revised, in order to get everybody aligned. For example, building a culture of quality and differentiating the company from its competitors requires frequent clarification to identify the distinctive value proposition to customers, define pricing and service policies, and to set the company's products and services apart from the competition.

As one of the ways in which we implant our organization's values and ideas, this type of feedback needs to be reinforced through meetings, memoranda, personal meetings, and even through everyday language. Establishing an organizational culture is achieved over time, through systematic and repeated activities, in the same way that water eventually shapes stone.

The second type of negative feedback comes in the form of feedback on behavior, which has to be given to an employee to address attitude problems or personal difficulties with other members of the organization, for example when somebody doesn't know how to delegate properly, is constantly negative or critical, or has failed to see how certain goals fit with the company's strategic vision. This is of particular interest to me because it is related to the task of developing talent that we assign to companies' leaders.

An interesting academic study by Fishbach, Eyal, and Finkelstein on the impact of negative and positive feedback in achieving personal results offers some relevant conclusions.[20] Generally, young people or new arrivals to a company tend to react more positively when given positive feedback along the lines of "the glass is half-full," which motivates goal pursuit when it signals an increase in goal commitment, reinforcing commitment.

Conversely, older employees, or those who have worked for the company for longer, tend to react appropriately when given negative feedback, recognizing that the effort to reach certain goals has not been properly focused—the glass is half-empty—perhaps because their commitment to the organization is assumed. The authors conclude: "beginners increased their efforts in response to success (versus failure) feedback, but as they advanced toward their goal, they tended to increase their efforts in response to failure (versus success) feedback."[21]

These findings are based on a range of experiments, and are borne out by our own experiences. For example, beginners in language courses will persevere when shown that they are progressing, however limited that progress may be. On the other hand, students with a certain degree of proficiency in a language are looking to have their weaknesses or mistakes pointed out and corrected.

There are other examples we can see in our own lives that confirm this general rule. When we begin a friendship, both sides tend to praise and flatter each other, generally avoiding negative comments. But old friends with a solid bond will look for positive criticism, accepting unfavorable opinions if they help to correct perceived weaknesses or defects. Similarly, long-standing partners tend to value criticism that in the early stages of a relationship might generate distance or misunderstanding: "relationship partners give each other more negative feedback, seek more negative feedback, and respond more to negative feedback by increasing their efforts, the deeper they perceive their relationship to be."[22]

Having established some of the situations in which we need to provide negative feedback, what is the best way to go about it? Butler explains that negative feedback is most effective when provided over three time frames.[23] The first requirement is to establish a "positive frame," which means transmitting a positive message, establishing trust, confidence, and recognition of the recipient's dedication and achievements. The next step is to transmit the message about what needs to be corrected or stopped, trying to be descriptive, specific, and concise. The third phase is to normalize the situation, reiterating the trust and confidence held in the employee and that he or she has a great future in the business.

Generally, negative feedback related to behavior should be given face to face and constructively. In any event, it is generally a good idea to avoid negative feedback during an argument or disagreement, and in circumstances in which the recipient is clearly upset or when they have already recognized their error and apologized or explained what happened.

Needless to say, positive feedback should prevail. In my own experience, which is backed up by a great deal of research into the impact of positive psychology, building managerial skills is best done over time through positive feedback.

A very different question is whether it is a good idea to give negative feedback to bosses. I would suggest that this should be done upon invitation only, and then in private. Some of us like to think that we're paid to "tell it like it is," but we still need to be careful about how and when we do this. That said, there are times when it is our duty to tell the truth, regardless of the consequences. How many of us will have found ourselves, over the years, in situations when we recall Hans Christian Andersen's tale of the emperor's new clothes, and wishing for a small boy to step forward to tell the truth?

To sum up, the following are a few pointers for honing our skills in providing negative feedback:

- There is no universal rule about when it is best to provide negative feedback. In general, experience shows that positive feedback motivates and deepens commitment to an organization, while negative feedback is discouraging, generates disaffection, and even a sense of alienation.
- That said, there are occasions when it is not only recommended, but essential to give negative feedback. New employees tend to react badly to negative feedback compared to longer-term employees.
- There are two types of negative feedback: one is on perceptions and outcomes, which can be done on the spot and in groups; and the other is on behavior, which is best done face-to-face and in a constructive manner.
- Positive feedback encourages people to work harder, while strengthening employees' commitment to the company

A final recommendation: our personal and professional lives are ongoing learning processes, and a certain amount of modesty and humility are necessary if we are to progress. Sometimes the last thing we want to hear is criticism, and in those moments particularly, it's not a bad idea from time to time to quietly repeat to ourselves Socrates' words: "All I know is that I know nothing."

Notes

1. C. Zillman, "Hillary Clinton joins LinkedIn because she's looking for a new job," *Fortune,* May 21, 2015.
2. "Manpower Talent Shortage Survey," 2014. http://www.manpowergroup.com/talent-shortae-explorer/#,VYal7Fzn7ww.
3. Stephen Powers, Mark Grannan, and Anjali Yakkundi, "The Forrester Wave," *Digital Experience Delivery Platforms, Q3 2014,* July 22, 2014.
4. Study by LinkedIn, quoted in McKinsey Global Institute, "A Labor Market that Works: Connecting Talent with Opportunity in the Digital Age," June 2015. http://www.mckinsey.com/insights7employment_and_growth/connecting_talen.
5. Ibid.
6. A. Headworth, *Social Media Recruitment: How to Successfully Integrate Social Media into Recruitment Strategy* (London: Kogan Page, 2015).
7. http://www.cnbc.com/id/101710272.
8. http://wired.com/2013/04/the-real-reason-you-should-care-about-linkedin/.
9. J. Wald, "What the Rise of Freelance Economy Really Means for Business," *Forbes,* January 7, 2014.
10. Deloitte University Press, *Global Human Capital Trends 2015: Leading in the new world of work.* http://dupress.com/periodical/trends/human-capital-trends-2015/.
11. Quoted in Headworth, *Social Media Recruitment.*
12. http://www.economits.com/news/business/21654083-industry-under-pressure-finding-new-services-sell-headhunters-culture-vultures.
13. B. Reeves, T. W. Malone, and T. O'Driscoll, "Leadership's Online Labs," *Harvard Business Review*, May 2008.
14. A. Pandey, *The Top 6 Benefits of Gamification in ELearning*, ELearning Industry, June, 17 2015.
15. K. M. Kapp, *The Gamification of Learning and Instruction: Game Based Methods and Strategies for Learning and Education* (San Francisco, CA: John Wiley & Sons, 2014).
16. B. Reeves, T. W. Malone, and T. O'Driscoll, "Leadership's Online Labs."

17. Aristotle, *Politics*; Book VIII, Part V.
18. J. Esteves, "Imagineering 2015: Turn Work into a Game," *The Economic Times*, January, 2 2015.
19. C. Lamb, "Mrs. Battle's Opinions on Whist," in *Essays of Elia*. http://www.gutenberg.org/cache/epub/10343/pg10343.html.
20. A. Fishbach, "Tal Eyal and Stacey Finkelstein: How Positive and Negative Feedback Motivate Goal Pursuit," *Social and Personality Psychology Compass*, Vol. 4 No. 8 (2010): 517–530. http://onlinelibrary.wiley.com/doi/10.1111/j.1751-9004.2010.00285.x/abstract.
21. Ibid.
22. Ibid.
23. T. Butler, "Delivering Difficult Feedback," *HBR Guide to Effective Feedback* (Boston, MA: Harvard Business Publishing, 2012); p. 46.

7

Challenges and Opportunities of Implementing Diversity and Inclusion

7.1 Embracing Diversity Enhances Leadership Skills

A woman pretending to be a man pretending to be a woman: the central character of Blake Edwards' 1982 musical comedy of errors *Victor Victoria*. Set in 1930s Paris, Victoria is a starving soprano played by Julie Andrews who comes up with the idea of posing as a gay man named Victor who in turn is a female impersonator. The ploy is an immediate success and Andrews' character attracts both men and women. As well as being very entertaining, the movie invites us to explore our prejudices by putting ourselves in somebody else's shoes, an exercise that some companies and business schools now include in their programs to raise awareness of diversity.

How do we form our identity? We first begin to identify with the family, a group, a country, and a region in infancy. This bond of attachment is then consolidated over the course of our lives, manifesting in preferences for the customs, interests, tastes, and even the cuisine of our particular group. For many of us, feeling that we belong to a group is

© The Author(s) 2016
S. Iñiguez de Onzoño, *Cosmopolitan Managers*,
DOI 10.1057/978-1-137-54909-9_7

part of our self-identity, of the collection of things that answer the question, who am I?

Interestingly, for children who have grown up in different countries, such as the offspring of diplomats or executives posted abroad, this sense of belonging to a single culture or to a group tends to be more tenuous. Furthermore, people who have spent their childhood or younger years traveling are often more interested in different cultures, even those that are distant from their own. Research shows that children exposed to different cultures, or who show an interest in other societies, tend to have a greater capacity for leadership than those brought up in the same place and who feel tied to their domestic environment.[1] A powerful example of this in recent history is Barack Obama, who spent much of his childhood in Indonesia and then grew up in several American cities. Our sense of belonging to a group is fundamentally cultural, a habit we acquire through education from infancy onward, and is something that, curiously enough, can also be seen in the behavior of our primate cousins. But what does our sense of belonging necessarily have to do with our entrepreneurial and leadership qualities?

Firstly, because it's a cultural—not innate—habit, our sense of belonging can be modified, for example by stimulating awareness that we live in a global community in the early years of education, by traveling or living abroad, or by cultivating in children an interest in different or unfamiliar cultures. Extending this broader sense of belonging, I believe, stimulates our leadership skills and capacity for interpersonal and intercultural socialization later in life.

The second consideration is that we can continue to modify our sense of belonging throughout life, up to and during adulthood, for example by studying abroad as part of university exchange programs, or, during our career, by being sent to work in another country or on another continent to do business with people from other cultures.

Another way to overcome the feeling of belonging is to at some point change the sector or company we work in. In my case, I first took a Law degree, then a doctorate in Moral Philosophy, and finally, an MBA—three very different areas. At the same time, I have taught at university—again in a range of subjects, from philosophy to business strategy—as well as having worked as a consultant, sat on boards, and been an academic manager. I don't consider myself a lawyer as such, nor purely an academic, and am aware that my professional background is blended, unorthodox. When asked my profession, I tend to reply "educator," an answer people can sometimes find puzzling.

In any event, I believe these different facets of my career have helped me gain a multidimensional perspective on an activity I have always wanted to embrace since childhood: teaching. I can also see the advantages enjoyed by professionals with a varied background—in education as well as in other areas—because I believe that a wide variety of professional experiences, particularly in relation to different cultures, stimulates creativity, innovation, and an attitude that encourages out-of-the box thinking.

Rather than going for specialization, my advice to young professionals would be to opt for semi-specialization, an approach that allows us to be open to other professional opportunities. For example, I would say that somebody with a Ph.D. in finance who only publishes in related academic journals, only attends conferences related to his or her discipline, and that only talks to other academics in the same field will have an extremely narrow and conventional professional world view, which can only inhibit innovation.

At the same time, I'm not suggesting we do away with the traditional channels of recognition and promotion within academia or in other professions, but I do think we need to be open to approaches that can help transform our jobs at the same time as the environment we operate in changes. Excessive standardization of careers based on immutable promotion structures tends to suppress creativity, which in turn leads to stagnancy and patterns that can only be disrupted by the appearance of an occasional genius within the system.

The third consideration here is the extent to which young people's sense of belonging has been diluted by the Internet and the social networks. Being able to communicate with friends and colleagues from different, often distant, places through platforms such as LinkedIn promotes awareness of and respect for different cultures, while at the same time helping us to see our own society and its values more objectively.

On this point, the reader might well ask why I am so interested in encouraging us to think about widening our sense of belonging beyond our traditional groups. After all, isn't the search for sameness conditioned by biology and nature, as shown by the behavior of primates? Isn't it perhaps normal to look for similarities with others in the world of work, as well as for commonalities in our personal lives?

My belief, which is based on ample research, is that embracing diversity, cultivating a sense of belonging to humanity regardless of other people's religion, culture, ethnicity, gender, sexual orientation, or class, helps to develop emotional intelligence, and in the process strengthens our openness to innovation and creativity and any other number of virtues, all of which can only facilitate personal relationships and professional success. At the same time, this approach spreads tolerance and encourages respect for the many ways there are to understand the world and to live what the Greek philosophers understood as the good life.

As already mentioned, I believe it is possible to cultivate a wider sense of belonging throughout our lives. To do so, we can apply a few useful practices to help broaden our personal horizons:

- Keep up to date with overseas events through international media and by reading books on distant cultures, as well as by watching documentaries that bring us closer to diverse contexts in the world.
- Establish relationships, either in person or through the social networks, with people from other cultures and environments who seemingly think and live differently to us.
- Take on a different role or propose alternative ideas to our own in discussions. This approach is increasingly used in education, whereby participants in debates are assigned alternative identities to those they occupy in real life, such as being from a distant culture, assuming another gender or sexual orientation, or being required to defend personal interests markedly divergent from their own.

Embracing diversity will enrich your identity and enhance your interpersonal skills. The search for sameness impoverishes personality, restricts our knowledge, and, moreover, is dull.

7.2 Diversity Policies: Stop Flirting and Commit

Recent literature on diversity policies in business has tended to focus on the benefits in terms of innovation, creativity, a better working environment, lower staff turnover rates, access to a broader cross-section of potential employees, and reaching out to more stakeholders. One oft-cited source is a 2007 survey by consultants McKinsey which showed that publicly traded companies with a higher number of women on their boards had better return on equity (ROE) (11.4%) than the average in their respective sectors (10.3%).[2]

Nevertheless, some analysts have questioned the science behind these conclusions, suggesting that the cause and effect between adopting diversity practices and ROE has not been fully established. For example, perhaps there is more direct causal relationship between the size of a company and its growth rate and concomitant ROE. As it happens, there is a higher percentage of women in medium-sized companies than in large corporations; we might perhaps conclude therefore that the relationship between ROE in medium-sized companies and greater gender diversity is circumstantial rather than causal.[3]

I raise these points because it is important to understand the reasons for implementing diversity policies in a company. In most cases, there are two main arguments for doing so:

- *The business case*. In short, diversity policies are beneficial for companies both in economic terms and in less tangible areas. This approach is supposedly more "scientific," given that it is based on empirical evidence of the impact of diversity on companies' financial results.
- *The moral case*. This line of reasoning argues that directors should encourage diversity in their companies as a way of promoting greater equality in the business and wider world. In other words, such policies are the outcome of moral and ethical decisions, regardless of what the economic impact on a company might be, although obviously, the hope is that it will be positive.

Most of the CEOs and CLOs I know subscribe both to the moral and to the business cases, using them to validate their diversity initiatives. They try to find evidence of the profitability of such measures and need to show their shareholders that these initiatives have direct positive influences on their companies' activities. If they couldn't justify these positive outcomes they would find it very hard to impose diversity policies.

But, as said, hard evidence of the relationship between implementing diversity policies and a healthier bottom line is elusive, and studies supporting this tend to be anecdotal or circumstantial.

Something similar happens when we try to establish links between CSR policies and a company's annual financial results. The problem, as several surveys have highlighted, is that it simply isn't possible to establish a definitive causal relationship between the two, because most of the time it is precisely the most profitable companies that tend to implement CSR programs, rather than the other way round. In other words, it might be argued that adopting CSR measures is actually an effect of a company's profitability rather than the cause.

Maria Riaz Hamdani and M. Ronald Buckley, two US-based researchers, have recently written about the impact of diversity on organizations, drawing the conclusion that: "What we have now is a morass of conflicting data, both anecdotal and empirical, which has failed to enable us to come to unequivocal conclusions regarding this important issue."[4] They point out that most studies on the ways in which diversity policies affect companies' bottom lines are not carried out over sufficiently long periods of time, use relatively superficial diversity variables, or fail to take into account other factors that might play a bigger role in how the company performs.

To further confuse matters, studies on diversity provide both negative and positive empirical evidence as to the effects of diversity policies. There are cases where greater diversity sparks innovation, experimentation, and a more global vision of the challenges facing the business, as well as boosting its reputation with different stakeholders. At the same time, diversity can also provoke interpersonal conflict and make it harder to recruit, train, and integrate new hires, as well as sometimes inhibiting or demotivating some members of the workforce.

Two recent pieces of research with very different conclusions about diversity illustrate the complexity of the question.[5] A survey by Virtom Consulting associated greater racial and gender diversity on corporate boards with an ROE 16.2% higher than the average for other publicly traded companies. Yet another study carried out in Norway between 2003 and 2008 into the impact of legislation there which stipulates that at least 40% of the members of boards must be made up of women concluded that those companies with the largest number of women directors saw their share price fall, as did their operating profits. The researchers also noted that these companies' boards tended to be made up of younger, less experienced people.

Are the conclusions of either of these studies sufficiently conclusive as to base a decision on whether to implement diversity policies? In my opinion, while they obviously provide insight into the way that real companies have tried to improve diversity on their boards and the impact in the medium term of quotas, neither provides evidence that can be extrapolated for all companies, all environments, and all circumstances.

In sum, the key factors that determine whether measures to promote diversity have a positive outcome are how they are implemented in the long run, how integration and communication is carried out, and how such practices are incorporated into the company's culture.

A growing number of businesses now find themselves on the horns of a dilemma. Nobody could reasonably oppose implementing diversity measures on either moral or practical grounds. But how might they overcome the problem that the empirical evidence as to the economic benefits of doing so just doesn't seem to be strong enough?

Faced with a shortfall of empirical evidence, Hamdani and Buckler decided to look at the question from a different angle. In reality, it is successful companies that adopt diversity practices, and they do so in response to social demands and at the behest of their shareholders and other stakeholders. Businesses are social institutions whose activities are influenced by their environment, and that in turn contribute to the nature of that environment. As social institutions they are obliged to change any practices that are out of step with the times, while at the same time they are expected to lead change that has a meaningful impact on society.

Irrefutable evidence about the positive economic impact of diversity has yet to be presented, but I would still argue strongly in favor of pursuing such policies, being absolutely convinced as a result of my own experience as to the tangible and intangible benefits to companies from implementing these kinds of measures.

To conclude, the reasons companies implement diversity policies are institutional, not economic, and are the result of businesses' relationship with the rest of society. If a company is going to pursue diversity, it should do so on ethical, moral, and social grounds rather than for economic reasons. In any event, it is likely that the correct application of these kinds of measures will result in a more efficient, better-run company.

Furthermore, it is not enough to simply take measures that generate greater diversity in a company in terms of gender, ethnicity, and background, for example. They must be accompanied by integration and training, as well as by evaluation as to how diversity is being aligned with the strategy of the company and with its objectives.

Finally, diversity is a mindset and a process, rather than the achievement of a cause in terms of recruitment and promotion, and its impact can only be fully appreciated in the long term. Short-term pressure that ties diversity to improved financial results will only cloud the issue.

Management should be considered many times more as an art than as a science, and decisions should often be based on firm intuition and conviction, rather than on irrefutable evidence. I recall here a maxim written by the British leader Winston Churchill in one of his early works: "I pass with relief from the tossing sea of Cause and Theory to the firm ground of Result and Fact."[6] This may also be applied to the domain of diversity.

7.3 Real Diversity Is About Bringing Together People with Different World Views

"We can't innovate without being diverse and inclusive,"[7] explained Denise Young Smith, Apple's Worldwide Human Resources president, when the company announced it was to invest $50 million in not-for-profit organizations that promote the integration of women, minorities, and older people into the technology sector. The news came out the same week Apple unveiled its smart watch, and is just one of many such initiatives that some Silicon Valley companies are undertaking to increase diversity, particularly in terms of hiring more women.

Using data on the number of women and minorities employed by tech companies at all levels, in early 2015 *Fortune* magazine compiled a list ranking LinkedIn, Apple, and eBay in the first three positions respectively, followed by Cisco, Hewlett-Packard, and Microsoft at the bottom in 12th, 13th, and 14th place.[8] As was reported widely when the survey was published, the majority of people working in the tech sector are still white American and Asian males.

The same picture emerges in many other sectors where innovation is also a key factor in generating value. For example, women make up the majority in education overall, but in the tertiary sector, and particularly the upper echelons of universities, diversity falls off rapidly.[9]

From talking to CEOs, CLOs, and my fellow deans of business schools, one of their main concerns when recruiting new staff is how to promote diversity in their organizations, particularly in key leadership positions. A 2014 Forbes survey on diversity notes: "When it comes to the strategy and implementation of a diversity program, responsibility for the success of company's diversity/inclusion efforts lies with senior management."[10] In the same report, 69% of multinationals surveyed had committees or boards whose job it was to supervise diversity strategies and initiatives. In 61% of cases, the CEO was a member of these diversity committees, while in 72% of them, so was the head of human resources. In the opinion of all those questioned, responsibility for promoting diversity in companies is the responsibility of the CEO or the head of human resources.

But a concurrent survey carried out by Deloitte reached a very different conclusion, suggesting that diversity was not considered a priority by human resource departments compared to, say, attracting and retaining talent, or leadership.[11] It is possible that the methodology used did not see diversity as a cross-cutting issue related to managing talent or recruitment and promotion.

It must be said that while diversity has become something of a buzzword, difficulties in understanding the cross-cutting nature of its impact on businesses has to do with its very definition. This difficulty is further highlighted by the assorted meanings attached to it by different cultures, for example what the management considers a minority, or how ideological and religious differences are interpreted. To provide a better understanding of the concept of diversity, perhaps we could apply an academic definition of corporate diversity: "A management philosophy of recognizing and valuing heterogeneity in organizations with a view to improving organizational performance."[12]

In which case, what kinds of diversity should companies be looking to manage? Any number of proposals have been put forward, but we can get a general idea by dividing them into two broad categories:

7.3.1 Demographic Diversity

This would include race, ethnicity, gender, sexual orientation, age, physical ability or disability, and other related factors that can be assessed on a yes or no basis: you are or you aren't. Demographic diversity is perhaps best understood in the context of organizational justice. For example, it is unjust that women be paid less for doing the same work as men, or that somebody is passed over for promotion because they are Hispanic. Similarly, inclusion policies directed at minorities or the disabled are the result of integration and non-discrimination principles, originating in an ideal of social and organizational justice.

In a bid to create greater demographic diversity, some countries, at different times, have implemented positive discrimination policies and quota initiatives, usually supported by public institutions. In the United States, a large number of universities have positive discrimination policies for applicants from minorities. These are helping provide access to higher education for a growing number of people who otherwise would have found it difficult to do so.

The Scandinavian countries have had quota policies to increase the presence of women in all kinds of organizations for decades, and so it comes as no surprise to learn that Norway, Sweden, Iceland, Finland, and Denmark occupy the top five positions in Forbes' composite gender diversity index.[13] This ranking assesses a range of factors related to female employment, among them the number of women in positions of authority, sitting on boards, and in parliament. As might be expected, countries such as Turkey, the United Arab Emirates, and Pakistan are at the bottom of the list.

Positive discrimination and quota policies have been criticized, with some analysts arguing that they can have a negative impact in the short term. That said, over time, they lead to greater social and organizational justice, which translates into a more healthy economy.

A very different question is the speed that diversity measures can really be implemented. For example, one of the problems facing the technology companies mentioned above is the low number of women who are graduates in STEM (Science, Technology, Engineering, and Mathematics) subjects, qualifications that Silicon Valley businesses require. The *Irish Times* recently commented: "Many suggest it is a mystery why this gross imbalance exists, why men so outnumber women when it comes to Stem, particularly maths and engineering, but it seems perfectly clear to me. It is the system. It is the way the odds of the game are stacked. It is like the Las Vegas casinos who know they are going to win no matter how many nickels you feed into the slot machines."[14]

To change the system we need to implement structural measures with medium-term impact to promote greater diversity on the most sought-after degree programs, backed by other measures to support women and ethnic minorities while they are studying, which is what Apple, Microsoft, and Google are helping to fund, reflecting a collective awareness of diversity in the tech sector.

7.3.2 Diversity Reflected Through Values and Personality

This second category of diversity applies to issues such as religion, beliefs, personal values, education, aptitude and abilities, cognitive faculties, and so on. Conceptually, this is more challenging, and it is also harder to identify in individual cases.

I would say that this type of diversity is directly related to a group or organization's capacity for innovation. Real diversity is about bringing together people who think differently—who have different views about the world and what the good life means. Diverse values can spark culture clashes, debate, and controversy, all of which feed innovation. Dialectic and discussion are a good way to generate new ideas. This is certainly what has traditionally taken place in the academic world, as well as in many companies.

The only limit that should be put on ideological, religious, and cultural diversity is respect for human rights. Within this framework, as UNESCO notes, cultural diversity becomes "the capacity to maintain the dynamic of change in all of us, whether individuals or groups."[15]

In short, what conclusions can we draw about diversity in organizations?

- Diversity is a concept with many meanings, depending on the country and the typologies governments and businesses establish. But it falls into two main categories: demographic on the one hand, and value- and personality-based on the other. Both types of diversity have the potential to drive innovation in all kinds of organization.
- The ultimate responsibility for driving and managing diversity in businesses falls, in the majority of cases, to the CEO and the head of human resources. That said, given the cross-cutting nature of diversity, middle managers will also need to be empowered to drive diversity in their respective teams. The most frequently cited barriers to implementing diversity programs are that middle management fails to execute them adequately, followed by budgetary constraints.[16]
- Implementing real diversity takes time, and cannot necessarily be imposed from above. As with any business policy, it needs to be accompanied by measures related to recruitment, development, promotion, and education in the workforce.
- Adopting diversity means respecting many different values and perspectives, as long as they are compatible with human rights.

"Diversity is the art of thinking independently together," said Michael Forbes once. Diversity strengthens companies, not the opposite.

7.4   Managing Diversity Is a Process of Permanent Evolution

Here's what the CLO of a top bank recently told me about the challenges of implementing diversity policies in his organization: "It's not about ranking, ratios, or percentages. Neither is it about reaching specific goals. No, it's about a culture of organization, an ongoing process of permanent evolution, change and adaptation, and you can never say: I've done it." As I told him at the time, I couldn't agree more.

That said, establishing quantifiable objectives and percentages, along with mechanisms to oversee the attainment of objectives, are an important part of measuring the success of diversity policies. Furthermore, communicating achievements to the wider world helps to improve the company's reputation, which in turn helps to attract and retain talent, arguably the biggest challenge any CEO faces. We shouldn't forget that one of the aspects increasingly valued in surveys about a company's reputation or in rankings of the best companies to work for is diversity.[17]

A pioneer in the field, American Express launched its groups for women's inclusion and underrepresented minorities 22 years ago. At present, the company has 16 such groups, representing not just women, but ethnic minorities, war veterans, LGBT, and even multi-tasking moms, with more than 100 chapters whose mission is to create a feeling of community while at the same time exploring ways to generate more value for the business. As a result, it comes as no surprise that AmEx occupies the 11th position in Fortune's Most Admired Companies list.[18] At present, 39% of AmEx's vice presidents and senior management are women, while in 2014, 69% of the corporate executives it hired were women. "Nobody said we had to do this. It's just smart business," says Susan Abbot, President of Global Corporate Payments.[19]

But just how many companies have a special unit or department responsible for designing and supervising diversity practices? A 2014 Forbes Insights survey analyzed more than 300 multinationals from around the world, revealing that 69% had a board or committee whose job was to oversee diversity.[20] Some companies have responded to the need to implement diversity policies by creating the post of vice president for diversity and inclusion. Similarly, many US universities now have a vice provost for diversity who oversees the promotion and hiring of teaching staff. Such measures reflect a gradual but steady shift toward the systematic implementation of diversity policies in large organizations.

Nevertheless, I would argue that creating teams or posts specifically to deal with diversity policies is just a first step toward implementing real diversity. A parallel can be drawn with the international departments of companies with no meaningful presence abroad, and where one person or a small department can deal with anything related to overseas markets. But truly multinational companies don't bother with international departments; they instead set up affiliates in the countries where they are active or create their own global business units.

Managing diversity should be the same. When it is truly embedded in a company's culture, it is a natural part of how it operates and is reflected in all its practices—it's on the priority list of the CEO, the CLO, and the head of human resources. These companies have management systems that guarantee the empowerment of the main business units, including middle managers, allowing them to implement diversity at all levels and in many different ways. At the same time, diversity management should be part of the incentive and recognition mechanisms of the main directors, and not limited simply to human resources.

One possible virtuous cycle for managing diversity might consist of the following core phases (reproduced in Fig. 7.1):

- Mapping an organization's diversity and establishing medium-term objectives
- Supervising recruitment and promotion within the company while fine-tuning diversity objectives
- Training and development of employees to instill a diversity culture within the company
- Internal and external communication of diversity achievements

These phases are cyclical, but need not necessarily be implemented sequentially, given that each is related and feeds off the others.

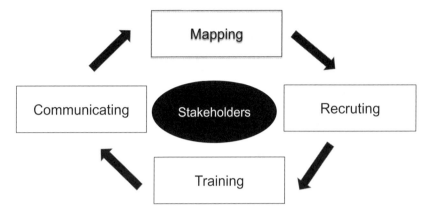

Fig. 7.1 The virtuous circle of diversity

Similarly, a 2012 report by the European Commission provides a useful benchmark for implementing diversity policies and measures in companies.[21] Drawn up by experts in the area to compare diversity practices in different countries throughout the EU, it identifies a range of actions in different sectors, from recruitment and promoting talent to diversity and inclusion training programs, as well as how to compensate and give recognition to directors and employees for promoting diversity, and the best approaches toward internal and external communication, including that with stakeholders such as suppliers.

The Forbes Insights report mentioned earlier identified five main areas for developing diversity. Among the main methods companies reported were professional development programs supported by training, which were implemented by 62% of those surveyed. Mentoring and employee resource networking groups were carried out by 61% of companies surveyed. Many companies or their staff were members of professional organizations focused on diversity, or had reached out to communicate their policies to different minority groups.

But we can go still further in creating a culture of diversity in our organizations, beyond demographics and practices to avoid discrimination and favor inclusion, and take the time to analyze and get to know diversity in all its forms. This is where the development of humanities courses, cross-cultural studies, and related disciplines taken on special meaning and acquire particular value. As will be discussed in Chap. 9, the humanities and liberal arts provide the cement to integrate the knowledge and skills of any profession, as well as to understand our complex world and societal interaction. In a diverse organization, knowledge of other civilizations and religions, and other ways of thinking about and understanding the world, is the best medicine for overcoming culture clashes and promoting tolerance.

Forbes' survey also revealed that the main places companies look for talent are universities and graduate schools, followed by search firms. This presents a particular challenge for business schools, where many companies recruit the next generation of directors. If one of the key requirements of companies is talent of this caliber, what can business schools do to attract greater diversity in their programs and equip their graduates as adequately as possible to be able to understand and manage diverse working environments?

One of the main virtues of the yearly rankings carried out by the *Financial Times* of MBA and EMBA programs is to assess the diversity of the schools that participate.[22] The criteria applied relate to gender and the internationality of the various types of stakeholders in each center, including teaching staff, pupils, and board members. European business schools lead in terms of internationality and cultural diversity, occupying the first 15 positions of global MBA rankings.

Obviously, the way diversity is managed in different organizations will depend on many factors, but we can draw a number of useful conclusions from this brief discussion:

- Managing diversity in organizations is a long-term project. We need to establish specific objectives and measure their implementation, but real diversity only happens when it is embedded in the organization.
- The existence of boards, committees, or specific posts to address diversity is a key step toward designing and supervising diversity policies, but the best situation for implementation is when diversity is present and shared by all units of the business and at all levels.

– The main areas of activity for promoting diversity in businesses is through recruitment and promoting talent on the one hand, and by training and development of personnel on the other. At the same time, internal and external communication initiatives contribute to establishing a culture of organizational diversity and improving a company's reputation.

Managing diversity is a key component in the strategic agenda of successful companies. It is not a bolt-on; it is instead a necessary condition for innovation and generating value.

Notes

1. H. Gardner and Emma Laskin, *Leading Minds. An Anatomy of Leadership* (New York: Basic Books, 2011), Chap. 2.
2. G. Desvaux, S. Devillard-Hoellinger, and P. Baumgarten, *Women Matter: Gender Diversity, a Corporate Performance Driver* (New York: McKinsey and Company, 2007).
3. UK Government, Department for Business Innovation & Skills, "The Business Case for Equality and Diversity: Survey of the Academic Literature," BIS Occasional Paper No. 4, January 2013. http://www.raeng.org.uk/publications/other/the-business-case-for-equality-and-diversity.
4. M. Riaz Hamdani and M. Ronald Buckley, "Diversity Goals: Reframing the Debate and Enabling a Fair Evaluation," *Business Horizons*, Vol. 54, No. 1 (2011), pp. 33–40 at p. 37.
5. Quoted in UK Government, "The Business Case for Equality and Diversity," p. 28.
6. W. Churchill, *The Story of The Malakand Field Force*, (New York, NY: Seven Treasures Publications, 2009), Ch. III, 1.2.
7. M. Lev-Ram, "Apple Commits More than $50 million to Diversity Efforts," *Fortune*, March 10, 2015. http://fortune.com/2015/03/10/apple-50-million-diversity/.

8. J. P. Mangalindan, "How Tech Companies Compare in Employee Diversity," *Fortune*, August 29, 2014. http://fortune.com/2014/08/29/how-tech-companies-compare-in-employee-diversity/.

9. https://twitter.com/Phil_Baty/status/582519455005167616.

10. "Global Diversity and Inclusion: Fostering Innovation Through a Diverse Workforce," *Forbes Insights*, July 2011. Based on interviews with 321 top executives from multinational companies. http://images.forbes.com/forbesinsights/StudyPDFs/Innovation_Through_Diversity.pdf.

11. Deloitte University Press, "Capital Trends 2014: Engaging the 21st-century Workforce." http://dupress.com/wp-content/uploads/2014/04/GlobalHumanCapitalTrends_2014.pdf and http://images.forbes.com/forbesinsights/StudyPDFs/global_diversity_rankings_2012.pdf.

12. M. F. Ozbilgin and A. Tatli, "Mapping Out the Field of Equality and Diversity: Rise of Individualism and Voluntarism," *Human Relations*, Vol. 64, No. 9 (2011), pp. 1229–1253.

13. E. Mannix and M. A. Neale, "What Differences Make a Difference?," *Psychological Science in the Public Interest*, Vol. 6, No. 2 (2005), pp. 31–55. These authors propose an interesting and large typology of diversity.

14. "Diversity & Inclusion: Unlocking Global Potential Global Diversity Rankings by Country, Sector and Occupation," Forbes Insights, 2012. http://images.forbes.com/forbesinsights/StudyPDFs/global_diversity_rankings_2012.pdf.

15. D. Ahlstrom, "Innovation Talk: What's Behind the Lack of Women in Science and Tech? UCD Report States that 'The Key Issue Appears to be Motivation'", *The Irish Times*, March 31, 2015. http://www.irishtimes.com/business/innovation-talk-what-s-behind-the-lack-of-women-in-science-and-tech-1.2085457.

16. "Global Diversity and Inclusion," p. 18.

17. "The Best Companies to Work For 2014," *Fortune*. http://fortune.com/best-companies/.

18. C. Fairchild, "Charging Ahead on Diversity," Fortune, February 1, 2015. http://fortune.com/2015/01/22/american-express-charging-ahead-on-diversity/.

19. Ibid.
20. "Global Diversity and Inclusion."
21. European Union, Commission, "Implementation Checklist for Diversity Management Support for voluntary initiatives promoting diversity management at the workplace across the EU," (2012). http://ec.europa.eu/justice/discrimination/files/checklist_diversitymanagement_en.pdf.
22. *Financial Times*, "Global MBA Rankings 2015." http://rankings.ft.com/businessschoolrankings/global-mba-ranking-2015.

Part II

Growing Cosmopolitan Managers

8

Creating Learning Communities

8.1 Why Friendship Has a Big Role to Play at Work

"Friends are God's way of apologizing for our families," is a quote attributed to the great American playwright Tennessee Williams. They are an important source of happiness in our lives, much of which we spend working, so perhaps it's worth exploring how friendship can play a positive role in our careers.

Or so you might think; in reality, most experts recommend caution, stating that we need to differentiate clearly between work and friendship, and to remember that the relationships we create within each sphere are subject to very different rules, and that, generally, it's not a good idea to mix the two. Friendship is, or should be, by its nature disinterested, they argue, while the relationship between colleagues at work is essentially about improving business, productivity, and efficiency, regardless of how we feel about each other.

At the same time, friendship in the workplace can generate conflicts of interest, and in some cases lead to cronyism, whereby decisions are often

© The Author(s) 2016
S. Iñiguez de Onzoño, *Cosmopolitan Managers*,
DOI 10.1057/978-1-137-54909-9_8

conditioned by the need to keep friends and family happy, rather than by merit, fairness, and the financial consequences. Notwithstanding, our own experience, intuition, and some research show that friendship in the workplace can have positive effects.

Adam Smith, the father of liberal capitalism, argued that the transition from a pastoral economy toward an industrial society meant that its members must stop depending on the close family and establish relationships based on their own interest and their talent. The relationships we form through economic exchange and business are voluntary, reflecting our innate propensity to "truck, barter, and exchange," as Smith put it.[1]

Smith's eighteenth-century contemporary, the Scottish economist and thinker David Hume, argued in a similar vein that the growth of trade and the markets widened the circle of people we could meet, and thus the number of potential friends we could make.[2]

This cosmopolitan conception of friendship, based on trade and business, is not necessarily solely utilitarian, say Smith and Hume, because, although it can result in reciprocal benefits, it is the outcome of free will and is based on trust and the qualities of our friends. Needless to say, like all personal contact, it requires trust and equanimity over the long term, something that cannot be reduced to utilitarian interests. Furthermore, a lot of friendships are formed as a result of doing business or working with others, and last over time in parallel with a working relationship.

Business and working relationships can create shared interests, visions, projects, and risks, and also mean spending a lot of time with other people, all sound bases for friendship. I firmly believe trade can help overcome problems between nations, providing an antidote to the mistakes our politicians sometimes make. We have seen this time and again at IE Business School, where the MBA programs attract a diverse range of participants.

At IE University, for example, the student body is made up of 106 different nationalities, representing a wide range of cultures, different world views, and creeds. The intake is also diverse in terms of gender. I have seen how students taking part in a discussion about business, or when working on a case study, usually come up with similar solutions, regardless of where they come from. This meeting of minds when it comes to finding solutions to problems even applies to culturally sensitive issues such as ethical dilemmas or questions where custom plays a key role in decision-making. Management thinking, the search for value generation or business solutions, encourages understanding and therefore friendship among participants.

So if doing business is a great way to make friends, why does it seem we have fewer and fewer friends at work? Adam Grant of Wharton Business School cites a survey showing that the number of Americans who think it is important to have friends at work as fallen over time: 54% in 1976, and 41% in 2006.[3] Cultural factors can also play a big role in this. Another survey shows that only 32% of Americans regularly invite workmates over to their house, while in Poland and India, the figure is 66% and 71% respectively.

Grant puts this down to a number of things. The so-called protestant work ethic, rooted in the Calvinist tradition, which has had a huge influence on Anglo-Saxon societies, sees social interaction in the workplace as interfering with getting the job done. We have also grown to see friendships in the workplace as temporary, given that more and more of us regularly move on, up, or away to other posts and sectors: long-term employment is increasingly a thing of the past. At the same time, more and more of us work from home or have flexible hours so we can attend to family needs.

But the fact remains that plenty of surveys confirm the positive effects of creating relationships at work. Some 51% of workers surveyed in a recent Gallup poll said having good friends at work motivated them to work harder and to identify with their company's mission, compared to the 10% who have no good friends at work.[4] There is also a growing body of work arguing that having friends at work improves an individual's performance, reduces stress, and increases cooperation, trust, and communication, thus helping people think more positively, as well as reducing uncertainty and anxiety, and thereby leading employees to stay with the company longer.[5]

In which case, what can we do to encourage camaraderie and friendship in the workplace?

1. ***Develop a shared organizational culture***. First, we need to detail the circumstances that can help create the right environment within

which camaraderie can flourish,[6] which means creating an inspiring corporate culture shared by everybody, one of the CEO's most important tasks. Sometimes, camaraderie can be confused with fun, which has led some corporations to create open-plan office spaces, even installing ping-pong tables, as well as providing chill-out rooms and kitchens to facilitate better contact within the workforce. More and more companies realize that a pleasant working environment is important, but we shouldn't forget that a company's culture is of greater transcendence, reflecting as it does its values, strategy, objectives, how it recognizes and rewards employees, and the philosophy of the company. The organizational culture is reflected in the narrative and the messages and attitudes shared by the workforce, and is what really holds an organization together.

For this culture to be effective means systematically applying it to the decisions the company makes, as well as communicating those values to all stakeholders, and particularly employees. This kind of culture cannot be implanted simply through decree, as it were; it has to be something that is an integral part of every aspect of life in the company and that over time begins to shape how people think, not unlike the way that water can change a rock's form.

A company's organizational culture brings employees closer; it invites them to share their hopes, dreams, and objectives, and to work together to achieve the company's goals. This sharing of ideals is the ideal way to generate friendships, which doesn't necessarily mean that everybody working for the company thinks alike or shares the same tastes. There are plenty of companies and institutions with solid shared cultures that have a highly diverse workforce.

2. *Encourage integration between different departments.* It's not uncommon for companies to create informal groups, which can morph into virtual clans, based on belonging to a particular department or working in a particular city. Sometimes groups are created by people of the same generation, through cultural reasons, or by having joined the company at the same time. But caution is advised: there is always the risk in such situations of "silo syndrome," with actually prevents cooperation and the exchange of information or synergies.

The best way to prevent silo syndrome is to start with internal communication, for example by using internal social networks such as committees and meetings. The imaginative solution that the founder of Zappos came up with was to provide off-site parking, so that employees would have to strike up a conversation on the walk to the office.[7]

On one occasion, teaching staff in one of the departments at IE Business School all asked to have their offices located on the same floor of one of the buildings we occupy in the center of Madrid. IE Business School's urban campus has the advantage of being in the center of the Spanish capital. You could say the downside is that it is relatively dispersed, meaning that we have to think harder about how to bring people together, particularly for informal activities. Putting all those academics in the same place, away from their colleagues in other departments, was not a great success. I'm not aware that it produced any major breakthroughs at the academic level, and my feeling was that it isolated them from the rest of the organization. Interestingly, some of these teachers even moved on shortly afterwards, bucking the trend in a school where teachers tend to stay. I've always thought that from both a personal and an organizational perspective, it would have been more fruitful to put them in with teachers from other departments.

3. *Retreats, clubs, and other informal events.* A lot of companies organize gatherings to help strengthen interpersonal relations between directors and the workforce. I'm not talking here about those dreaded cocktail parties at Christmas or suchlike, which sometimes have the opposite effect, but rather activities where staff can discuss strategy, approaches, their sector, and the future. Retreats with open agendas, or brainstorming sessions outside the workplace, sometimes assigning people different roles or using games, are another option frequently chosen by companies.[8]

Informal events that bring families into the equation, involving them in the company's plans or introducing them to key figures in the organization, can also be an effective way of balancing professional and personal lives. That said, I believe we need to have relationships outside work, as well as beyond our close circle: it's usually easier to talk openly and honestly with friends that have nothing to do with our professional activities.

4. ***Implement training and executive development and integration programs.*** Internal education programs specifically designed to develop participants' personal and organizational development can contribute to creating lasting friendships within the company. Learning together is a great way to establish disinterested ties with others, and given that people tend to be more open, participants often create friendships that will be of value in working together to reach common objectives.

5. ***Encourage blended relationships.*** As well as meeting people in person, contact via the social networks, intranet, video conferencing, chats, and websites can help create ties between members of different departments, or units based in other countries, that are deeper and more intellectual. At the same time, they can also strengthen a sense of corporate identity, helping to better understand how the company works.

I'm not sure how close Tennessee Williams and Henry Ford's thinking was on friendship, or to what extent the father of the production line would have approved of some of my suggestions about how to encourage friendship within the workplace, but the man who said "Coming together is a beginning; keeping together is progress; working together is success,"[9] surely understood the importance in business of those two close relatives of friendship, camaraderie, and fellowship.

8.2   When It Comes to Making Friends at Work, Take Aristotle's Advice

What makes a good boss? For some respected business gurus it's a somewhat dehumanized individual focused on results—typically measured over a short period of time through scorecards or dashboards—who is hypercompetitive and who never lets their feelings or instincts interfere with getting the job done. Furthermore, bosses can never have a friendship with their subordinates for fear of compromising their need to drive them harder, to correct them, or eventually to sack them.

This rather rigid interpretation is pretty much that of Harvard Business School's Linda Hill and veteran manager Kent Lineback, spelled out in their book *Being the Boss: The Three imperatives for Becoming a Great Leader*: bosses cannot be friends with their subordinates.[10] And while building friendships with employees, they argue, is a natural tendency among humans to look for the best in people, to avoid conflict, or to sympathize with the personal or family situation of others, they also warn that bosses can use friendships to secure support and better performance.

Instead, they say, professional relationships should be governed by other factors. To begin with, friendship should never be a means to end. Furthermore, true friendships can only take place between equals. Bosses are there to exercise pressure when needed so as to produce better results; friendship is about reciprocity. And, of course, as Hill and Lineback point out, it is simply not possible to be friends with the entire workforce. Which is all well and good, but as we know from experience there is always a utilitarian aspect to all friendships: we tend to have certain expectations from our friends, whether we seek their support, advice, or simply a good time when we see each other. At the same time, employees will have certain expectations from their bosses, and if these are not met, it may prompt them to leave the company. I think we all know by now that one of the main reasons people move on is because they can't get along with their boss.

"*Philia* [the Greek word for friendship], is the motive for society," wrote Aristotle.[11] "Society depends on friendship. After all, people would not even take a journey with their enemies."[12] I believe the same principle applies to the world of work, which is typically a microcosm of society. Aristotle believed that there are three different kinds of friendship, that of utility, friendship of pleasure, and virtuous friendship "for what the other is," because both "resemble each other in excellence." The first two types of friendship, said Aristotle, tend to be temporary, while the third includes elements of the first two and is the true friendship. This type of healthy friendship is found among virtuous people and "lasts as long as they are good, and excellence is something lasting."[13] But could such a friendship develop in a business context, for example between boss and employee? I think Aristotle would agree it can, provided that the relationship is built on "excellence." Either way, wrote the philosopher, such friendships are uncommon.

But when you think about it, why can't we be friends with our boss or our subordinates? As British contemporary thinker A. C. Grayling points out, history and literature are filled with examples of friendship between superiors and inferiors: Aeneas and Achates, Achilles and Patroclus, Orestes and Pylades, Cyrus and Araspes, or Scipio and Laelius—and that's just in the Ancient World. What characterized these relationships is that the senior partner needed somebody they could trust, somebody they could be at ease with, ask for disinterested advice, share their concerns, or simply seek solace. As for the subordinate, says Grayling, he or she "has to be able to comprehend the qualities of the superior, they must be able to discuss, to share attitudes and feelings about things, there must be confidence and trust between them; it will seem as if perfect equality subsists between them in their interaction."[14] This is how something can be created that is able to transcend the mismatch of power, something much more along Aristotelian lines.

You might be forgiven for thinking that this kind of friendship is a corporate utopia, but I would argue it provides a better template for how we should behave within an organization, even if it largely remains an ideal and is never fully realized. In short, it certainly offers greater hope than the dehumanized model previously mentioned.

Considered in Aristotelian terms, a friendship between boss and subordinate should be neither based solely on achieving shared objectives nor in having a good time together. Instead, it should also include a shared vision of excellence, of values, and of identifying with the company's mission and values. And this is where senior management's role is so important: leaders must create an organizational culture that promotes the company's principles, as manifested by the decisions it takes and the relationship between members. Without them, there is no question of friendship in the workplace.

Obviously, we're not talking here about a friendship that consists of going out after work, or of having the same tastes and hobbies and discussing personal matters. Instead, it should arise naturally. There are extrovert bosses who enjoy socializing with their employees, inside and outside the workplace. There are also more introverted people who look for a meeting of the minds.

I remember the CEO of a large multinational telling me that he preferred not to play golf or engage in social activities with the members of his board. On the one hand it allowed him to find a better balance between his professional and private lives, as well as disconnecting from work. At the same time, he was fully dedicated to his job and directors, with whom he met frequently outside the boardroom. His is an example of how it is possible to have a friendly relationship at work without the need for shared extracurricular interests.

It is also important to remember that our understanding of friendship depends in large part on what kind of society we live in. The way culture influences what kind of relationship we have at work with our bosses or subordinates has been termed the power distance relationship by Dutch social psychologist Geert Hofstede. Power distance measures the sense of hierarchy and the expectations that people in lower positions in organizations may feel about how they are treated by their superiors.[15] Interestingly, a lot of studies show that it is not just in Asia where the power distance can be considerable; it is typically the case in Latin America, for example. Although globalization is shortening power distances, deep cultural roots mean that change takes time. As might be expected, in countries with significant power distances, friendship between bosses and subordinates is uncommon and discouraged on the whole. That said, new organizational models are challenging traditional, vertical power structures in companies.[16]

The family-run business also raises some interesting questions about workplace relationships. Relationships between family members are obviously not based primarily on friendship, but there is usually an element of affection involved, and this can complicate dealing with professional issues. Many family enterprises fail during the handover from the founders to the next generation precisely because of a lack of professionalization or management ability. But I would say that those that pass the test, and that perhaps go on to become large corporations—the hospitality sector offers many examples of successful family businesses—can provide a model for other organizations.

You may not work with people who are interested in or able to create a relationship based on Aristotelian principles of excellence, but it is still possible to move toward this goal. In the first place, it's always a good idea to have friends at work and outside of the workplace. Within work this should be both within your department and in others, as well as with people of the same position and with those above and below you. Only seeking out friendships with your superiors or those of the same rank is a rather old-fashioned way of going about things, and in the long run probably isn't going to help your career much anyway.

The guiding principle in establishing a relationship between bosses and employees is to be natural, to be yourself, not that this means being an open book. It's certainly a good idea to cultivate good relations, which means treating others as they would like to be treated—by showing respect rather than fawning. The acid test here, as with all friendships, is to ask yourself whether you are loyal to your boss or to your subordinate. If you do establish a friendship with your boss, don't try to be their oracle, and much less so if your workmates are encouraging you to be so.

If you have established some degree of intimacy with your boss or subordinate and you discuss non-work-related topics, don't assume that this will translate into closeness regarding professional questions. The best thing is to draw a line between the two spheres.

Then there is the question of friendships established prior to establishing a professional relationship. These can often be damaged by differences about how things should be done at work, and such conflicts can be difficult to resolve. As discussed above, as a rule, it's best to keep the personal and professional separate, although there will probably be some spillover. Getting past such obstacles requires understanding, time, and consideration, but in the long term it needs to be seen as an investment.

If you are friends with your boss, you certainly mustn't expect any special treatment at work; bosses cannot be seen to favor subordinates who are also their friends, particularly in public. In fact, they will expect greater discretion from you, coupled with a truly professional approach. Expressing jealousy or anger when our boss-friends require the conversation to be purely professional will simply be interpreted as a sign of immaturity.

Overall, I believe it's a good thing to cultivate friendships between bosses and subordinates; it is a fundamental sign of our humanity. If you work in an organization where the favorite topic of conversation is criticizing the boss, then it is clearly a place where these kinds of friendly relations are absent. But rather than getting home in the evening and playing *Whack the Boss* or re-watching the movie *Horrible Bosses*, perhaps your time would be better spent reading Aristotle. Or you could just change job.

8.3 Corporate Alumni: An Oxymoron?

There was a time when leaving a company meant leaving behind the friendships that had been made there. This was particularly the case for those who had been sacked or lured away by the competition; their former colleagues would generally keep their distance, hoping to avoid any conflict of interest, misunderstandings, being seen as disloyal, or even about to follow the same route. Leaving the company was a bit like breaking up, and even when litigation was absent, it would result in cutting all ties with the person leaving. Sometimes, departures took place within a matter of minutes, with the former employee being asked to clear their desk there and then, having their Internet access cut off, and a security guard accompanying them down to reception.

But over recent years, these dramatic scenarios have become less frequent, in part thanks to part-time working arrangements, short-term contracts, flextime, working from home, and freelancing. As a result, joining and leaving a company is a more natural process, and it's increasingly common for professionals to continue to collaborate in one way or another with their former employer. In short, when we join a company, it's rarely till-death-do-us-part. At the same time, the social networks and the Internet have made it easier to keep in touch with former colleagues.

We are also seeing a trend whereby outgoing members of senior management play a transitioning role, helping pave the way for their replacement and even working with them for a short period of time while they find their feet. I would argue that this more measured approach makes sound management sense.

What's more, some organizations are going further, launching initiatives to maintain and build on relationships with former employees. Perhaps the best example of this new approach can be found in the alumni departments of many universities. Their job is to attract future alumni, particularly from the families of former students; they donate money, particularly in the United States, where there is a strong tradition of fund-raising; they can sit on boards or consultative bodies; and in short, represent the old alma mater socially and professionally.

Many companies have followed this model, seeking to maintain contact with former employees. The pioneer in this regard was McKinsey,[17] and the practice has since been extended to other consultants and professional service companies, among them law firms and auditors, as well as to other sectors. In the corporate sphere, the reasons for creating alumni communities are mainly driven by financial considerations. For example, former employees can help consolidate current projects or bring in new business, as happens with consultants and lawyers who go on to work for a client of their former employee. They can also help to identify and recommend talent.

Given that they tend to have kept in touch with their former colleagues, former employees can also be a reliable source of sensitive information, and are often open to new opportunities to collaborate. What's more, they expand a company's network of relationships beyond the existing stakeholders. Corporate alumni can also take on the role of proactive ambassador for their former employees and colleagues. For example, a significant number of former Goldman Sachs directors have been employed by the White House, regardless of the president's political affiliation.

Not that creating corporate alumni is without its challenges. In universities, it is often said that the stakeholders most opposed to change are the faculty and alumni. Alumni in particular tend to have an idealized image of the institution, and want to keep things as they remember them. Similarly, former employees may have a rather outdated view of where they used to work, which can make change or the implementation of new strategies difficult. This is probably the main problem with corporate alumni communities: they can become an obstacle to change, blocking the development of a new vision or business opportunities that have been created after their time.

Another potential problem that needs to be taken into account when thinking of developing a corporate alumni community is what those former employees are going to get up to once they have left the company. Media coverage of the case of Rajat Gupta, who was convicted of insider trading, continually referred to his former employers, McKinsey.[18] That said, this potential danger exists with or without a corporate alumni community.

Care would also have to be taken to prevent former employees leaking information about the company's plans, although in an increasingly transparent environment with real-time data flows, it's difficult to keep such information solely within a small community of stakeholders.

The existence of corporate alumni communities can encourage a greater turnover of staff; if the relationship between employee and employer is going to continue after the former's departure, there is no stigma attached to moving on. What's more, many companies run director development programs based on the principle "get promoted after some time or leave," and in such cases, having an alumni scheme makes it clear that leaving the company is about norms and isn't personal.

Finally, when considering setting up a corporate alumni program, companies should think first about the cost. Unless former employees are going to bring in new business, the other benefits are pretty much intangible and hard to put a figure on. Businesses also have groups of stakeholders that are closer to the company and whose interests are more crucial to its mission. That said, it is possible to maintain a community of some 3,500 alumni per facilitator.

A noteworthy study commissioned by Xing identifies three types of corporate alumni communities based on their involvement in the company:

(1) Independent grassroots, which, as their name suggests, are informal, set up outside the auspices of the company, and tend to be used as a directory of members. Estimates suggest there are more than 118,000 alumni groups of this kind on LinkedIn.

(2) Company-supported grassroots associations, which usually have some kind of corporate support, particularly in terms of information and technological support. Procter & Gamble is a good example of this kind of hybrid community.

(3) Company-managed associations, created, financed, and run by the firm. These used to be found mainly in the professional services field, although many multinationals have copied the model. Around 98% of Fortune 500 companies have a community of this kind or the former.[19]

Xing's survey shows that most people who join alumni communities do so to boost their employment prospects and generate executive development opportunities, largely for the same reason that other professionals join networks. For companies, it's a good way to identify talent and implement a recruitment network.

Below are a series of pointers, both for companies already running alumni programs and for those thinking about doing so.

Setting up an alumni community needs to follow a clearly defined strategy, and can't be simply the result of wanting to keep in touch with former employees. As we've seen, the main reasons for setting up an alumni community are to boost business and generate new opportunities through networking. This requires close monitoring to measure whether these objectives are being reached.

In some companies, under some circumstances, setting up an alumni program probably isn't going to work. For example, when large companies merge, it can be very difficult to manage highly diverse groups made up of people who identify with their former employers rather than the outcome of the fusion. In such cases, creating a community of alumni is more likely to prevent, rather than facilitate, the development of a shared vision of the company's mission or finding new business opportunities.

The same applies when a company is going through a bad patch, or when there is conflict between different stakeholders. Setting up an alumni community to deal with internal crises is a mistake. Far from resolving the conflict, it may well fan the flames.

Similarly, for companies with fewer than 500 employees, or where turnover is low, setting up an alumni community may well prove costly and ineffective. Alumni communities make sense for large, international companies, particularly those working in the professional services sector, where the advantages of global networking can be fully leveraged.

Alumni communities can take on a life of their own, so it's important to keep their mission aligned with that of the company. If the company manages the community, those in charge will need to report to the board, which will be responsible for decision-making and communication.

Provided they aren't direct competitors, companies with less experience in relationship management can join forces with other businesses to manage alumni groups. They can also team up with business schools experienced in the field that can provide continuous training to members; one of the best ways to keep alumni in touch with the company is through professional development.

Finally, while the benefits of creating alumni communities are clear, companies will need to exercise discretion. Not every former employee will be a natural candidate. Needless to say, the rules governing membership need to be established by the company; it's not unknown for some alumni groups created via the social networks to undermine the organization rather than supporting it.

Today's reality is that most professionals will work for several companies over the course of their career. But this doesn't mean that employers can't have a long-term relationship with their employees, one that, through corporate alumni communities, continues to be mutually beneficial, even after the latter has moved on. After all, if both parties have invested time, energy, and resources in the relationship, surely it makes sense to look for synergies into the future.

8.4 Corporate Universities: The Case of Mazars

Over the last couple of decades, more and more corporations have set up their own universities, and there are now more than 4,000 around the world.[20] The main job of corporate universities is to train managers in line with the company's corporate culture, to identify and promote internal talent, and to align executive development with the firm's strategy. One of the best examples is General Electric's Crotonville campus, which over the last 50 years has offered programs internally, as well as in conjunction with a number of business schools.

The advantage of corporate universities is that by carrying out training internally, they are able to align training with the company's strategy, as well as reduce costs. Among the disadvantages is that they can be too inward-looking, meaning that they miss out on the opportunities for innovation that comes from contact with the wider educational world. Equally, the qualifications from corporate universities are sometimes seen as being less desirable than those from independent business schools or universities.

In any event, we are going to see more corporate universities established over the coming years, which will likely result in strategic alliances with other players in the executive education sector.

For a better insight into the future of corporate universities, I talked to Laurent Choain, the Chief People & Communication Officer at Mazars, who has overseen the development of the global accounting firm's corporate university.[21]

Question What makes Mazars University different to other corporate universities?

Answer Firstly, our university is embedded in our global positioning, strategy, and business model. We are a professional services firm, in other words a talent-intensive organization, mostly composed of young graduates who will spend three to ten years with us. What they look for is more employability, exposure to complex business issues and top executives, and fast-track access to managerial responsibilities. Our profession gives them technical excellence, but we need to sharpen their business acumen and leadership skills.

One of our particularities is to be the one and only integrated partnership in our industry, which is dominated by the "network of firms" model. Mazars is a partnership of individuals, all truly united in a worldwide mutualized profit-sharing system. Lastly, our university itself is a key differentiating factor; as a profession, we cannot beat the leaders.

Therefore, we need to differentiate ourselves as a smart(er) organization; training is not a shared service, it's the heart of our HR policy and we want to be at the vanguard of innovative practices in learning with our university.

Question Why did you launch the Mazars MBA?

Answer The original need was to help create a community of leaders to succeed a great leader who, over 30 years, had developed Mazars much beyond any foreseeable expectation: Patrick de Cambourg. In a partnership, succession is definitely an internal game. But with 70+ countries, and almost 20,000 professionals worldwide, we thought that it would make sense to pioneer new forms of what we call "shared leadership." To build a community of leaders, we thought that the best medium would be executive education, learning together instead of being told by an external consultancy what to do.

We reviewed what the market was offering, but we rapidly came to the conclusion that the current offer in executive MBAs is not matching the new demand for shorter, cheaper, and more disruptive education for executives in office.

Question What have been the main achievements and how do you envision the future of the Next MBA?

Answer The program takes place all over the world, starting in California, and is taught by top academics with a strong executive education background and covers in total 12 core courses. The simple fact that companies have immediately bought into the project, and that they are repeat clients, is a first significant achievement.

The second achievement is the high level of satisfaction expressed by the participants, all graduates from the best business and engineering schools and having followed the top exec programs in their respective companies. Having alumni of LBS or HEC putting the Next MBA (which is the master's offered by Mazars University) on top of their LinkedIn profile is definitely an achievement, the "proof of the pudding."

Finally, the program is "low cost–high value." With tuition fees ranging from €30,000 to €40,000, accommodation included, our Next MBA shows the way to a different approach of executive education. As far as the future is concerned, the best thing that can happen to the Next MBA is that it is widely copied and is seen as an alternative.

Question What are the main trends in executive development today?

Answer The difficulty today with executive education is that business schools are pursuing inward-looking goals—essentially diversifying their revenue streams to balance the loss of traditional shareholders and to finance the expensive demands of accreditations systems. At the same time, executive education is booming because of a growing middle-class in emerging markets and the disruption in management practices induced by the digital economy.

Hence, business schools make a very poor offer to an incredibly favorable demand. New actors in executive education will emerge. Charles Handy calls this "Davy's bar" syndrome. If you are not able to change your direction early enough, you'll end up drinking beers at Davy's bar.

Question Are you confident in the use of technology-assisted programs in executive development? Do you run blended programs, combining face-to-face with online courses at Mazars University?

Answer Yes we do. We've gone from an LMS-based approach to a learning platform featuring a full digital mindset. Yet, there are two digital illusions:

(1) You cannot go directly from contact to trust; you need to transit through a conversation. Conversation builds trust. And so far, the most productive conversation you have [is] in person, not in written [form]. Live video is an option.
(2) The digital world tends to be more "transactional" than relational, even if it is very social.

Question Have you developed assessment schemes inside Mazars for the evaluation of executives and participants?

Answer Absolutely. For example, all our Next MBA participants go through an "external" assessment center. But when selecting our partner for this, we made a deal; we are now developing with them a new type of assessment center, targeted at revealing the leadership potential of Generation Y members, not based on Generation X criteria.

Notes

1. A. Smith, *The Wealth of Nations*, (ed. by A. Skinner) (London: Peuguiu, 1990) P. 118.
2. D. Hume, *Essays Moral, Political and Literary* (1977): "Of the Jealousy of Trade", (New York, NY: Cosimo luc, 2006) p. 334.
3. A. Grant, "Friends at Work? Not So Much," *The New York Times,* September 4, 2015. http://www.nytimes.com/2015/09/06/opinion/Sunday/adam-grant-friends-at-work-not-so-much.html.
4. http://www.gallup.com/services/178514/state-american-workplace.aspx.
5. A. Kacpercyk, J. Sánchez Burs. and W. E. Baker, "Social Isolation in The Workplace: A Cross-Cultural and Logitudinal Analysis," University of Michigan. http://sitemaker.umich.edu/kacperczyk/files/social_isolation.pdf.
6. J. (Jay) Lee and C. Ok, "Effects of Workplace Friends on Employee Satisfaction, Organizational Citizenship Behavior, Turnover Intention, Absenteeism and Task Performance," Scholarworks, University of Massachusetts, Amherst, 2011. http://scholarworks.umass.edu/gradconf_hospitality/2011/Poster/123/.
7. See C. M. Riardon, "We All Need Friends at Work," *Harvard Business Review,* July 3, 2013. https://hbr.org/2013/07/we-all-need-friends-at-work.
8. http://www.forbes.com/sites/kareanderson/2015/04/16/four-ways-to-speed-shared-learning-and-camaraderie-at-work//

9. http://www.forbes.com/sites/erikaandersen/2013/05/31/21-quotes-from-henry-ford-on-business-leadership-and-life//.

10. L. A. Hill and K. Lineback, *Being The Boss. The Three Imperatives for Becoming a Great Leader* (Boston, MA: Harvard Business Review Press, 2011), pp. 49–57.

11. Aristotle, *Politics*, 1280b38-9.

12. Ibid., 1295b23-5.

13. Aristotle, *Nichomachean Ethics*, 1156b5-15.

14. A. C. Grayling, *Friendship* (London and New Haven, CT: Yale University Press, 2013), p. 109.

15. G. Hofstede, "Dimensionalizing Cultures: The Hofstede Model in Context," ScholarWorks@GVSU. Online Readings in Psychology and Culture. Retrieved 6 September 2015. http://scholarworks.gvsu.edu/cgi/viewcontent.cgi?article=1014&context=orpc

16. Tim Kastelle, "Hierarchy Is Overrated," *Harvard Business Review*, November 20, 2013.

17. McKinsey Alumni Centre. https://alumni.mckinsey.com. See also: http://www.economist.com/news/business/21597935-more-firms-are-seeking-stay-touch-former-staff-gone-not-forgotten.

18. Rajat Gupta. http://www.nytimes.com/2013/05/19/magazine/rajat-guptas-lust-for-zeros.html?_r=0.

19. Xing, "Corporate Alumni Networks: Leveraging Intangible Assets," August 29, 2006. https://corporate.xing.com/fileadmin/image_archive/survey_corporate_alumni_n.

20. P. McAteer and M. Pino, "The Business Case for Creating a Corporate University," *Corporate University Exchange*, September 12, 2011.

21. Interview held via questionnaire in November 2015.

9

Management and the Humanities

9.1   Don't Knock the Humanities

"Could a seventeenth-century novel bring down a twenty-first-century presidency?"[1] This question, raised in *The New Yorker* in 2012, alluded to the imbroglio sparked by former French president Nicolas Sarkozy in the wake of his comments about *The Princess of Clèves*, a seventeenth-century French novel. At a campaign event in 2006, Sarkozy was of the opinion that only "a sadist or an imbecile—I leave the choice to you—had put *The Princess of Clèves* on the syllabus used to test candidates."[2] This was no verbal faux pas; Sarkozy continued comment on the matter for years after. Perhaps as a result, his government reduced the number of questions on literature in exams for access to low-level civil service positions. Andre Santini, secretary of state at that time, justified this decision on the grounds that entrance exams to public administration should avoid "overly academic and ridiculously difficult questions which reveal nothing about real aptitudes to fill a position" and expressed a preference for the inclusion of common-sense questions.[3]

© The Author(s) 2016
S. Iñiguez de Onzoño, *Cosmopolitan Managers*,
DOI 10.1057/978-1-137-54909-9_9

We are all entitled to our opinions, and in mine, *The Princess of Clèves* is an enjoyable piece of literature, particularly for lovers of historical novels. Its author, Madame de Lafayette (1634–1693), was one of the most active intellectuals and writers of her time and a friend of other illustrious writers such as Racine and La Rouchefoucauld. She regularly attended the salons, the cultural gatherings where guests discussed and gossiped about politics, literature, religion, and philosophy. As lady-in-waiting to Queen Anne of Austria, mother of Louis XIV, the Sun King, she had first-hand access to court affairs, an insider's perspective vividly described in her works.

The Princess of Clèves has been described as one of the first psychological novels, describing the opposing sentiments of love and duty experienced by the protagonist. The action takes place during the reign of Henry II of France in the mid-sixteenth century, when opposing factions were struggling for power, and political relations were intertwined with personal and sexual affairs: "Grandeur and gallantry never appeared with more luster in France," begins the novel.

Sarkozy's charge seems inept, even from a political perspective. Not surprisingly, it caused one of the most intense cultural debates in France in recent times and was picked up internationally.[4] Was this an overreaction driven by the French cultural establishment against Sarkozy's anti-elitist demagoguery?

Whatever his failings, Sarkozy is no anti-intellectual: government spending on increased by more than 20% during his mandate, while analogous budgets declined across other European countries over the same period.

The former French president's comments on the need for job skills rather than a knowledge of general culture attracted some popular support. In my view, the mistake lies in seeing the two options as mutually exclusive. Nurturing the necessary practical skills to implement a job does not preclude cultivating general knowledge. Furthermore, I believe the exercise of any profession in today's knowledge society requires a cultural background. The humanities and the liberal arts provide the glue that joins together the knowledge and the skills of any profession, as well as providing an understanding of our complex world. Moreover, it would be unfair to ask immigrants applying for citizenship to answer general knowledge questions that are not applicable to the civil servants who examine them.

Furthermore, job training that is too practical or applied, or centered mostly on procedures or providing the right answers to set questions, may become obsolete quickly and replaced by technology. In fact, the difference between interacting face-to-face with a person and filling in forms through the Internet is our human and cultural resourcefulness.

In short, it is misleading to consider the humanities useless for practical jobs. Oscar Wilde's famous comment that "all art is quite useless" should be understood in the sense that being cultured isn't the same as learning a procedure or preparing for a test of ready-made answers. But it does provide us with a rich cultural heritage that is essential for any profession involving contact with other people.

Sarkozy's attack on the unfortunate princess was also a hugely populist move; being cultured is generally associated with the middle and upper classes, and general knowledge exams probably do discriminate against those who have not had the privilege of a good education, which tends to be the lot of the poorer in society. While there may be some truth in this argument, it is also perverse. The challenge is not to lower the bar for accessing jobs, but to provide universal access to formal education and university, as well as highlighting the value of the humanities in all our lives. I believe that technology-based education, open courseware and MOOCs, along with other promising new developments, may be part of the solution to this challenge.

The humanities and the liberal arts should be part of our lifelong learning. Not only do they provide more meaning, color, and joy, but they will also help us to face the uncertain complexities and demands of tomorrow's jobs.

9.2   Taste and Management Skills

"Nothing is so improving to the temper as the study of the beauties, either of poetry, eloquence, music, or painting," wrote David Hume, one of the most influential philosophers of all time. His brief essay *Of the Delicacy of Taste and Passion*, published in 1777, is an easy read, and

I would recommend it, particularly for managers.[5] The main tenet of the Scottish thinker's essay is that the cultivation of the liberal arts and the humanities leads to sound happiness and builds the necessary resilience to face the adversities of life.

To develop his point, Hume distinguishes between two types of delicacy that shape humans' personalities. The first is delicacy of passion, which refers to the degree of emotional intensity experienced towards fortuitous events and misfortunes. Those with a higher delicacy of passion may feel much happier in joyful circumstances and much sadder in the face of adversity than those with cool and sedate tempers. The "passionate" humans may forge ardent friendships at the smallest attention and value enthusiastically honors and recognitions. However, they may also become severely dejected and offended when criticized even slightly. At the opposite end of the spectrum are the tempered and cool, who react with detachment through life's ups and downs. Hume concludes that, all things considered, it is better to be tempered than passionate, given that life is filled with more sorrow and pain than pleasure and joy, and that we don't necessarily make our own luck.

The second type of delicacy Hume proposes is the delicacy of taste, which is developed by cultivating knowledge and the liberal arts. Those with a deeper delicacy of taste are able to value and enjoy good literature or music, for example, and experience real emotional pleasure from it. At the other extreme, people lacking delicacy of taste may feel indifference when exposed to works of art or poetry.

Hume states: "delicacy of taste is as much to be desired and cultivated as delicacy of passion is to be lamented, and to be remedied, if possible."[6] His conclusion is based on the fact that we can choose the objects of taste, while the ill or good fortunes affecting our delicacy of passion are uncontrollable by us. Moreover, delicacy of taste can be cultivated voluntarily, as philosophers have long argued that wise people depend on themselves for happiness and not on chance or external circumstances.

The most interesting proposal in Hume's essay is that the cultivation of delicacy of taste can counteract and even suppress the negative effects of delicacy of passion: "Nothing is so proper to cure us of this delicacy of passion, as the cultivating of that higher and more refined taste [...] a new reason for cultivating a relish in the liberal arts. Our judgment will strengthen by this exercise: We shall form juster notions of life: Many things, which please or afflict others, will appear to us too frivolous to engage our attention: And we shall lose by degrees that sensibility and delicacy of passion, which is so incommodious."[7] At the heart of this is the belief that education and the nurturing of knowledge improves one's character and develops an autonomous and freer personality.

Obviously, achieving delicacy of taste is a lifelong journey; it would be ridiculous to expect instantaneous effects from just reading a classic or attending an opera. For example, I have a collection of notebooks where I write about what I have read, collect quotes, elaborate on ideas, and simply include names and facts.

Expanding our delicacy of taste also improves cross-cultural management skills. In another of his essays, Hume explains: "You will never convince a man, who is not accustomed to Italian music, and has not an ear to follow its intricacies, that a Scotch tune is not preferable."[8]

I believe that the joint development of delicacy of taste with one's partner, spouse, and family members strengthens intellectual affinity and friendship among participants and contributes to a sustainable and durable relationship. In the words of Hume: "a delicacy of taste is favorable to love and friendship, by confining our choice to few people, and making us indifferent to the company and conversation of the greater part of men."[9]

Educational programs at business schools and corporate universities, and executive education programs could include courses on the liberal arts and the humanities. I can say in all honesty that seven years of doing so at IE Business School has been amazingly positive.

9.3   Strategic Intent and *Moby Dick*

"A whale-ship was my Yale College and my Harvard," confesses Ishmael, the narrator of Herman Melville's *Moby Dick*.[10] Given the intense human interaction and the rigid hierarchy on board, the adverse weather, combined with challenging and peremptory missions, it's little wonder that life at sea has inspired many studies on management and leadership. Melville taught himself the wonders of sailing first-hand while spending much of his youth at sea; his experiences are widely reflected throughout his works.

However, I am more interested here with Captain Ahab, the central character of the novel, and his obsession with killing Moby Dick, the white whale that bit off his leg in a previous voyage. Ahab's obsession with Moby Dick reminds me of the business concept of strategic intent proposed by Hamel and Prahalad in their 1989 paper analyzing how several Japanese multinationals were able to catch up in the 1980s with the US and European leaders of their respective industries by focusing persistently on very clear strategic objectives.[11] Strategic intent, explained the authors, is "an obsession with winning at all levels of the organization and then sustaining that obsession over a 10- to 20-year quest for global leadership." Some examples of this strategic intent were:

- For Komatsu: "Encircling Caterpillar"
- For Canon: "Beating Xerox"
- For Honda: "Becoming a second Ford"

Strategic intents should be clear, accomplishable, and match the resources of companies and the opportunities brought by the environment. Was Captain Ahab's strategic intent of killing Moby Dick a sound one? I will respond to this question through an analysis of the main features of strategic intent.

Strategic intent should focus the organization's attention on the essence of winning. Clearly, killing Moby Dick did not capture the essence of winning. Instead, it was Ahab's obsession, and one not shared by his crew. At one point Starbuck, the chief mate, argues with Ahab and suggests that the ship's purpose should be to hunt whales for their oil, with luck returning home profitably, safely, and quickly. Think about the following alternative strategic intent for the vessel Ahab commands, the *Pequod*: becoming the champion whaler of New England. Of course, adopting this alternative goal would have changed the entire plot and the point of the novel, but it could have still retained its sea epic nature.

Strategic intent should motivate people by communicating the value of the target. This is not the case aboard the *Pequod*. Ahab only tells the crew about their mission after the ship has left Nantucket and they cannot abandon the ship. Instead, he nails a gold doubloon to the mast and promises that whoever sees Moby Dick first can have it, but at the end of the novel he says he has won it himself.

Strategic intent should leave room for individual and team contributions. Ahab does not leave much room for dissent or for the ideas and suggestions of others. As mentioned, Starbuck unsuccessfully tries twice to convince him of the recklessness of his mission. Another enigmatic character in the novel, Elijah, predicts the disastrous end of the *Pequod* should they meet Moby Dick, but Ahab ignores the prophecy.

Strategic intents should sustain enthusiasm by providing new operational definitions as circumstances change, using intent consistently to guide resource allocation. But the obedience paid by the *Pequod's* crew to their captain is based more on fear than on enthusiasm. Moreover, Ahab adheres fanatically to his goal without considering the information gathered from the officers of other ships when they encounter them at gams, those meetings of two or more ships on the open sea. At one of these gams he meets Boomer, captain of the *Samuel Enderby*, who despite having lost an arm in an attack by Moby Dick, remains sane and reasonable. Boomer tries to dissuade Ahab from pursuing Moby Dick but this only infuriates him even more.

Given Ahab's mental state, it is hard to understand how he is able to hold his power over the crew and why they don't mutiny. It is amazing how fear and blind obedience may lead to organizational disaster, as happened when the *Pequod's* crew, except for Ishmael, disappear while their ship sinks during the epic battle with Moby Dick. This and other similar episodes from real business life lead me to conclude that the practice of true leadership should be a rational exercise and that those who follow leaders are not exempt from questioning the orders they are being asked to execute. In fact, one of the challenges of business schools is how to prepare good leaders and managers who can be loyal to their organizations and their bosses, while also developing critical skills that reveal their true commitment to their stakeholders.

Strategic intent should balance ambition and a proper understanding of the risks faced by the company. "I will have no man in my boat who is not afraid of a whale," says Starbuck referring to his captain. Ishmael explains: "By this, he seemed to mean, not only that the most reliable and useful courage was that which arises from the fair estimation of the encountered peril, but that an utterly fearless man is a far more dangerous comrade than a coward."[12]

9.4   What *King Lear* Can Teach Us About Family Businesses

An aged father wishing to retire summons his descendants to announce how his properties will be distributed. His plans consist of transferring his businesses, achieved after a long and laborious existence, while he is still alive. The beneficiaries will be his children, who, he is convinced, will continue his legacy and further expand it. In doing so, he acts according to his own principles, respecting tradition, and trying to being fair to each, but without first asking his successors about their wishes and aspirations. To his surprise, he learns that one of his daughters rejects her assigned inheritance, preferring to look after her ailing father. He reacts angrily and not only excludes her from his will, but expels her from the family domains. Shakespeare understood that the tragedy of King Lear is often repeated in real life, particularly where family businesses are concerned.

Lear mistakes his daughter's generosity for ingratitude, an error that subsequently causes a tragic sequence ending in his ruin and solitude. His other two daughters, who pretended to respect his desires and to care about him, leave him in abject poverty. Interestingly, I have found that some business founders also believe an offspring's refusal to work at the family business is a sign of ingratitude.

I remember an unfortunate fellow who, after finishing his MBA, declined his father's job proposal and explored other opportunities in consulting. His father not only opposed him but even tried to dissuade potential recruiters from hiring him. What's more, the father believed he was protecting his son's future. Succession is a key time in family businesses, and experience shows that parents should not take for granted what their descendants want to do as professionals.

Property and management are two particularly complicated areas. Company heirs should ideally decide whether to unite both functions or leave executive positions for the more competent and willing. At the same time, second and later generations would do well in acquiring managerial experience before taking over the family business.

Finally, I'd like to pose the following question: how many books should we read each year? To a large degree, the answer depends on how quickly we read, our personal tastes, and how much effort we put into our reading, but I'd say it is a good idea to aim for a book per week, which is to say, around 50 each year. That said, when it comes to reading, quality is more important than quantity.

The next question we might ask ourselves is whether we should finish every book we start. Traditionally, finishing a book has been seen as a duty, a task almost along Kantian lines, and in the case of literature courses, an academic obligation.

Furthermore, as experience often shows, persevering with a seemingly impenetrable book can have its rewards, as over time the author's meaning and intentions begin to dawn on the reader. I will admit that I started and then dropped James Joyce's *Ulysses* three times before mustering the required determination and time to finish it. And I must now say that my efforts have borne considerable fruit in the form of reflections and references to the book, ideas and associations that crop up in everyday life, as well as interesting ideas and topics to discuss with friends and colleagues.

That said, some people have argued that the best thing to do with a book we're not enjoying is to stop reading it; as British writer and critic Tim Parks noted: "Schopenhauer, who thought and wrote a great deal about reading, is on [Dr] Johnson's side. Life is 'too short for bad books' and 'a few pages' should be quite enough, he claims, for 'a provisional estimate of an author's productions'. After which it is perfectly okay to bail out if you're not convinced."[13]

Parks continues that as adults we should have developed an instinct by now as to when we can bail out from a bad book, and furthermore that we should feel free from the obligation we might have felt when we were younger to finish what we have started. Perhaps, over time, as consumers of all cultural output, we have become more demanding and time-conscious, more prone to abandon a book, walk out on a film, or turn a piece of music off when we lose interest in it. Parks even goes so far as to say we should stop reading a book at the point when we have enjoyed it enough, adding that some masterpieces are unfinished anyway, and that it might even be more enjoyable to speculate as to possible alternative endings for some of the classic works of literature. From my own experience, I must say I believe that the endings of some of the most widely praised works in the literary canon are disappointing and could definitely be improved on.

Another reason we might feel ourselves free from the obligation to finish every book we start is that our objective of getting through 52 tomes over the course of a year becomes a distinctly more realistic goal.

A very different question to that of consciously and perhaps justifiably dropping a book is whether our loss of interest is because we're simply unable to concentrate. We live in an age of interruptions, when much of our time is taken with carrying out multiple tasks at the same time: checking emails and text messages, and dealing with background noise and the activities of those around us.

There are, of course, those enviable souls able to read several books at the same time. In my opinion, this is a practice dependent on how deep one wishes to delve into a book, as well as the level of our multi-tasking skills, and which requires the capacity to be able to shift attention from one undertaking to another without losing focus.

But the simple truth is that reading is one of those things that cannot be done in conjunction with another activity: it requires exclusive dedication if we are to fully enjoy and appreciate it, which is why so many people say they enjoy reading when traveling by plane, which is one of the few places where we are disconnected from the world and can enjoy our isolation.

Digital technology now expands our reading experience through e-books or audiobooks. I am a big fan of audiobooks, and listen to them while I travel or while I'm in the gym. And critics of audiobooks, who say the experience of listening cannot be compared to reading, should be reminded that in the many centuries prior to the invention of printing, and even for long afterwards, reading out aloud in groups was the norm.

Whether we read alone or are read to, as Mark Haddon, author of *The Curious Incident of the Dog in the Night-time*, points out, reading is "primarily a symptom. Of a healthy imagination, of our interest in this and other worlds, of our ability to be still and quiet, of our ability to dream during daylight."[14]

It's always a good idea to discuss with friends and family the books we are reading or have just read. Conversations about how books have impacted on us are not only entertaining, but increase our critical faculties and ability to put forward an argument.

When starting a book, we should set ourselves a time limit, which can always be extended if we decide to take a more leisurely approach. Setting time frames also obliges us to think about whether to drop a book that we're not enjoying.

We should also try to read as many genres as possible. Fiction stimulates the imagination and can give us insight into the world and the behavior of others; poetry stimulates our sense of the lyrical and augments our sensitivity; and biographies and history help us to relate to people from other periods, seeing commonalities over the centuries that help us to understand the world around us today.

Recommendations from friends and colleagues are always welcome, but it is a good idea not to allow others to exercise too much influence over what we read, and that we choose books that reflect our own criteria and preferences. Regularly check the bestseller lists, as well as reading the book reviews in the leading international newspapers. But also make time to browse the bookshops or specialist websites. Equally, there is nothing wrong with judging a book by its cover; if somebody has taken the trouble to come up with an attractive, eye-catching design, it is probably because the book itself has some merit.

And while I'm a fan of the classics, I believe we should also pay attention to contemporary works that might help us better understand the world around us, particularly those by writers from other cultures that can help connect us with people from worlds different to our own. Opening ourselves up in this way can provide us with insight into diversity, perhaps making us more tolerant of alternative world views to our own. In so doing, we increase our cosmopolitan sensibilities and our ability to operate as global citizens.

9.5   Meditation as a Way to Achieving Balance

Few Roman emperors were much interested in writing. Among the exceptions is Marcus Aurelius (121–180 CE) whose colossal equestrian statue can still be seen at Capitol Hill in Rome because the early Christians believed it represented St Peter. Marcus Aurelius lived at a time when Rome faced internal and external threats. Internally, there were several political and cultural opposing forces. At the same time, the fight between defendants of the old faith in Roman deities and Christians was starting to erode old beliefs associated with traditional Roman customs and law; in philosophy, Stoics, Epicureans, and supporters of the imported doctrines of Plato and other Greek philosophers sought to establish their superiority. Marcus Aurelius was, by education and self-cultivation, a Stoic. Essentially, the Stoics believed that in order to achieve perfection self-control was necessary, along with the subjection of the senses to the mind, and acceptance of nature and the given state of things.

This world view influences Marcus Aurelius' *Meditations*.[15] The Internet Encyclopedia of Philosophy explains that, "by reflecting upon philosophical ideas and, perhaps more importantly, writing them down, Marcus Aurelius engages in a repetitive process designed to habituate his mind into a new way of thinking."

This is something many of us can easily do. Writing a blog or a diary that reflects your ideas and thoughts is a beneficial practice for at least two reasons: first, by describing your actions you may give further meaning to your decisions and your behavior; second, it is an excellent way to formulate explicitly your beliefs and values, and reshape and interiorize them.

Many of the maxims in the *Meditations* seem repetitive, but they can help when managers have to face disappointment, failure, and other setbacks. I include a selection below:

– II.1. Begin the morning by saying to yourself: I shall meet with the busybody, the ungrateful, arrogant, deceitful, envious, unsocial [...] I can neither be harmed by any of them [...] for we are made for cooperation, like feet, like hands, like eyelids, like the rows of the upper and lower teeth.

- The following advice is for those who look for places to retire and recharge the batteries—I declare myself guilty of this, since, at the time of writing, I am at my little house in the country:
- IV.3 Men seek retreats for themselves, houses in the country, sea-shores, and mountains, and you too are wont to desire such things very much. But this is altogether a mark of the common sort of man, for it is in your power, whenever you shall choose, to retire into yourself.

  Greater self-awareness, meditation, mindfulness, call it what you will, but more and more executive education courses are encouraging managers to get in touch with their spiritual side as a way of improving their performance in the workplace.

9.6 Developing a Cosmopolitan Attitude

How many continents did you visit last year? Which languages are you competent in beyond English? Have you ever lived and worked abroad? You may not have had the opportunity or time, but a cosmopolitan outlook is as much a question of mindset as earning frequent flyer points. Immanuel Kant, a highly influential philosopher and author of *Perpetual Peace*, one of the first essays on globalization, never left Königsberg, his hometown, in his entire life.

Indeed, globalization has embraced cultures, social relations, the economy, and particularly business over the past decades. The question is not whether your industry is global but rather how global is your industry.[16] Interestingly, globalization has fostered two opposing trends: on the one hand, the standardization of products and services; and on the other hand, increased differentiation and the booming of local and regional identities.

In this context, the need for managers to develop a global mindset is a must. In order to practice this mindset, I offer the following advice:

- **Nurture a global vision for your company**
  Think international first—about exports, not about local markets. Where can your products and services be distributed outside your

country? Who are your international competitors? Remember that maxim that was suggested by Gary Hamel, the renowned strategic guru: "Out there in some garage there is an entrepreneur who's forging a bullet with your company's name on it. You've got one option now—to shoot first." I would add that the referred garage could be located in Asia or Africa.

– *Consider alternative strategies for growing your company internationally*

Can you distribute your services or your products using one or several or the following strategies: (1) internal growth; (2) acquisition of another company; (3) franchise; or through (4) strategic alliances. The choice of any of those strategies should be conditioned by how technology—social, mobile, analytic, and cloud-based—is impacting your business model.

– *Cultivate an interest and concern about international issues*

Express your opinions, without being opinionated, about matters that are happening abroad and affecting the economy and business. You may not be able to travel frequently, but following the international press, reading foreign literature, and watching international movies might be constructive habits in beginning to become acquainted with people and customs of other cultures.

– *Develop diplomatic skills*

In other words, live by the credo of when in Rome, do as the Romans do. The clichés held by most people about other cultures are exposed when they learn about those cultures in depth. Indeed, the main obstacle for doing international business successfully is having an attitude of cultural superiority. Open-mindedness is one of the most in-demand skills as multinational CEOs search for talent globally.

At this point I would like to mention one of the first accounts on global business: *Description of the World*, dictated by the thirteenth-century Venetian trader Marco Polo to his prison companion, Rusticello de Pisa, after they were both incarcerated together.[17] The book is interesting from a business perspective on at least three accounts.

First, it shows how business promotes geographical exploration and knowledge of foreign cultures. The protagonists, Marco Polo, his father, and his uncle, "were men of good family, remarkable for their wisdom and foresight. After talking things over, they decided to cross the Black sea in the hope of a profitable venture," according to the first pages. Indeed, they went far. From Crimea they moved to modern-day Uzbekistan and further to Cathay (today's China) where they served the Kublai Khan, King of the Mongols. The book charts Polo's return to Europe through India, the Arabian Sea, and the Crimea. In each place they visited, business played a key role and we are offered multiple anecdotes evidencing the importance of trade in their relations with native peoples.

Second, the book illustrates how diplomatic skills are central to cross-cultural management and essential for today's global managers, as they were to Marco Polo in his international venture.

Third, the book illustrates that what we imagine is no less real to us than supposed reality. We are told about the wall built by Alexander to keep the Tartars out, a region where shadows appear and disappear, a tower filled with treasures where a king starves, a desert where demons mimic the voices and features of friends to disorientate travelers, and Adam's tomb on a mountain summit, to cite just a few of Marco Polo's incredible adventures. Many of his contemporaries did not believe Marco Polo and questioned whether his travels were real or fictitious.

9.7   What Makes a Great Manager: Idealism or Pragmatism?

Idealism and pragmatism, as opposed but complementary and mutually beneficial visions of the world, are eloquently illustrated in Cervantes' masterpiece *Don Quixote*,[18] acknowledged by many as the first modern novel. However, some literary scholars suggest that the novel should have been entitled *Don Quixote and Sancho Panza*, for the two main protagonists of this book deserve equal recognition, representing two facets of the personality that, if combined into one, may achieve a perfect equilibrium.

Don Quixote is otherworldly, idealistic, has fallen on hard times, and is a victim of delusions of grandeur. A skeletal figure, he is duty-bound by honor to restore chivalry.

Sancho Panza, working unpaid as Quixote's squire, is the very opposite: short and stocky, with his feet on the ground and a pragmatic approach to life. His job is to take care of the day-to-day needs of this prototypical odd couple. He even has capitalist instincts, rare in sixteenth-century Spain—when he discovers the properties of the supposedly magic balsam of Fierabras that heals whomever drinks it, he wonders how to mass produce it.

The two protagonists represent yin and yang, making them one of the most complementary couples in world literature. They are fond of each other regardless of their differences. Quixote and Sancho characterize the personality poles that many companies need in their top management. In fact, idealism and pragmatism are not easily found together in a single person. Some managers are the embodiment of strategic vision, possessed of a passion for innovation, while others have a marked orientation towards finance and performance. Some are risk-averse and conservative, and well suited for times of crisis, whereas others drive their organizations in times of growth.

There are many cases of companies run by an idealist and a pragmatist, like Quixote and Sancho. A paradigmatic example of this was the initial management at Philips, the Dutch electronics conglomerate. During the first decades of expansion the company was co-driven by the two founding brothers: one focused on innovation, and the other the needs of the market.

Another example can be seen in Apple during the period under Steve Jobs and John Sculley, then CEO of PepsiCo. Jobs' combination of idealism, strategic vision, and perfectionism matched Sculley's marketing talent and performance-oriented style. But the tandem ended with a power struggle that Jobs lost. Indeed, Jobs' quixotic traits and his erratic and temperamental attitude—some witnesses even referred to a sort of reality distortion—veered toward the extreme at that time.[19] Unfortunately, Sculley was no supportive Sancho Panza either.

Given your past experience and feedback from your colleagues and coaches, do you consider yourself an idealist or a pragmatist, a Quixote or a Sancho? You probably combine elements of the two, but if you are naturally inclined to one end of the spectrum, perhaps you should think about counteracting the undesirable effects of this inertia in your company by appointing a senior manager with a complementary profile. Steve Jobs, who acknowledged his previous error, did this during his successful second mandate as CEO at Apple.

"Did not I assure you, they were no other than windmills? Indeed, nobody could mistake them for anything else but one who has windmills in his own head?" Sancho tells Don Quixote at one point. Was Sancho right or did he not understand his master's vision? Perhaps we need to remember that sometimes our perception of reality is as important as what is really going on around us, and that having somebody to provide an alternative perspective is not a bad idea.

Notes

1. E. Zerofsky, "On Presidents and Princesses," *The New Yorker*, November 8, 2012. http://www.newyorker.com/books/page-turner/of-presidents-and-princesses.
2. h-france.net/fffh/princesse-of-cleves/.
3. Ibid.
4. www.theguardian.com/commentisfree/2011/mar/23/sarkozy-murderer-princess-of-cleves.
5. www.davidhume.org/texts/etv1.html.
6. Ibid., DT 3.
7. Ibid., DT 4.
8. "The Sceptic," in *The Philosophical Works of David Hume*, edited by T. H. Green and T. H. Grose. 4 vols (London: Longman, Green, 1874–75), p. 217.
9. www.davidhume.org/texts/etv1.html, DT 7.
10. H. Melville, *Moby Dick* (New York: Bentham Classics, 2003).
11. G. Hamel and C. K. Prahalad: "Strategic Intent," *Harvard Business Review*, May–June 1989.
12. Melville, *Moby Dick*, Chap. 26.
13. Tim Parks, "Why Finish Books?," *The New York Review of Books*, March 13, 2012.

14. Mark Haddon, "The Right Words in The Right Order," in *Stop What You're Doing and Read This!* (London: Random House/Vintage Books, 2011), p. 90.
15. Marcus Aurelius, *Meditations* (London: Penguin Classics, 2003). http://www.iep.utm.edu/marcus.
16. Cornelis A. De Kluyver, "Fundamentals of Global Strategy: The Globalization of Companies and Industries," Harvard Business Publishing, August 2010.
17. Marco Polo, *Description of the World*, edited by A. C. Moule and Paul Pelliot (New York and Tokyo: Ishi Press, 2010).
18. See Carole Slade's 'Introduction' to M. de Cervantes, *Don Quixote* (New York: Barnes & Noble, 2004), p. xvii.
19. Andrew Hertzfeld: "Reality Distortion Field." http://www.folklore.org/StoryView.py?project=Macintosh&story=Reality_Distortion_Field.txt.

10

Creating a Virtuous Learning Environment

10.1 Is Teamwork Overvalued?

"Insanity in individuals is something rare, in groups, parties, nations and epochs, it is the rule" wrote German philosopher Friedrich Nietzsche,[1] who himself suffered from episodes of dementia in the final years of his life, tragically converting himself into the exception to his own rule.

He would have been unaware of the term, but in part, what Nietzsche was talking about was *groupthink*, a dynamic that's been variously defined as that which happens when group members trying to avoid conflict reach a consensus decision without properly evaluating other viewpoints, whether by isolating themselves or suppressing dissent.

Due to the complex nature of the tasks companies must carry out—the need to integrate specialist activities or to internationalize operations— most work within them is carried out by teams. Teamwork is part of the DNA of all types of organizations, and business schools are keen on getting their students to work in small groups with the aim of preparing leaders able to lead them and make them productive.

But I sometimes wonder if we don't overestimate the results of teamwork and that maybe there is something to be said about letting

© The Author(s) 2016   **169**
S. Iñiguez de Onzoño, *Cosmopolitan Managers*,
DOI 10.1057/978-1-137-54909-9_10

somebody who prefers working alone to do so more often. Sometimes, teamwork's very virtue can also be the seed of its destruction. Tightly knit teams, flexible, with a strong spirit of cooperation and a winning spirit, all positive in themselves, can also generate a feeling of invulnerability and a tendency to converge, which often leads to rejecting other opinions, information, and data that contradicts supposedly agreed positions, as well as demonizing anybody who disagrees, while blinding the team leader to undesired outside ideas.[2]

Have you ever seen a sales team "unanimously" reject the launch of a popular product, using the excuse for example that it might cannibalize existing products, or perhaps resisting raising the price of a clearly differentiated product? Or perhaps you have come up against the wall of resistance that the IT department can show when it refuses to outsource a particular service.

Critics of teamwork say that the great works of art, along with many scientific discoveries, were the work of one great person, even though they may have benefited from the collective efforts of their culture or society. None of the 100 greatest novels of all time was written collectively,[3] and neither were any of the great paintings or symphonies.[4] Some might argue that Mozart's collaboration with master librettist Da Ponte produced his finest work, but his creative talent far outshone that of his librettists.

Susan Cain writes in *Quiet: The Power of Introverts in a World That Won't Stop Talking*, "research strongly suggests that people are more creative when they enjoy privacy and freedom from interruption. And the most spectacularly creative people in many fields are often introverted (…) They're extroverted enough to exchange and advance ideas, but see themselves as independent and individualistic. They're not joiners by nature."[5]

Cain is referring to the Coding War Games survey, which analyzed the results of the work of 600 computer programmers in 92 countries, showing that the companies with the best results were not those that with the oldest or that paid the best, but those that provided their employees with privacy, personal work space, and who interrupted their programmers less often.

Cain also quotes Apple co-founder Steve Wozniak, who writes in his autobiography: "Most inventors and engineers I've met are like me … they live in their heads. They're almost like artists. In fact, the very best of them are artists. And artists work best alone.... I'm going to give you some advice that might be hard to take. That advice is: Work alone … Not on a committee. Not on a team."

Another criticism frequently leveled at teamwork is that it can encourage some members to sit back and let others do the work, as well as providing a great excuse for when things go awry. In Japan, if a team gets something badly wrong, then it is expected to resign as a unit, taking collective responsibility, but in the West, at worst, the group leader will stand down, while the other members of the team are somehow protected by their having taken decisions jointly.

Despite its inherent weaknesses, teamwork can generate excellent results, and seems unavoidable in the current corporate world. What practices could be adopted to avoid the risks of groupthink, as well as to promote individual creativity, and to empower the team to assume collective responsibility, for success as well as failure?

- *In the first place, decision-making procedures need to be effective and avoid oversimplifying issues so as to reach agreement.* They must also involve the search for a common denominator, as well as looking for innovative solutions. I tend to recommend groups that are taking big strategic decisions not to do so by majority, because this approach can often lead to conventional outcomes or the continuity of the status quo. Instead, I believe they should designate a leader from the group according to their specialist skills, give them all the input necessary, let everybody have their say, and then allow that person to decide.
- *It is a good idea to rotate leadership of the group frequently or on an agreed time frame.* Regardless of whether some of the team's members have more evident leadership skills, rotating leadership can add a new dimension, highlighting unexpected ideas. It is also an opportunity for those with greater leadership skills to learn from their colleagues.
- *Diversity is essential in successful groups.* The presence of women in groups tends to lead to more empathy and consensus, but it is also important for the mix to be cultural and ethnic. The point of a working group should be to bring together people who think differ-

ently from one other, and with a range of views on business or a particular sector. Logically, the role of the leader is to make as much as possible of this diversity, and to be able to propose specific solutions that the others in the group will sign up to. Sameness among team members is one of the leading contributors to groupthink.

— *The Three Cs*. Benjamin Voyer of the London School of Economics calls for three Cs when working in teams: Collaboration, so that all are working toward the same goal, regardless of individual viewpoints; Coordination, which tends to be the job of the leader, and so that the tasks in hand are carried out according to schedule, and that everybody contributes; and Communication, which is essential to avoid misunderstandings, which can be the cause of conflict between group members.[6]

— *Working in a team means taking a constructive, can-do approach.* One of the main risks is that some members will sit back, something the team leader needs to keep an eye on. It is important for leaders to cultivate a spirit of generosity, empathy, diplomacy, and avoid being brusque and talking too much, and instead find a way to implement the decision that has been taken, even if not everybody was initially in agreement.

On occasion, when talking to the members of a team on our MBA programs that hasn't gelled properly, or that is underperforming, they tell me that this group is worse than the others and that its members are not contributing equally. I tend to reply that their group was potentially just as good as the others, and that the problem lies with the capacity of each of its members to lead. At IE Business School, when assigning groups, we always aim for diversity in the hope of sparking learning synergies and personal interaction. The training and background of its members, along with their academic merits and admission tests, are also taken into account.

We also work with our groups, particularly in the early stages of the program, through exercises, role playing, feedback, and sessions on team work, with the aim of boosting their chances of success. Nevertheless, on occasions, some teams just do not work, either due to personality conflicts or because of common errors. In such cases I usually remind those involved that the problem was not the team itself, but the lack of leadership and emotional intelligence.

– *Finally, a proposal to help strengthen highly diverse teams.* Our experience at IE Business School is that working in a blended format, combining classroom sessions with online studies, generates better results in work teams than purely face-to-face teaching. Teams that work online develop a series of skills and tend to be more respectful than those that work together in the classroom. Each member's contribution tends to be more balanced, perhaps because it is more tangible and permanent in a digital format. In a traditional face-to-face classroom situation, it is easier to take a back seat. Online interaction also allows for a deeper intellectual experience between members, which helps cement relationships and encourage greater openness.

Unsurprisingly, Susan Cain is also an advocate of the advantages of working online, such as getting the most out of the diversity, given that "introverts are more likely than extroverts to express intimate facts about themselves online."[7] A lot of companies could benefit from hybrid or blended programs that combine face-to-face teaching with an online teaching component as a way to identify introverts with leadership potential. Cain adds that brainstorming in online groups produces better results than individual work or face-to-face groups. It is the best combination of individual work with a team effort.

Albert Einstein wrote: "I am a horse for single harness, not cut out for tandem or team work. I have never belonged wholeheartedly to country or state, to my circle of friends, or even to my own family."[8] But for many of us, given that teamwork is probably unavoidable at some time, and while we mustn't give up our right to work alone sometimes, knowing how to work well in a team can be a highly rewarding experience. In short, why not enjoy the best of both worlds?

10.2 Developing an Entrepreneurial Mindset

Moving forward and into the future, among the many topics Professor Chris Impey, Deputy Head of the Department of Astronomy at the University of Arizona, looks at in *Beyond: Our Future in Space,*[9] his highly readable examination of space exploration, is the role that genes have played, and continue to play, in mankind's eternal drive to discover new places, whether on earth, or... beyond.

Impey cites the 7R variant of the DRD4 gene, carried by a fifth of humanity and that controls dopamine, the chemical associated with risk-takers, extroverts, and explorers. The gene variant is believed to have emerged around 40,000 years ago, around the time our forebears began migrating out of Africa, and has been identified in their descendants in far-flung places. For Impey, the will to explore is "built into our DNA," meaning we will establish a presence in space, sooner or later.[10]

That's how an astronomer sees genes, but the geneticist who actually discovered DRD4-7R, Professor Kenneth Kidd of Yale University, plays down the role of genetics in behavior, noting: "You just can't reduce something as complex as human exploration to a single gene. Genetics doesn't work that way."[11]

I'm inclined to agree with Professor Kidd, that environmental factors such as family and work, opportunity, and even luck are probably more important when it comes to developing our entrepreneurial or leadership skills than the genetic hand life deals us. As science writer David Dobbs argues in a *National Geographic* article about explorers: "our genetic traits evolved to the point where we could create them, and we reshape them constantly. But this changing culture can likewise shape our genetic evolution, sometimes in stunningly quick and direct ways."[12]

To be fair to Impey, he's not really saying that everything comes down to genetics, as his choice of space entrepreneurs shows. What do Richard Branson, founder of Virgin Galactic, Peter Diamandis, who set up the Zero Gravity Corporation, and Elon Musk, creator of SpaceX have in common? We don't know if they possess the DRD4-7R gene variant, but we do know that they all started businesses around the age of 20, and that they are now the heads of global corporations active in a range of areas. What's more, they all had difficult childhoods that may well have contributed to their propensity for adventure and ability to overcome challenges.

Branson was dyslexic, and on one occasion, he says his mother left him in his pram three miles from home so that he would have to find a way to communicate with strangers if he wanted to get back. At age eight, Diamandis built rockets in his back garden and gave his family and friends lectures about space exploration. In a recent biography of Elon Musk we learn that he was an avid reader as a child growing up in South Africa, didn't like sports, was bullied at school, and was subjected to lengthy reading sessions by his father during which he couldn't speak or move.[13] At the age of 17 he decided to escape the claustrophobic confines of Pretoria where he had grown up, heading for Canada, and making a new life for himself there.

Another thing these space entrepreneurs have in common is their view of the future, which is long term, anticipatory, and one in which they see themselves changing the world.

Musk currently runs three companies with highly ambitious goals: Tesla, which makes electric cars; Solar City, the largest provider of solar power systems in the United States; and SpaceX, an aerospace manufacturer and space transport company with the long-term goal of colonizing Mars.

Diamandis is the founder of the International Space University and Singularity University, which provide alternative approaches to higher education.

These three entrepreneurs also share the same approach to strategy, focusing more on their projects, products, and services than the financial aspects of their businesses. This is the difference between an entrepreneur, somebody who has a deep personal stake in their projects, and a manager, who is more concerned with meeting deadlines, evaluating contingencies, and handling resources. "I don't complicate my life with financial reports," Branson once famously said, admitting he didn't know the difference between net and gross profit. It is said of Musk that he isn't motivated by money, but by ideas.

Another characteristic of these kinds of entrepreneurs is their restlessness, their determination, and even their obsession with getting a project off the ground. They are perfectionists, and have a seemingly limitless capacity for work. Branson's passion for aviation and space travel led him to sell Virgin Records, the label he had founded with three friends in 1972 at the age of 22, and which had made his fortune, in order to keep Virgin Atlantic in the air at a time when it faced unfair competition from British Airways, along with soaring fuel costs.

Musk, who works a 100-hour week, spent most of his fortune on SpaceX and Tesla, a move considered at best risky, and by some to reflect questionable sanity.[14]

Entrepreneurs of this caliber are, needless to say, very sure of themselves, but they are also aware of their limitations, which is why they typically surround themselves with the best professionals and highly qualified teams, of whom they then demand the impossible on top of the impossible. Branson hired Burt Rutan, one of the most respected aircraft and rocket designers in the world, to create SpaceShipOne, the first privately funded manned spacecraft, which carried out its first flight in 2004. Musk too knows how to pick the best, and to motivate them to perform beyond the normal.

And while we're on the subject of entrepreneurs demanding the impossible from their teams, how can we fail to mention Steve Jobs? Bud Tribble, Apple's chief software engineer, describes how Jobs would create a "reality distortion field," a term taken from *Star Trek*: "In his presence, reality is malleable. He can convince anyone of practically anything. It wears off when he is not around, but it makes it hard to have realistic schedules."[15] Jobs' intransigence had a very simple goal: to get his people to produce the best possible product, and sometimes that meant meeting deadlines that seemed impossible, or checking and rechecking information and data in pursuit of perfection.

In the absence of scientific proof of the presence of DRD4-7R in our DNA, but in a world in which entrepreneurial skills are more necessary than ever, below are a few takeaways that might even shape our genes, and who knows, help us to boldly go…

- We might ask ourselves what our childhood dream was, and what would we do with our lives if we had the money and the opportunity?
- We need to surround ourselves with the best talent, with people who know how to do the things we can't, and who can get them done.
- We need to be determined, without rushing, but without respite, until we reach our goal. There is no point looking for shortcuts or losing hope when things take longer than we thought they would.

That said, a certain degree of impatience is also necessary if we aren't to waste our time.

– We should focus more on strategy, on products and services, thinking always of the client rather than just financial questions. At the same time, it's a good idea to look for the best managers to look out for the health of our financial results.
– Look to the future by keeping up to date on what is going on in our sector, using the new solutions that technology can provide, as well as learning from disruptive competitors. At the same time, we can gain inspiration from the humanities and from literature.

A final reason why we shouldn't believe that our entrepreneurial abilities are rooted solely in our genetic makeup: by reading the biographies of the men and women who have taken risks and achieved great things, we can learn from their behavior, we can imitate them, and in so doing reach for the stars in our own way.

10.3 Mentors and Sponsors

Talent, ambition, leadership skills, luck, or perhaps simply opportunity: which of the above would you say is the key to making it to the top of the corporate ladder? Well, according to a recent survey by the American Society for Training and Development, 75% of executives surveyed credited their mentors with helping them reach their current positions.[16]

The same survey also shows that 71% of Fortune 500 companies run mentoring programs. In most cases, these are managed by human resources departments, and are tied to other initiatives to attract and retain talent, such as training and development programs, or to internal promotion policies.

Small- and medium-sized companies also use mentoring. A Sage survey carried out in 17 countries shows that 93% of SMEs see the value of mentoring practices in terms of improving their teams' performance, although just 23% actually hire mentors, most of them from outside the company.

Mentoring programs offer clear advantages for businesses. Aside from allowing them to identify and develop talent, they increase feelings of satisfaction with work, build loyalty, and encourage executives to identify with the company, and thus are a way to hold on to potentially valuable players. At the same time, mentoring is a way of passing on knowledge and key relationships from senior executives to younger professionals, who may have only joined the company recently, while helping to develop skills and abilities related to the organization's culture or that provide corporate advantages.

In an increasingly diverse environment for companies, mentoring programs also help to attract minorities, as well as helping with intergenerational integration. Many large corporations will have a workforce spanning up to five generations: those born before 1945; the baby boomers born between 1945 and 1960; Generation X, from 1961 to 1980; Generation Y—also known as the millennials—from 1981 to 1995; and Generation Z, born after 1996. The relationship between members of these different generations can generate interesting synergies for companies, mixing experience, reputation, and relationships on the part of older employees with the drive, technological affinity, and familiarity with the social networks characteristic of younger people. This has even led to what has been dubbed reverse mentoring, often attributed to Jack Welch at General Electric, by which younger executives take older members under their wing, as it were, teaching them about more recent consumer trends and how to make the best use of new technologies, for example establishing relationships via the social networks.

Alan Webber, co-founder of Fast Company, describes the potential of reverse mentoring: "It's a situation where the old fogies in an organization realize that by the time you're in your forties and fifties, you're not in touch with the future in the same way the young twenty-somethings. They come with fresh eyes, open minds, and instant links to the technology of our future."[17]

Comparisons have been made between mentoring and coaching, but there are a number of important differences between the two, says Management Mentors, a company with two decades of experience in the field. Coaching is essentially task-oriented, performance-driven, and largely aimed at achieving short-term goals. In many cases, the coach will be the boss of the company or a senior member of the management. In short, coaching is typically about developing specific skills, learning how a system or management program works, and preparing for taking on a new position or responsibility.

Mentoring, on the other hand, creates a lasting relationship between the two parties, and equally importantly, is as much about personal development as acquiring new skills. Furthermore, a mentor is, ideally, not a boss, but somebody from outside the mentee's frame of reference.

As a rule, mentoring programs are for directors or younger managers with major potential, although CEOs themselves are also increasingly turning to support figures, usually in the form of coaches. A Stanford Graduate School of Business survey shows that 66% of CEOs don't have external coaches, although all of those surveyed said they would like to have one. The survey also showed that in 78% of cases it was the CEO who initiated the search for a coach, and in 21%, it was the chairman of the board.[18] Most CEOs are looking to acquire extra skills in conflict resolution, given the many agendas of the different stakeholders he or she must attend to. Some board members, for their part, say that CEOs need coaching in developing a succession plan and talent development, as well as in improving their sharing and delegation skills.

As we've seen, mentoring programs tend to be institutionalized within large corporations. That said, freelancers also use coaches, and even mentors. The self-improvement industry is estimated to be worth around $10 billion, generating in recent years any number of spin-offs and other initiatives, such as websites that claim to match your personal development needs with the right coach or mentor. The social networks are also increasingly the place where people go to find mentors, with sites such as Facebook and LinkedIn offering advisory services.

There is no one-size-fits-all mentor, and as we have seen with reverse mentoring, on occasions, a younger person can be the ideal adviser when it comes, for example, to understanding the latest trends. The key elements in a successful mentee–mentor relationship are mutual respect, logical fit, the absence of any political agenda, similar working and personal styles, and a commitment to making the relationship work.[19] At the same time, it is important that a mentor brings added value, fits in, and inspires trust and confidence. As INSEAD's Herminia Ibarra notes: "Chemistry is the key ingredient in true mentoring relationships."[20]

In her fascinating book *Forget a Mentor, Find a Sponsor: The New Way to Fast Track Your Career*, Sylvia Ann Hewlett proposes a new category of personal support, the sponsor.[21] These people are frequently bosses who believe in the personal value and potential of their protégés. Importantly, they have the direct ability to decide on their promotion and allow them to act independently and to take risks. These types of relationships are based on a quid pro quo: "sponsors seek furthering your career as an important investment in his or her own career." For their part, protégés assume a series of commitments, not necessarily explicitly agreed, along with demonstrating unshakeable loyalty, marking their personal stamp on the development and influence of their sponsor. Perhaps the important thing in these types of relationships is that the success of the protégé is almost built in, given that the sponsor also needs them for their own personal success.

The term mentor comes from Homer's *Odyssey*, when the goddess Minerva takes on the human form of Mentor to help Telemachus find his father and retake the throne of Ithaca. Minerva commits to helping her protégé every step of the way, allowing him to take risks and make mistakes, the true sign of a mentor: "But such was the affection of my friend, that he embarked with me for that voyage, which, in the folly of my presumption, I undertook contrary to his advice; and the gods, perhaps, permitted the fault, that the calamity which it drew upon me might teach me wisdom."[22]

10.4 The IBM Mentorship Program

During his time at the helm of IBM in 1993, Louis V. Gerstner Jr. brought about a decisive transformation within the company. The mandate of his predecessor, John Ackers, had ended with uncertainty over the competitive positioning of Big Blue and its future business areas, along with greater competition and a sharp fall in earnings. In a 1993 article about the upcoming CEO, the *Financial Times* invented a job advertisement that read: "Executive willing to take on the most challenging management job in the World. Must be a natural leader, able to make tough decisions, boost the morale of 300,000 employees and win the confidence of millions of shareholders and customers worldwide. Knowledge of 'computer-speak' helpful. Salary high and negotiable. Benefits include worldwide instant recognition. Wearers of white shirts need not apply."[23] The post required a visionary, and IBM chose Gerstner, the first outsider to occupy the post since 1914, and who had previously been CEO of RJR Nabisco, as well as holding senior positions at American Express and McKinsey & Company.

In his autobiography, *Who Says Elephants Can't Dance?*, Gerstner describes IBM at the time as an inward-looking, Balkanized company due to a strategy that consisted of dismembering the company's business units into "baby blues" that competed independently.[24] Gerstner ended this approach and inspired what would be IBM's future strategy of designing and offering integrated services to its clients. He would also reduce the workforce, as well as integrating business units to improve synergies.

Among the initiatives introduced to improve integration within the company was a mentoring program led by the 30 top executives of the company along with its 300 senior leadership team members. Federico Castellanos, then VP for Global Human Resources, has said that one of the main objectives of the mentoring program, once candidates had been selected, was to avoid these men and women who would eventually lead the company from "derailing" over the coming years.[25] This meant, for example, overcoming lack of confidence or the imposter syndrome— more common among senior managers than is generally recognized— and improving their ability to manage people, and to delegate. IBM identified 12 different personal traits that have gradually been addressed through a change of environment and management input. Another of the main objectives was to incorporate and promote members of minorities to senior positions.

IBM's mentoring program also aimed to "oil the system" of a highly diversified organization, with a global presence and with sophisticated but fragmented decision-making systems at all levels.

It goes without saying that the right mentors are crucial to a mentoring program. In the case of IBM, mentors were chosen from the top three levels of management, and the person chosen had not previously worked with their mentee. This is a key aspect in promoting trust and avoiding conflicts of interest. Mentors were, and still are, trained by coaches as well as by internal trainers.

Before joining the program, participants are evaluated by a team from Leadership Development. Candidates' files are consulted, along with 360-degree appraisals and any other feedback that might be considered relevant. One of the most important things for the heads of human resources is matching mentee and mentor, a proposal that would be approved by the senior management.

Mentors take on the role of coach, and are assigned to do so for life. They are regularly consulted by the board about promotions and appoint-ments, and they are asked about their mentees' progress. In effect, they take on the role of defending their charges. Castellanos says that during meetings with Gerstner there was always a "5-minute drill" that looked at any high-level openings, and which candidates might be suitable for them. The five minutes frequently turned into more than an hour, he remembers. Mentors' opinions were very important during such sessions.

Based on interviews carried out by IBM's human resources depart-ment, it seems that all involved in the mentorship program are happy with the initiative. As with similar programs, meetings are called as and when mentees request them.

Dating back to the 1880s, IBM is today one of the most admired and respected companies in the world, envied for its ability to attract and retain talent. Its business is global, but power and decision-making are decentralized. Its mentoring program also has a global reach and has become a central plank of the company's talent management strategy.

Notes

1. F. Nietzsche, *Beyond Good and Evil*, Chap. IV. http://www.guten-berg.org/files/4363/4363-h/4363-h.htm.
2. Harvard Business Press, *Managing Teams: Expert Solutions to Everyday Challenges*, Pocket Mentor Series (Boston, MA: Harvard Business Press, 2010), p. 45.
3. http://entertainment.time.com/2005/10/16/all-time-100-novels/slide/all/.

4. http://www.theguardian.com/artanddesign/jonathanjones-blog/2014/mar/21/the-10-greatest-works-art-ever.

5. S. Cain, "The Rise of the New Groupthink," *New York Times*, January 13, 2012. http://www.nytimes.com/2012/01/15/opinion/sunday/the-rise-of-the-new-groupthink.html?_r=0.

6. http://www.economist.com/blogs/prospero/2015/01/quick-study?fsrc=scn/tw_ec/benjamin_voyer_on_the_psychology_of_teamwork.

7. S. Cain, *Quiet: The Power of Introverts in a World That Can't Stop Talking* (New York: Penguin, 2013), p. 88.

8. http://www.nytimes.com/learning/general/onthisday/bday/0314.html.

9. C. Impey: *Beyond: Our Future in Space* (New York and London: W.W. Norton, 2015). Locations in Kindle version: 277, 1295. Second quote attributed to Robert Goddard.

10. D. Dobbs, "Restless Genes: The Compulsion to See what Lies Beyond that Far Ridge or that Ocean—or this Planet—is a Defining Part of Human Identity and Success," *National Geographic*, January 2013.

11. Ibid.

12. http://ngm.nationalgeographic.com/2013/01/125-restless-genes/dobbs-text.

13. A. Vance, *Elon Musk: Tesla, SpaceX, and the Quest for a Fantastic Future* (New York: Ecco/HarperCollins Publishers, 2015). file:///Users/santiagoiniguez/Desktop/'Elon%20Musk,'%20by%20Ashlee%20Vance%20-%20NYTimes.com.html.

14. Ibid.

15. W. Isaacson, *Steve Jobs* (New York: Simon & Schuster, 2011), p. 117.

16. American Society for Development and Training http://www.investopedia.com/articles/personalfinance/022315/best-fortune-500-mentorship-programs.asp. And a Sage report: http://www.sage.com/businessnavigators/research.

17. L. Quast, "Reverse Mentoring: What is it and Why it is Beneficial," *Forbes*, January 3, 2011.

18. http://www.gsb.stanford.edu/sites/gsb/files/publications-pdf/cgri-survey-2013-executive-coaching.pdf.

19. Harvard Business School Publishing, *The Right Match: Advice for Matchmakers from Coaching and Mentoring* (Boston, MA: Harvard Business School, 2006).

20. H. Ibarra, "Making Partner: A Mentor's Guide to The Psychological Journey," *Harvard Business Review*, March–April 2000.

21. S. A. Hewlett, *(Forget a Mentor), Find a Sponsor: The New Way to Fast Track Your Career* (Boston, MA: Harvard Business Publishing, 2013).

22. *The Adventures of Telemachus, the Son of Ulysses*. From the French of Salignac de la Mothe-Fenelon, by John Hawkesworth. http://openlibrary.org/books/OL19373286M/The_adventures_of_Telemachus_.

23. "IBM Needs a New Boss: Who's Got the Right Stuff", *Financial Times*, March 29, 1993.

24. L. Gerstner, *Who Said Elephants Can't Dance? Leading a Great Enterprise Through Dramatic Change* (New York: Harper Collins, 2002).

25. Interview with Federico Castellanos held in July 2015.

11

Nurturing Management Virtues

11.1 Leadership Virtues and Management Workouts

There is no magic formula for turning somebody into a consummate manager. Good managers have generally honed their skills over time, through the systematic exercise of good habits and routines, and as a result of accumulated experience of their role and of their relationships. To reach the heights of management excellence requires discipline, practice, and hard work. It is not achieved simply through the passage of time. The learning curve is steep.

Virtues are not innate but acquired. However, some people argue that it is not possible to learn or develop basic traits of character beyond a certain age. This view is based on outmoded Freudian theories, according to which the basic features of personality are acquired and fixed before reaching adolescence—more extreme versions of this say that they are formed in the womb. But a growing number of contemporary education theorists and cognitive psychologists accept that many skills and character traits can be learnt and developed in maturity if the necessary attitudes

© The Author(s) 2016
S. Iñiguez de Onzoño, *Cosmopolitan Managers*,
DOI 10.1057/978-1-137-54909-9_11

are cultivated. Indeed, at business schools we work on the premise that junior and senior managers cannot only update their knowledge of the latest business tools but also perfect their skills and further shape their personality—hopefully for the better—through education and practice, and socializing.

One of the most promising avenues for becoming a better manager is to practice management virtues, those operative good habits achieved through constant exercise, in a similar way to how muscles develop with fitness training.[1]

Firstly, remember that the list of managerial virtues is large and diverse. The more appropriate virtues to practice depend on your aspirations and how they match your responsibilities or your company's values. Some of the virtues traditionally associated with management include wisdom, resilience, courage, temperance, justice (fairness), and sociability.

Secondly, focus on the practice of those virtues which you are strong in. Traditionally, one of the objectives of education was to correct deviations from standard behavior, to overcome personal weaknesses, to teach lefties to write with their right hand. Fortunately, modern educators have evolved and respect and value individual intrinsic diversity. In this vein, one of the interesting contributions of Positive Psychology, whose aim is to "find and nurture genius and talent" and "to make normal life more fulfilling,"[2] is precisely to show that it is more productive, potentially successful, and fulfilling to enhance one's strengths than to try to strengthen one's weaknesses.

Thirdly, identify what are your two or three more outstanding virtues. Here the diagnosis from friends is more helpful than self-analysis. Knowing your distinctive strong points may help you to round your personality and to build up your personal brand.

Fourthly, keep track of your evolution in the practice of managerial virtues. Sometimes writing a diary or keeping an account of your personal evolution may be helpful and reinforcing. Benjamin Franklin's candid account of his progress on the 13 virtues basic to him,[3] along with an evaluation chart, is a very vivid illustration of this effort and has been commented on extensively.[4]

Fifth, remember that the main purpose of practicing managerial virtues is to become a better person, not just a more perfected management technician (see Fig. 11.1).

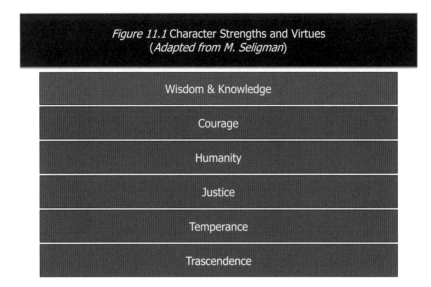

Fig. 11.1   Character strengths and virtues (Adapted from M. Seligman)

11.2 Call It Presence, Call It Gravitas: Just Be Yourself

It's a cliché, but there's more than a grain of truth in the maxim that first impressions count.[5] What's more, if we didn't know it from personal experience, innumerable surveys confirm we have just a few seconds to impact positively, whether in a one-on-one interview or when delivering a presentation to a crowded conference.[6]

Our concerns about self-perception and how others see us has now been conceptualized as executive presence, spawning a plethora of books and courses over recent years aimed at identifying the qualities that will set us apart from our peers and using them to put us on the path to leadership. But identifying the ingredients of executive presence, the things that seemingly make some people natural leaders, is far from easy.

As good a place as any to begin identifying the key traits of executive presence is by observing people who have already reached the top. Of course, these people have a natural advantage in that they are already ringed with the aura of power, prompting respect, interest, and even admiration when they appear in public.

For example, when a new pope is elected and makes his first speech from St Peter's in Rome, the faithful are not measuring his height, listening to the tone of his voice, or gauging the quality of his Italian. Something similar happens at our first meeting with the CEO of a major corporation, the dean of a major university, a successful artist, or a prize-winning novelist. We may know nothing about their life or earlier achievements, but the fact that they hold high office or enjoy universal acclaim gives them the glow of success that generally invites respect and recognition.

Going back further, the Romans, who knew a thing or two about power, executive or otherwise, distinguished between *potestas*, or power, and *auctoritas*, authority: *potestas* was the attribute granted to magistrates, and that they enjoyed regardless of whether they were good or bad at their job. Then, as now, power in itself generated respect.

But *auctoritas* was the influence or ascendency associated with senators, based on reputation, experience, and tried and tested wisdom. Ideally, both *potestas* and *auctoritas* would be melded in politicians with the most responsibility, although this was not always the case. Of the two attributes, the second is preferable, conferring greater legitimacy and acceptance on the bearer.

In today's corporate world, CEOs have *potestas*, an important starting point, and in most cases are assumed to enjoy *auctoritas*, given that they will have built up careers before taking on their responsibilities.

In her 2012 book *Executive Presence*, British writer Sylvia Ann Hewlett, the founder and CEO of the Center for Talent Innovation, uses another concept invented by the Ancient Romans, gravitas, as the key quality that sets successful business people apart, with 67% of executives she interviewed identifying this quality, along with communication skills (27%) and appearance (5%).[7]

Hewlett says that gravitas manifests itself as self-confidence and the ability to maintain grace under fire at moments of crisis, as well as determination and knowing when to bear one's teeth, along with integrity and the strength of character to speak truth to power. Emotional intelligence and charisma are also features of gravitas, says Hewlett. In short, it is pretty much the repository of all the qualities we associate with leadership.

The fortunate few imbued with gravitas need not worry too much about our communication skills or what we look like, says Hewlett, although the three qualities tend to go together. Great leaders will be forgiven for their lack of oratorical skills or dress sense, for example Napoleon, who was short, balding, and spoke French with a strong Corsican accent.

For communication expert Karen Friedman, Napoleon had the "wow factor," what she calls "magnetism," and that allows them to easily influence others: "They often speak up, use strong and clear language, communicate with passion and energy, and display positive body language by standing tall, making eye contact, offering a firm handshake, and using an authoritative tone of voice."[8]

Call it the wow factor or call it gravitas, but in my experience, the best way to get people's attention and hold it is by presenting to the world what we might call the best version of ourselves, which simply means just being genuine, being prepared, and being empathetic.

Sometimes we confuse being genuine with being spontaneous, although the effect of the two on other people can be very different. Spontaneity is acting without thinking, improvising, and can sometimes be amusing, and sometimes awkward; what's more, while it may get you a laugh, you're unlikely to be taken seriously at meetings.

But behaving in a genuine way, presenting that better version of yourself to the world, will give your words and actions authenticity, projecting a natural, straightforward image of somebody who thinks clearly and who can express themselves with ease.[9]

Presenting this better version of ourselves cannot be left to chance, and requires some preparation when going into meetings. Mark Twain once said: "I was never happy, never could make a good impromptu speech without several hours to prepare it."[10] We should know our subject well before discussing it with others, anticipating questions and responses, and even researching our listeners, what their expectations are, and of course what we want out of the meeting. It may seem boring, but going over a presentation until you are absolutely comfortable will always yield better results.

In being genuine, and after we have prepared what we are going to say, we also need to be able to project empathy toward those around us. As a rule, and depending on the context, applying a little humor can help connect with our audience, but what really makes the difference is knowing how the people we're talking to do things: assertiveness is expected when you're talking to a roomful of British or American executives, but might be counterproductive in China or Japan.

Just as spontaneity isn't the same as being natural, extrovert behavior isn't necessarily a sign of true leadership. Western culture is keen to divide us up into extroverts and introverts, and most of us will have taken the Myers-Briggs test at some time. Nobody is entirely extrovert or introvert, and we all have facets of both qualities within us. A common mistake is to assume that people who are more introverted are timid, and that therefore, extroverts make better leaders.

But in her bestseller *Quiet: The Power of Introverts in a World That Can't Stop Talking*, Susan Cain explains that up to a third, or even half, of Americans say they are introverts.[11] So if the United States is the most extrovert country in the world, we can only assume that there are many more introverts in other areas of the world, and that even in the West, around half of senior management will be introverts, even if they are trying to hide it.

Cain bolsters her argument by citing a survey carried out by Adam Grant of Wharton School of Business showing that research often attempts to establish a link between leadership and extroversion. We tend to measure our leaders as much by their charisma and personality as we do by their achievements in heading companies, or perhaps more so. Grant's work shows that it is often the case that extrovert leaders perform better when they have passive teams under them, while introverts do better with proactive employees, meaning that introverts may do better when it comes to innovation.

In conclusion, what are the leadership qualities we can identify in executive presence?

- First of all, to lead people, to have executive presence, you don't need to be an extrovert. Some of the most successful corporations today are led by people who fit the profile of what Jim Collins calls Level 5 Leaders.[12] These are professionals who have worked they way up to the top, are modest, but have a deep knowledge of their sector, are dedicated, and happy to delegate to their colleagues.

- Gravitas, arguably the most important element of executive presence, is acquired over the course of a career, and is the fruit of the prestige and reputation derived from being a true professional.
- There is no one-size-fits-all executive presence: understanding cultural context is essential.
- If, unlike Caesar, your reputation doesn't precede you, it is still possible to project gravitas by communicating clearly, from your appearance, and even your dress.
- If you have any doubts about how to project executive presence, particularly in terms of your appearance and communication skills, then it's certainly worth hiring the services of an adviser to give you a few pointers.

And finally, some advice from a man who knew a lot about appearances: Franco Moschino used to say "if you can't be elegant, at least be extravagant."[13] But thinking about it, perhaps this is not the best approach to take in the world of management, regardless of the Italian fashion designer's unquestionable *auctoritas*.

11.3 Look to the Future: Increase Your Empathy

Writing at a time when science seemed to promise a solution to all of humanity's problems, H. G. Wells was fascinated by the question of how technology would affect mankind's behavior in the coming centuries. In his 1924 novel *Men Like Gods*, a collection of middle-Englanders suddenly find themselves transported through time and space to Utopia, a society much more technologically and culturally advanced than that of early twentieth-century Britain.[14] This is a place whose inhabitants have long ago left behind "the days of confusion," a time of social and political upheaval, interrupted by constant wars and characterized by social inequality and rampant individualism—a place not much different than that which we find ourselves in a century later.

The reason Utopia is so peaceful a society is that its inhabitants have developed their empathy to such a degree that they are now able to communicate non-verbally. In one particularly amusing scene in Wells' book, the Utopians attempt to explain to their new guests, via telepathy, their history and customs. But not all are able to "hear" what is being said, and some are even left completely in silence. Among the few who pick up everything they are being told is a character called Barnstaple, and the reason is simple: he is among the few of his peers who unthinkingly makes the connection between his own experiences and knowledge and that of his hosts. In other words, he is naturally empathetic.

Empathy is the capacity to identify and respond to the feelings of others. Neuroscience and psychology have established that empathy, just like all intellective faculties, is physiologically rooted in our brains. It's hard-wired. Furthermore, the brain's plasticity allows us to adapt it and to train it through certain exercises and habits, not just in the first years of our lives, but into adulthood. Daniel Goleman's celebrated book, *Emotional Intelligence* lists several experiments that support this. The roots of empathy are not just genetic, but also cultural.[15]

The point Wells is making is that it is only through knowledge and education that different cultures and civilizations can overcome the barrier of communication (let's not forget he was writing less than a decade after the slaughter of World War I and a time of upheaval throughout Europe). Ignorance, he argued, and I would agree, is the biggest obstacle to understanding between us, and particularly in the case of understanding those from other cultures.

This is a principle that the Utopians have embedded in their society. Their education system is so sophisticated that they do not need governments or other power systems. Life in Utopia is based on the "five principles of Liberty": privacy, free movement, unlimited knowledge, truth, and the freedom to discuss and criticize. Having reached this advanced stage of intellectual development, conflict is resolved through reason, which has won out over the Utopians' earlier, more basic instincts.

Now, while I certainly believe in the transformative power of knowledge and education, my intention here is not to speculate on whether we could ever aspire to a society like H. G. Wells was describing. But what I do believe is that we can strengthen the relationship between education and empathy, which would certainly help promote better understanding between people. What's more, I think that cultivating our empathy can even heighten our receptiveness to other people's needs and wants: call it telepathy if you like, the point is to help us all communicate better. I am sure you've heard somebody say that there are moments with their partner, their friends, or even their boss when neither needs to say anything, and that a look or a gesture is enough—it may even have happened to you.

Empathy is essential for success in relationships, at work, in the family, and with friends and acquaintances. It allows us to know and understand other people's feelings, not just through conversation, but by interpreting non-verbal forms of expression through gestures, body language, and other signs. Most children, from an early age, show empathy by copying the mood of those around them, for example by crying when they hear other children cry, or laughing when their peers are laughing. As we get older, we feel sorry when our family members are unhappy, or pleasure when things go well for them.

Similarly, in *The Empathic Civilization*, Jeremy Rifkin argues that it is precisely our relationships with other people that gives meaning to our lives: "Empathy conjures up active engagement—the willingness of an observer to become part of another's experience, to share the feeling of that experience."[16] For Rifkin, humanity has by now reached a degree of empathy and biosphere-wide consciousness thanks to wireless and cellular technology that we can now connect with anybody anywhere on the planet, regardless of linguistic or cultural barriers. This will lead to a system of what he calls distributed capitalism that will allow us to collectively solve the major problems facing humanity, such as climate change or pandemics, and that will be focused on improving the quality of our lives and in working together rather than competing.

Rifkin's book includes many examples of how empathy between individuals and groups has overcome conflict and misunderstanding. He cites the famous incident during World War I when German and Allied soldiers facing each other across the trenches called a truce on Christmas Day 1914, meeting in no-man's land to exchange gifts and share photographs of loved ones. True, the generals soon put an end to the fraternizing, but the event showed how collective empathy between people in close physical contact was able, albeit briefly, to overcome confrontation.

There are still many in management who believe in Machiavelli's dictum, outlined in *The Prince*, that it is better to be feared than loved,[17] but

I believe that one of the essential characteristics of leadership is knowing how to cultivate empathy with one's colleagues and subordinates. Empathy motivates people and helps them to understand and share an organization's missions. What's more, it improves productivity.

As US academic Jason Boyers pointed out in an article a couple of years ago: "Though the concept of empathy might contradict the modern concept of a traditional workplace—competitive, cutthroat, and with employees climbing over each other to reach the top—the reality is that for business leaders to experience success, they need to not just see or hear the activity around them, but also relate to the people they serve."[18]

We may not be able to aspire yet to Utopia, but here's what H. G. Wells might have recommended the business leaders of the twenty-first century do to cultivate a little more empathy around them.

- An optimistic and constructive attitude is fundamental. I'm talking here about optimism tempered by realism, not the dreams that people are likely to dismiss or turn away from. A sense of humor, one of the optimism's sisters, is also a good idea, and can help generate intimacy, a good atmosphere, and a positive spirit in the workplace. Given how much time we spend at work over a lifetime, it's very convenient to enjoy ourselves there.
- We should take the time and interest to know more about our colleagues and subordinates: what their worries are, whether they have family problems or are faced with illness. Equally, let's find out what makes them tick and how they amuse themselves outside of work. A simple but rewarding practice is to send a birthday card.
- Passion for what we do, for the organization, and its goals also generates empathy, because passion is contagious. Enjoying our time at work and thinking constantly about how to improve on what we do inspires others to take the same approach.
- Be trustworthy and predictable, project reliability, and don't allow yourself to be brought down by moods.
- Read—particularly novels that give us insight into other people's characters, portray realistic situations, and depict how people like us respond to the things life throws at us.

– In general, we should always be looking to learn new things, to be
open to new ideas throughout our careers; this will better equip
us to understand those around us by seeing life from different
angles.

H. G. Wells was a far-sighted man who understood that it would take
humanity many centuries, if ever, before reason would overpower brute
force. In the meantime, we can make our contribution to Utopia by trying to understand each other better and working to overcome our collective problems. In a word, empathy.

11.4 Sense and Sensibility in Management

In today's developed world, the majority of us are lucky to live at a distance from external violence. Although our chances of suffering a violent
attack or an accident may vary, depending on countries, lifestyle, or jobs,
they are not comparable to the defenselessness experienced by our ances-
tors, centuries ago. The evolution of institutions, the rule of law, and the
moral progress achieved in our societies make the experience of external violence an improbable event. However, we can still witness violent
phenomena through TV and other media, watching the news on wars,
terrorist attacks, murders, natural disasters, and similar horrible events,
which happen elsewhere.

When learning of those human atrocities, such as the many cruel kid-
nappings of children, I recall Simone de Beauvoir's splendid *Les Belles
Images*, where the French protagonist, a conscientious mother, is concerned by her daughter's sadness over the evils occurring abroad—hun-
ger, epidemics, natural disasters—and causing devastating effects among
huge numbers of poor.[19] The mother believes that her daughter's suffer-
ings are useless because these calamities cannot be solved solely by one
person, if at all. This impotence of the single individual to solve big evils
produces a natural, psychological reaction in many humans. People like
"belle images"—beautiful images—and prefer them to scenes of hor-
ror. Additionally, most people are not prepared to coexist with permanent images of evil or suffering. The natural reaction of the mother in

Beauvoir's novel is, then, to change the television channel, or the subject I should say, in order to impede her beloved daughter's continuous exposure to the cruelest aspects of life. The extreme version of this "belle image" syndrome is just not talking about or not showing pictures of some particular disaster, minimizing the exposure to calamities, or even pretending that they do not exist. I am sure you can identify with the syndrome I am talking about.

In a similar vein, sometimes I hear that managers should avoid being sensitive or compassionate, since they should take hard decisions that may affect thousands of people, while keeping themselves calm and unaffected at the same time. This is encapsulated by the widely used expression: "It's nothing personal; It's just business."

Imagine that you have to fire half of your team as a consequence of a merger or a company downsizing. How could you cope with the personal tensions derived from such measures without detaching yourself enough to avoid suffering personally? Indeed, some managers, and humans in general, develop some sort of self-defense mechanism to protect themselves from mental disruptions in times of crisis, a sort of automatic reaction to elude thinking about the harmful consequences of our decisions on others.

However, sensitiveness and compassion have a place in business relations as virtues to be practiced. The challenge for managers is how to take hard decisions and at the same time keep their humanity. I can only think of a way out in those cases: hard decisions should be subject to rational scrutiny and managers who adopt them should be capable of defending them in the public arena through reasonable arguments. Contrary to what Machiavelli stated, I believe that, in business it is better to be loved than to be feared.

Going back to atrocities and how people react to them, I recently read Susan Sontag's *Regarding The Pain of Others*,[20] a forceful essay on the imagery of warfare, a wake-up call at a time when we are witnessing, every day, countless attacks on human lives everywhere, more than that which headlines can tell, and sometimes very close to home. Sontag explained: "the understanding of war among people who have not experienced war is now chiefly a product of [war photographers'] images." So far as we feel sympathy, Sontag wrote, "we feel we are not accomplices to what caused the suffering. Our sympathy proclaims our innocence as well as our impotence."[21]

Sontag was also realistic about what intellectuals can do about warfare: "Who believes today that war can be abolished? None, not even pacifists. We hope only (so far in vain) to stop genocide and to bring to justice those who commit gross violations of the laws of war (for there are laws of war, to which combatants should be held too), and to be able to stop specific wars by imposing negotiated alternatives to armed conflict."

Good Business is the best antidote to bad international politics. Good Education is the best equalizer across humans and societies. Working as a teacher in a business school is a privilege, as we get the opportunity to enhance our students', and our own, sense and sensibility, and contribute in some way to avoiding the "belle image" syndrome and try to keep our humanity.

11.5 Get into Shape Socially

Do you consider yourself more social than asocial? The response may not necessarily be related to whether you are more introverted than extroverted. Actually, it is facts that matters here and counting the time spent in social activities or interacting with others, beyond your closest family members, could quickly ascertain your degree of sociability.

Since one of the basic components of management is leading other people, socializing becomes a key part of our jobs. Henry Mintzberg, the renowned management academic, rightly criticized what he called the "folkloric" view of management, consisting in planning, organizing, coordinating, and controlling, and he showed that top managers spend most of their long work days dealing with people: in meetings, conferences, gatherings, and the like.[22]

Socializing has been and is essential for life, and not just for business, but also the arts and the sciences. Allow me to refer to the salons, the very selective social gatherings held in France in the second half of the seventeenth century. Salons—in French, living rooms—were meetings attended by aristocrats, artists, and intellectuals who engaged in lively discussions and gossip about politics, literature, religion, philosophy, and other related issues. Attendance at salons was by strict invitation, and apart from frivolous and social aspects, the gatherers aimed at engaging in elevated conversation. Prominent writers such as Molière, Racine, François Duc de La Rouchefoucauld—our featured writer here—and many other celebrities of the time showed up at the Salons to rehearse their works, perfect their thoughts, or just provoke the audience. The two most exclusive salons in Paris at that time were the houses of Madame de Montpensier and Madame de Sévigné.

Today, cocktails and other evening social events play a similar role. Interestingly, interaction in digital social networks, such as LinkedIn groups, has replaced many selective gatherings held face-to-face and are playing a significant role in the spreading of ideas and the expansion of business globally. Two of the differential advantages of interaction via social networks, as compared to traditional meetings, are asynchrony and remoteness. Maybe the salons of today and tomorrow will take many new virtual forms.

Socializing is the flip side of formal connections happening inside companies and ambitious managers realize the need of expanding the range of their personal exposure beyond the company landscape. Admittedly, many of today's social gatherings lack the profoundness of French salons and people may rather engage in "small talk" rather than discuss philosophy.

Given the long working hours of many managers, many find it difficult to reconcile professional and family responsibilities with social gatherings. I recently met a graduate of my school, currently CEO of a major company, who told me that he had given up on his social agenda. "How do you cope with increasing demands that managers become public figures?" I asked him. "Well, I have opted for a multiple but extremely methodical interaction with my company's stakeholders." I can vouch from experience that it works, given his sustained social prestige.

Despite La Rouchefoucauld being a regular attendee of salons—and many would imagine him enjoying being permanently surrounded by others—he was not fortunate in love nor in friendships, and his fate runs in parallel with the pessimistic reflections contained in his classical book *Maxims*.[23] He shows deep skepticism towards the meaning and the practice of virtues: "Our virtues are usually only vices in disguise" he anticipates at the beginning of the book.

The fact that most maxims are ironic does not preclude some comfort in reading them, as an exercise of detachment from vacuities and tantalizing human aspirations. Indeed, the reading of *Maxims* may be beneficial in enhancing humility, though some think it prompts nihilistic feelings. The following is a sample:

3. Whatever discoveries have been made in the land of self-love, many regions still remain unexplored.

Other reflections inspire more courageous and positive feelings from readers, such as the following, which is reminiscent of Socrates:

405. We come quite fresh to the different stages of life, and in each of them we are usually quite inexperienced, no matter how old we are.

Managers spend a lot of their time socializing, whether in the workplace or in the wider world. It goes with the territory, because, as discussed throughout this book, management is about leading people. And to be able to lead people, social skills are fundamental.

11.6 A Proven Technique for Reducing Stress at Work

Visual exposure to natural landscapes reduces stress, improves attention capacity, and induces behavioral changes that improve mood and general well-being. It even facilitates recovery from illness: this is evidenced in the findings of cognitive psychology, confirming the experiences of many of us.[24]

Some of us run to the countryside for the weekend in search of placid bucolic views; others to the coast to enjoy the boundless immensity of the sea. In the meantime, if your office is located in an urban area lacking views over nice gardens, the best means to experience a similar sensation is to hang a picture or a photo of one of your favorite landscapes that you may glance at in moments of fatigue or boredom. I have two photos visible from my working desk: one of Capri Island's silhouette, in Italy, and another of the red cliffs surrounding the white sands of Pipa beach, in Brazil.

In addition to those beneficial psychological effects, the contemplation of nature and the environment's allure has been a central object of the work of artists and writers through human history. In fact, as the British art historian Kenneth Clark observed: "the appreciation of natural beauty and the painting of landscape is a normal and enduring part of our spiritual activity."[25]

Appreciation of beauty can help release stress, improve mood, increase imagination, and contribute to recharging the batteries: "Considered from the perspective of the cognitive approach, landscape perception becomes a process of interpretation, mediated by emotional responses to sites, perceived meanings, and physiological reactions (e.g. stress reduction)."[26] According to research: "Generally, the natural landscapes gave a stronger positive health effect compared to urban landscapes," and the greener, the better.[27]

In short, a landscape hung in the office or as a screensaver will not only show off your erudition, but make you feel better.

Notes

1. An interesting approach in this way is: A. Rego., M. Pinha, M. Cunha, and S. R. Clegg, *The Virtues of Leadership: Contemporary Challenges for Global Managers* (Oxford: Oxford University Press, 2012).
2. C. Peterson and M. Seligman, *Character Strengths and Virtues: A Handbook and Classification* (Oxford & New York: Oxford University Press, 2004).
3. en.wikipedia.org/wiki/The_Autobiography_of_Benjamin_Franklin.
4. G. Rubin's LinkedIn post: "How You, Too, Can Copy Benjamin Franklin," January 3, 2014. See also: S. Shank's LinkedIn post: "The Autobiography of Benjamin Franklin: There Will Be Sleeping Enough in the Grave," November 19, 2013. https://www.linkedin.com/pulse/20140103185636-6526187-how-you-too-can-copy-

benjamin-fanklin?articleId=86666121591371368#comments-86666612159138371368&trk=seokp-company_posts_primary_cluster res_title.
5. http://www.businessinsider.com/only-7-seconds-to-make-first-impression-2013-4.
6. B. Kasanoff, "Nailing a Presentation in the First 60 Seconds," LinkedIn Pulse, September 18, 2013. https://www.linkedin.com/pulse/20130918033719-36792-nailing-a-presentation-in-the-first-60-seconds.
7. S. A. Hewlett, *Executive Presence: The Link Between Merit and Personal Success* (New York: Harper Business, 2014).
8. See J. Goudreau, "Do You Have Executive Presence?," *Forbes*, October 29, 2012. http://www.forbes.com/sites/jennagoudreau/2012/10/29/do-you-have-executive-presence/.
9. Ibid.
10. http://quoteinvestigator.com/2010/06/09/twain-speech/.
11. S. Cain, *Quiet: The Power of Introverts in a World That Can't Stop Talking* (New York: Penguin 2013), p. 69.
12. J. Collins, "The Level 5 Leadership: The Triumph of Humility and Fierce Resolve," *Harvard Business Review*, July–August 2005.
13. Attributed to F. Moschino, *Independent Revolution*, November 7, 2014.
14. H. G. Wells, *Men Like Gods* (New York: Ferris Printing Company, 1923).
15. D. Goleman, *Emotional Intelligence: Why It Matters More than IQ* (New York: Bantam Books/Random House, 1995).
16. J. Rifkin: *The Empathic Civilisation: The Race to Global Consciousness in a World of Crisis* (New York: Penguin, 2009).
17. N. Machiavelli, *The Prince*, Chap. 17.
18. J. Boyers, "Why Empathy is the Force That Moves Business Forward," *Forbes*, May 30, 2013.
19. S. de Beauvoir, *Les Belles Images* (Paris: Gallimard, 1964).
20. S. Sontag, *Regarding the Pain of Others* (New York: Penguin, 2004).
21. Ibid.
22. H. Mintzberg, "The Manager's Job: Folklore and Fact," *Harvard Business Review*, March–April 1990.

23. La Rouchefoucauld, *Maxims* (New York and London: Penguin, 1982).
24. M. D. Velarde, G. Fry, and M. Tveit, "Health Effects of Viewing Landscapes—Landscape Types in Environmental Psychology," *Urban Forestry & Urban Greening*, Vol. 6 (2007), pp. 199–212.
25. K. Clark: *Landscape into Art* (London: Penguin, 1961), pp. 15–16.
26. B. Kara: "Landscape Design and Cognitive Psychology Procedia: World Conference on Psychology and Sociology 2012," *Social and Behavioral Sciences*, Vol. 82 (2013), pp. 288–291.
27. Velarde, Fry, and Tveit, "Health Effects of Viewing Landscapes."

12

Talent Management and Sustainable Companies

12.1 How Transparent Should a Company Be?

"Transparency is fake and it's overvalued," the CEO of a food company told me once. We were discussing demands for businesses to be fully transparent, as well as the trend on the social networks for people to share their experiences and thoughts in real time *urbi et orbi* with friends and strangers alike. The CEO added that what he called the digital strip-tease some people perform on their Facebook or LinkedIn blogs was simply an act, the projection of a fictitious identity, and that all they were really doing was creating a personality to please an audience, rather than truly reflecting what was going on in their lives. What's more, he said, hammering home his point, businesses typically respond to demands for complete transparency by launching overloaded and unconvincing marketing and communication campaigns that quite frankly are not in shareholders' interests.

I am sure this largely negative analysis of transparency in business is shared by many other CEOs uncomfortable with the idea of constant

© The Author(s) 2016
S. Iñiguez de Onzoño, *Cosmopolitan Managers*,
DOI 10.1057/978-1-137-54909-9_12

and total scrutiny of their actions and decisions. Let's be honest: few of us find the idea of being under a microscope very appealing.

But if we're not going to dismiss the question of transparency out of hand and want to discuss it in any depth, then we have to start with some basic questions: first of all, what do we mean by transparency in business? And secondly, does transparency help make companies more profitable?

To begin with, transparency means different things to different people. On the basis of compliance requirements, it can simply mean that a company will provide full, accurate, and timely disclosure of information, mostly to the company's shareholders.[1]

But some advocates of corporate transparency want to go far beyond just observing the requirements of traditional reporting, and argue that compliance alone is not enough. Sustainability-in-business pioneer Adam Werbach, for example, writes: "True transparency itself [...] is the one that most companies miss and the one that makes all the difference. Beyond bringing operations into compliance, share the information broadly inside and outside an organization. This will allow a company to open up to further improvements and innovations."[2]

To attain this degree of openness, Werbach recommends companies develop a quadruple bottom line that, as well as weaving together environmental protection, social equity, and economic health, also incorporates cultural vitality. Werbach explains that these practices should not be seen by the company as a public relations exercise, but should also drive and support internal transparency, which is in turn reflected in what the company says to the wider world.

That said, research finds many companies wanting as regards internal transparency. According to one recent survey, 71% of employees said they felt their directors didn't spend enough time communicating the company's objectives to the workforce.[3] "When asked what was holding their company back, 50% of these employees pointed the finger at a lack of company-wide transparency."[4]

To improve internal transparency, senior management has three options at its disposal:

- *Internal communication based on interactive platforms* such as Yammer, Chatter, Jive, or Telligent to facilitate contact between employees. Managed properly, these can improve interaction at different levels, spark discussion between formal and informal groups, contributing to information flows, as well as demonstrating best practice. Needless to say, transparency will increase as senior management shares information about the key issues facing the company.

— *Recognition of individual or group contributions via incentives* that promote new ideas and innovation. It is important not just to recognize those ideas that are implemented, but also to recognize those that have not been able to be carried out for whatever reason, whether cost or opportunity.

— *Installing an open-plan office system* that facilitates access and interaction between different departments.

In regard to the latter, on a recent trip to the United States I had the opportunity to visit a number of buildings that best exemplify the principles of transparency applied to architecture. The Ford Foundation's headquarters, created by Kevin Roche in 1963 in Midtown Manhattan, has at its heart a huge, tree-filled central atrium from which all the floors run, and from where it is also possible to see just about everything that is going on in the building, except for the directors' offices. The design, using glass, symbolizes the transparent practices of a not-for-profit organization such as the Ford Foundation through its programs and communication initiatives.

I was also impressed by Evans Hall at Yale School of Management in New Haven, Connecticut, where Norman Foster has created a four-story building with exterior and interior glass walls built around a courtyard, just like the Ford Foundation, although open to the sky. The library, the cafeteria, the auditorium, and access to the classrooms and passageways all run round the courtyard, making it possible to see what is going on in most parts of the building. Again, the design is meant to reflect the ideal of transparency in the corporate environment.

So should this ideal of physical transparency be applied across the board? Should all companies adopt the open-plan office?

The Apple campus, which I have also had the privilege to visit, is located at the intriguingly named 1 Infinite Loop, in Cupertino, California. Apple is now the world's leading company in terms of its share value, and is also considered to be among the most innovative. At the same time, the corporate culture that founder Steve Jobs imposed was one that restricted communication, saying nothing about its products and services until the moment of their launch. Jobs' obsession with keeping projects strictly under wraps is well known, and employees who discuss company business with the media are still likely to find themselves looking for a new employer.

The design of the Apple campus, which dates back to 1993— a spectacular new headquarters is being built, also designed by Norman Foster, a few miles up the road—very much reflects the culture of secrecy that has come to characterize the company. Access to the central atrium is through a single entrance flanked by security guards who check everybody's identity, whether visitors or employees, turning anybody away who doesn't have permission to be there. It is forbidden to take photographs inside the building. The sancta sanctorum is the research laboratory run by Jony Ive, and it is a closed space, with tinted windows, and to which access is extremely limited.[5]

Interestingly, the design of Apple's headquarters is very much in contrast to its retail outlets, which are open to the world, with glass staircases and open-plan floor space, brightly lit, and where it is possible to see everything that is going on. Surely there's a contradiction here?

Not really. Apple's culture of secrecy applies to the early stages of its value chain: design, production, and distribution. Its goal is to protect innovation up to the final moment, keeping the element of surprise about its products until they are launched, a strategy that makes perfect strategic sense. But once the product is out there, Apple is the very model of transparency when it comes to providing information about its creations, as well as in terms of customer service. Apple reveals very little about its corporate policy, its strategies, or its research, but says a lot about its products and what they can do. Steve Jobs was a born communicator, a skill that Tim Cook shares.

In short, Apple is proof that full transparency in all areas of a company's activities is not necessarily the best way to generate innovation and profitability. Ethan Bernstein's article "The Transparency Trap" convincingly argues that complete transparency is not advisable, at least in three areas of a company's activities.[6]

In the first place, open-plan offices where everything is on view can actually inhibit innovation and employees' ability to carry out their tasks, as they may feel that they are essentially under surveillance. This is particularly the case when different work groups are sharing the same area, with each seeing the task in hand from very different perspectives. A friend of mine who is a chef has told me that many cooks feel more comfortable working in a kitchen that is away from public view than in restaurants where the cooking area is open to diners, a tendency that has become fashionable in recent years. Areas set aside for a department to work in can often lead to greater productivity, freeing employees from the feeling that Big Brother is watching.

Secondly, Bernstein argues that while transparency is great for letting the workforce know about key decisions, it is not so beneficial for generating feedback about employees' performance. Some departments, for example, use a whiteboard for charting success in meeting objectives. Bernstein warns that sometimes it's better not to publicize what individual members of the team have accomplished. Somebody may be going through a difficult time, or may have contributed to the collective effort to their personal detriment, and the feeling of being named and shamed is hardly the best motivator.

The final area where transparency is ill-advised is during certain stages of the innovation, experimentation, and development process—as seen with Apple—or when delicate negotiations are underway. For example, it would be unwise to let anybody other than the close circle of directors and the legal department know about a merger or acquisition with another company. The workforce may feel they have been kept in the dark when they hear about the takeover in the media as a result of leaks. This can be avoided by having an internal communication plan ready that can be implemented at short notice.

In short, transparency is not an absolute for all companies at all times. Corporate transparency is a matter of degree. We must establish which groups in the company need to be more transparent and what the objectives are, which will mainly be to drive innovation, share knowledge about the company, and to promote best practices. It is always a good idea for the workforce to understand the company's strategy and goals. The CEO's involvement in this, through the channels and means that are appropriate to each company's size and activities, help employees feel more involved.

It is also important to establish a balance between transparency and privacy, in relation both to the workforce's activities and to the individual, as well as in collective information. We live in a world where access to information about businesses and people, true and false, is universal and immediate. In such an environment, directors can feel that they are permanently on stage. We need to respect people's personal space.

Companies will benefit from implementing transparency practices that go beyond compliance, while at the same time respecting the confidentiality that provides its competitive advantages. A proactive external communication policy, one that is ahead of the curve, will create a better perception of transparency by the company's different stakeholders. At the same time, transparency generates trust and loyalty among customers.

The acid test of transparency is authenticity. What counts in the final analysis is that, when necessary, the people running a company can reasonably justify their decisions, even when they are controversial, in the public arena.

To conclude, imperative transparency is excessive and counterproductive. As General de Gaulle famously said: "Mystery is the essence of prestige," and in part, he was right.

12.2 Building Our Own Personal Narrative

Imagine that a Hollywood producer wants to make a movie of your life—not only covering your lived experiences, but also anticipating your future. If you accept the deal, you may start working with a scriptwriter, or decide to write the script yourself. The resulting story should recreate your life in the best possible light, appealingly and attractively, even entertainingly, for the general public. This is regardless of whether your personal story is composed of only happy moments or whether it contains drama and even tragedy: the lives of most of us have light and darkness, ups and downs, happiness and sadness.

Additionally, in order to build a good personal narrative, the script should depart sometimes from actual events and recreate reality with epical and poetic elements.

Let's get back to reality. It's quite improbable that our lives will reach the screen, but we may agree that the exercise of developing the story, the narrative, of your life makes sense, both for you and your family members and friends, and even for a wider array of stakeholders if you are a leading manager or hold a prominent social position.

"One of the puzzles of the human personality is our virtual compulsion to storify our reality: we love stories," says strategic narrative expert Amy Zalman.[7] Indeed, since childhood we grow attached to stories, fables, family anecdotes, local tales, and epical narrations of remote civilizations. Those stories bring meaning to our environment, simplify the complexity of the world, facilitate our integration in society, and provide us with behavioral references and role models. Furthermore, stories enhance our sense of belonging to the broad and diverse constituency of human beings.

The early philosophers used myths to explain some of the major issues affecting our lives since they were mindful of the formidable pedagogical power of stories. Plato, for example, will be remembered by many for his myths of the Cavern and of the Ring of Gyges: the first addressing whether true knowledge is possible, and the second considering, with less fortune in my opinion, the duty to just be, regardless of external pressure.[8]

Stories are also essential to bolster social organizations and to gain both internal and external supporters. The origins of states, religions, institutions, some family sagas, and of course companies rely on stories, based either on reality or fiction, which recreate their genesis and evolution and make them stand out as unique and distinctive.

Furthermore, storytelling is essential for learning and personal development and widely used in the education of children. Some of the fondest memories of my childhood are the stories that my mother told us after watching movies together. Her emphasis was not just on the plot, but also on the visual and evocative aspects of what she had observed, which stimulated our imagination and awareness, and our desire to further our knowledge.

However, the use of stories is not only restricted to the education of the young. Experience shows that stories are also very useful for teaching adults and even senior managers. The case-study methodology, commonly used at business schools, employs a characteristic strategic narrative that gives meaning and unity to facts and data on a company or management situation. Interestingly, according to the feedback from executive programs' directors, managers, especially those with greater responsibilities, increasingly demand shorter case studies, perhaps due to their lack of available time and their distinctive orientation to action, with less time for reflection, a common feature of manager's work.

In fact, the analysis of stories and narratives has flourished across the social sciences in recent years, from international relations to business strategy and political science, and has led to the creation of the cross-disciplinary field of narratology, the theory of how narratives are structured and related issues.

In this context, a concept that has gained increasing ground is "strategic narrative." The fundamental assumption behind strategic narrative is that telling stories is a purposeful activity, and that those who relate narratives want to cause some effect in listeners or recipients, for example increasing motivation, aligning people around some cause or value, strengthening a community and even to influence the future behavior of others. Indeed, strategic narrative is associated with linking the past and the future: "Narrative imagining was fundamental both to our ability to explain and our ability to predict," explains Mark Turner.[9]

In the same vein, Sun Tzu's *The Art of War*—essential reading for all managers—states that: "true leaders create magic in all their strategies."[10] My interpretation of this is that the strategic narrative employed by business leaders can provide the appropriate, almost spiritual, conditions to motivate others.

Indeed, in business communication, stories are carefully selected by top managers to describe their company's key milestones, or to illustrate their organizational culture and stakeholder's values, their strategic mission and essential features. Those stories add true value to their companies and conceptualize their main strategic advantages.

Also, CEOs use stories in their presentations to justify or mystify key strategic decisions and to provide context for corporate transformations.

"Stories are the latest fad to have hit the corporate communication industry. Experts everywhere are waking up to the something that any child could tell them: that a story is easier to listen and much easier to remember than a dry string of facts and propositions," explains *Financial Times*' columnist Lucy Kellaway.[11]

That said, strategic narratives are not pitches. The latter are those discourses prepared for short, quick presentations, either of your company or of yourself, usable at cocktails, elevators, at the beginning of business meetings as well at some other social events. A strategic narrative takes longer than a pitch and provides more nuances and references to provide a complete picture about you or your company.

While building a narrative, I suggest you follow the golden rules of American publicists: first, tell a meaningful story; second, be concise—even brief; third: emphasize the emotional over the conceptual.

It is advisable to develop a strategic narrative of your own company if there is not one in place already. This narrative should portray the company's institutional values, the fundamental milestones in its history, its main activities, products or services and the key features of its members. Stories have protagonists, and it may be helpful that the main characters are company figures. At the same time, the more anchored a narrative is in past characters and former episodes, the less future-oriented and innovative it may be. Of course, it depends on how forward looking and futuristic are the stories that form the narrative.

It is a good idea have your own strategic narrative about yourself: an attractive and seductive story about your origins, your background, your key personality traits, showing how your personality was formed. Your story may also include your principal mentors, or alternatively you may emphasize your growth as that of a self-made person.

Your own story, of course, evolves as time passes. Some personal narratives emphasize the consistency and unity of one's life, whereas others may highlight the discontinuity and juxtaposition of different facets or stages in a life (like when we refer to the first Wittgenstein or the second Picasso).

I am convinced that taking the effort to produce your personal narrative will help you to give more meaning to your own life, even if it lacks coherence and you find that the dots of your experience are disperse.

12.3 Is Retirement Still an Option?

Medical progress means that compared to even a few decades ago, for more and more of us, our age no longer necessarily reflects our health or our ability to work. Somewhere along the way, it seems we have gained at least an extra decade of useful life.

Until now, we have tended to assume that our minds followed our bodies' aging processes, and that each stage of life deeply affected our outlook on the world and our ideas of ourselves. That was until what has become known as modern aging challenged these conventions, forcing us to rethink what it means to be older, now that we are living longer. Soon, the over-50s will make up the majority of the population in many countries, particularly in the developed world, and this will prompt major changes, some of which are already underway, with implications for us as individuals and as societies.

From my own perspective, my expectations of living longer will inevitably mean delaying retirement, along with new cycles of personal and professional renewal. We can probably expect new educational initiatives focused on the over-sixties, along with seeing greater numbers of older people attending university either to retrain or reorient themselves toward new careers or professional projects.

Society too, will change the way it sees and treats older people, if only because they will make up a sizeable demographic that governments will want the support of. We can expect to see more novels and movies about adult life, we will have more older role models, and there will be more services and products aimed at older people; the needs of seniors will even be reflected in fashion. In fact, modern aging is one of the most promising areas for entrepreneurs, generating any number of start-ups.

Becoming old is a "privilege" and a "special favor" wrote French philosopher Michel de Montaigne in the seventeenth century.[12] Today, at least in developed societies, passing the age of 65 confers the right to retire on a pension, whether state, or accrued through savings.

But what we now need to ask ourselves, given that we are going to be living longer is whether it's a good idea any longer, whether it's healthy, appealing, or simply possible to retire, at least at the current benchmark age, especially if it means doing nothing other than playing golf into the twilight years (assuming one's pension is up to it).

One solution that comes to mind is continue with voluntary retirement at the same time as gradually raising retirement age in line with extended longevity so that our societies are able to continue paying pensions, whether private or public.

Of course, different countries have different voluntary retirement ages. In Sweden and the United States people can retire when they wish, and cannot be forced to step down from their job based solely on their age. But a recent survey by Randstad shows that one in three people would like to retire between the ages of 62 and 63.[13] At the same time, countries such as Spain and Italy are raising retirement age to 67, while in Germany there is talk of extending it to 69. In China and India, it's 60. And the country with the highest retirement age is Australia, where it's 70, which is what the European Commission is recommending that EU do, arguing that this will help keep us more active into old age.

But if we're going to have a discussion about retirement, why not take the opportunity to rethink the nature of work along more radical lines, making for a more continuous working life in which we achieve more, and that rather than just stopping, we scale down our professional activities once into our sixties, but continue contributing? For many people this is simply another way of preventing us from exercising our seemingly fundamental right to rest after a long, hard working life. Seen from another perspective, working in this way can actually improve our quality of life in old age, while at the same time keeping our bodies and minds healthier. Carlos Slim, the Mexican businessman who shows no signs of slowing down at 75, has suggested raising the retirement age to 70, at the same time as introducing a three-day week with longer hours.[14]

Needless to say, such an approach wouldn't work for people with professions requiring sustained physical effort, such as athletes or manual workers.

Returning to our central issue: when is a good time to retire? For most of us, this is largely a financial question: do we have enough money to do so? Retirement is not a time to be faced with economic worries and we want to make sure that we have saved up sufficient funds to allow us to pursue whatever plans we might have made. It's not a good idea to retire when you still owe a lot of money, or if you still have major outgoings such as the education of your children.

Aside from finance, there are other questions to be addressed. Firstly, as management guru Robert Sutton points out,[15] the idea is to step down gracefully, particularly if you want to be remembered as a "selfless steward" rather than a selfish narcissist. This means dealing effectively with succession, transferring your knowledge and your contacts with major stakeholders to the rest of the team, and being prepared to help out if needed.

It is also essential to have your own plans and projects for this new age in which you will no longer be working. In particular, do not stop learning new things, and continue developing the skills that you put into practice during your professional life, keep up to speed on technology and the sciences, and keep your network of personal relationships active.

More and more of us are opting to retire to places where there is developed world medical treatment available, along with a benign climate, low prices, and where older people are safe. The globalization of financial services, coupled with agreements between countries, such as within the EU, that allow access to the state health service is seeing growing numbers of pensioners head to countries such as Spain, or some enclaves within Latin America.

Philosophers have largely seen old age in two lights: the most optimistic view is perhaps that of Cicero, whose essay On Old Age takes a stoical approach to aging, explaining that we gain in experience as we enter our final stage of life, and that we can compensate for our physical decline by living in the mind. He uses the analogy of a ship's captain, who is able to direct operations even though he no longer able to shin up the mast any longer.[16] But what Cicero is really doing is praising the members of the Roman Senate, made up of older, experienced men, as opposed to Julius Caesar and his successors, who imposed an autocratic system of empire.

Two millennia later, Simone de Beauvoir, the doyenne of existentialism, wrote in *The Coming of Age* of entering a stage of decline, and that society sees the process as negative, regardless of how we ourselves feel about it. "No one ever speaks of a beautiful old women," she writes, but only of "a charming old woman."[17]

Employers also face the important responsibility of managing their senior staff. It's a good idea to create a company demographics map to help handle this challenge, given that an aging population can impact on the talent coming through the pipeline, as well as productivity.[18] At the same time, to get the most from what older staff have to offer, it is a good idea to introduce more flexible working hours, as mentioned above.

One of the things I have always admired about China's large corporations is that many of them have special departments, led by vice presidents, whose job is to look out for the interests and wellbeing of retired workers. This reflects China's traditional respect for older people, and a way of thanking them for their contribution to the collective good. For example, the policy of state oil company Sinopec toward its 400,000 former employees, is: "Retirees have won colleagues' respect and recognition with their integrity, hard work and contributions to the company in the history of Sinopec. We are doing what we can to care for their living and health condition, add comfort and joy to their life, such as visiting them from time to time."[19]

Of course there are also people who do not want to retire. In the information society, anybody who is still in possession of their mental faculties can make a contribution. And if you are the owner of your own business, then you probably aren't thinking of retiring any time soon. It's part of the reality of being an entrepreneur. Perhaps some of us should think about becoming entrepreneurs as we enter our sixties, after all, it's never too late, and what better way to enjoy the final stage of our lives than by putting all our experience to good use?

12.4 The Good Life

One of the moments that remains most vividly in my memory from my time at Oxford University was attending a class given by Ronald Dworkin about The good life. The University College classroom was packed with attentive students, some of them sitting on the floor. Dworkin loved debate: he was a magnificent speaker, eloquent, sometimes provocative, and never indifferent toward his audience. Referring to his ability to argue a point during his many years in the legal profession, he was once described as "that lawyer that beats them all." On one occasion he came to Madrid, and I had to transcribe a talk he had given without any notes. The text required virtually no editing, reflecting his mental discipline and oratorical skills.

Dworkin was a great lover of art, and the analogy he used to describe what to him was a good life was creating the best work of art possible, depending on our personal opinion. He explained that assessing the success of this artistic endeavor should not focus solely on the outcome, the work of art in itself, or our achievements in life, but more importantly on the process that has led up to that outcome. In the same way that in the artistic world what matters is the genesis of a work of art or a style—for example, Picasso's move from his blue period to cubism, rather than a particular painting, which after all can be copied by somebody else—when evaluating our lives, we need to focus on the itinerary, on the path we take through life: "We value human lives well lived not for the completed narrative, as if fiction would do as well, but because they too embody a performance: a rising to the challenge of having a life to lead. The final value of our lives is adverbial, not adjectival—a matter of how we actually lived, not of a label applied to the final result. It is the value of the performance, not anything that is left when the performance is subtracted."[20]

An important part of what gives our lives meaning is work: it takes up an important amount of our time, provides us with the means to live, and hopefully can be a source of satisfaction and personal development. That's why it's so important we like our profession. Sadly, most people in the world do not enjoy their job. But if you are reading this, then in all likelihood you're among those lucky few who have chosen their profession. This freedom of choice comes with the responsibility of carrying out that profession to the best of our ability; in short to be a consummate professional.

Fortunately, we live in a diverse world, one that offers us the opportunity to choose how we want to work, as well as to reach our own conclusions about what constitutes the good life, conclusions we must always reach as a result of our own experiences: others can tell us about their lives, we can follow their model, but in the final analysis, how we live is down to us.

Dworkin's advice that we see life in terms of a process rather than the outcome can be applied to any manner of topics, and has even become a mantra for many golf coaches in recent years. Regardless of the position we might occupy in an organization, or even if we have reached the pinnacle of a company, it is the experience and the development process that really gives meaning to professional endeavor. That's why there is no point in feeling frustrated if we don't get this or that position. What counts is what we have learned and experienced in trying.

In fact, many psychologists say that we get more pleasure from the effort of trying to achieve something than we do once we have it. The analogy of life as a journey, in which the more intense emotions happen along the way rather than when we arrive, may be a common one, but as we get older, the sense in it becomes ever clearer.

Clayton Christensen has been advising graduates of Harvard Business School about planning a career for many years, which he has distilled into an intriguingly titled article, *How Will You Measure Your Life?*[21] Before reading it, I assumed that it would provide a model, based on management theory, which would allow us to measure the personal worth of life itself. Can different people's lives be evaluated? Can we calculate the value of our own lives, assigning values to the lives of people we know?

Such an exercise would make little sense, because we put supreme value on any human life. Closer to home, we feel that the lives of the people we love are of incalculable value, and are even prepared to sacrifice ours in their place. At the same time, we consider our own lives to be beyond any price, and our experiences cannot be itemized according to the valuation models we apply to things, or even animals, although it has to be said that some people would definitely put their pet's life over that of many humans.

In short, human lives cannot, or should not, be subject to economic factors or transaction costs. At times over the course of history, humankind has practiced slavery and traded in people, and tragically, there are many places in the world today where human life seems to have little value and people are treated shamefully. All right-minded people feel that it is their duty to combat such practices, regardless of the perverse arguments sometimes used to justify them, and to eradicate them forever from our world: little wonder that we admire those who dedicate their lives to fighting inequality and poverty.

Surely few right-minded people would accept the idea of measuring a life in terms of accruing a fortune and amassing material goods? Money can be an instrument of freedom, and having the necessary resources means being able to live in relative comfort and to provide well-being and access to opportunities for our loved ones. But most intelligent people understand that once our basic needs are met, happiness is dependent on other factors, and mainly on the relationship with those we love.

Returning to Christensen's advice. Aside from recommending his graduates to design a personal strategy focused on talent, time, and the energy required to implement it, he offers particularly wise counsel in assessing our personal lives: "I've concluded that the metric by which God will assess my life"—Christensen is devoutly religious—"isn't dollars, but the individual people whose lives I've touched. Don't worry about the level of individual prominence you have achieved; worry about the individuals you have helped become better people."

Perhaps one of the golden rules for living the good life is never to see those around us as a means, but instead as ends in themselves. This can apply to all kinds of contexts: with loved ones, friends, work colleagues, as well as everybody we deal with.

If we see existence as evolution, then thinkers such as J. David Vellerman, believe that life is better if over time it improves rather than drifting into difficult situations: "Consider two different lives that you might live. One life begins in the depths but takes an upward trend: a childhood of deprivation, a troubled youth, struggles and setbacks in early adulthood, followed finally by success and satisfaction in middle age and a peaceful retirement. Another life begins at the heights but slides downhill: a blissful childhood and youth, precocious triumphs and rewards in early adulthood, followed by a midlife strewn with disasters that lead to misery in old age."[22]

Vellerman believes the second is the better, although I imagine he would accept that his thinking is flawed. No life is that lineal: we experience ups and downs at different periods. At the same time, although it is possible to describe somebody's life in terms of progress or decline, to do so is more an exercise in literature than a reflection of how we ourselves see our lives. David Copperfield and King Lear are powerful characters, but much of their older lives bears little relation to our own experiences. What's more, the good life is one that develops by weighing up the important things, as well as knowing how to mature and grow old regardless of adversity, health problems, or the loss of those we love.

Looking back over our lives, there are two feelings we should avoid at all cost. The first is regret, particularly as regards how we have treated others at certain times. Regret is best countered by asking for forgiveness. Saying you are sorry is healthy, and helps us to overcome guilt, and sometimes can even win back relationships we thought were lost forever. In turn, to forgive, to truly forgive, brings inner peace. Let's not forget that forgiveness was a power once reserved for the gods.

The second feeling that we tend to fall prey to as we get older is nostalgia. But unlike memory, which can revive experiences, particularly happy ones, nostalgia is simply the feeling that time has passed us by, and holds us hostage to the past, preventing us from facing the future with optimism. Cultivating it is ill-advised and quite simply a futile exercise that will take us nowhere.

The Ancient Greeks wrote three kinds of biography: the *enkomion*, which was originally sung to honor the winners of the Games; the peripatetic biography, influenced by Aristotle, focused on the virtues and characteristics of the subject and based on the belief that a person's character was reflected in their actions; and finally, there were scientific biographies, which outlined somebody's life in chronological order rather than exploring their character, and tended to be drier and more focused on the facts.[23]

As we look back over our lives, whether from the perspective of retirement, or as part of the new generation of senior managers working into their seventies and beyond, it's tempting to think about how we would best like to be remembered. At the same time, perhaps we should also take the time to share some of the wisdom we have acquired along the way with our younger colleagues, and help point them in the direction of the good life.

Notes

1. Elaborated after. http://blog.experts-exchange.com/ee-tech-news/transparency-in-business-why-it-matters/.
2. A. Werbach, *Strategy for Sustainability: A Business Manifesto* (Boston, MA: Harvard Business Publishing, 2009), p. 102.
3. "Cost of Poor Internal Communication." http://www.slideshare.net/ldickmeyer/cost-of-poor-internal-communications-912.
4. I. Pozin: "How Transparent Is Too Transparent In Business?," *Forbes,* February 4, 2014. http://www.forbes.com/sites/ilyapozin/2014/04/02/how-transparent-is-too-transparent/.
5. W. Isaacson, *Steve Jobs* (New York: Simon & Schuster, 2011), p. 345.
6. E. Bernstein, "The Transparency Trap," *Harvard Business Review*, October 2014.
7. e dostrategic-narrative.net/#sthash.imxNkl1c.dpuf.
8. Plato, *The Republic*. www.gutenberg.org/files/1497/1497-h/1497-h.htm.
9. M. Turner, *The Literary Mind* (New York and Oxford: Oxford University Press, 1998). pp. 14–20.
10. Sun Tzu, *The Art of War*, translated by L. Giles, (Stockholm: Chiron Academic Press, 2015).
11. L. Kellaway, *Sense and Nonsense in the Office* (London: Financial Times/Prentice Hall, 2000), p. 19.
12. M. de Montaigne, "De L'Age," in *Oeuvres Complètes*, edited by Albert Thibaudet and Maurice Rat (Paris: Gallimard, 1962), p. 311.
13. http://www.jubilacionypension.com/jubilacion/guia/cual-seria-la-edad-ideal-de-jubilacion/.
14. Ibid.
15. R. Sutton, "Stepping Down Gracefully," Harvard Business Review, June 2011.
16. Cicero, *Cato Maior De Senectute*, edited by J. G. F. Powell (Cambridge: Cambridge University Press, 1988).
17. S. de Beauvoir, *La Vieillesse* (Paris: Gallimard, 1970).
18. R. Strack, J. Baier, and A. Fahlander, "Managing Demographic Risk," *Harvard Business Review*, February 2008.

19. http://www.sinopecgroup.com/group/en/socialresponsibility/Care/
    scc.shtml.
20. R. Dworkin, "What Is a Good Life?," *The New York Review of Books*,
    February 10, 2011. http://www.nybooks.com/articles/archives/2011/
    feb/10/what-good-life/.
21. C. Christensen, "How Will You Measure Your Life?," *Harvard
    Business Review*, July–August 2010.
22. J. D. Vellerman, "Well-Being and Time," *Pacific Philosophical
    Quarterly*, Vol. 72 (1991), pp. 48–77.
23. Suetonio, *Vida de los Doce Césares*, edited by R. M. Cuevas (Madrid:
    Gredos, 1992).

13

Epilogue: Earthly Paradises and Satisfaction at Work

Who hasn't dreamt every now and then of saving up enough money and retiring to live contentedly in some earthly paradise? This was Tom Wilson's plan, the main character in Somerset Maugham's 1935 short story, *The Lotus Eater*.[1] Wilson is a hard-working bank manager in London, who at the age of 35 loses his wife and daughter, two of the worst setbacks anybody could suffer. Hoping to forget his sorrows, he travels to Italy, where he visits the island of Capri, an idyllic spot that bewitches him.

Upon returning to his routine job in London, Wilson begins planning early retirement in Capri. Now without familial responsibilities, he believes that his pension from early retirement, along with the sale of his house and his savings, will provide him with enough money to survive for the following couple of decades, given that the average life expectancy in the early years of the twentieth century for men was around 60. Wilson puts his plan into action and begins to enjoy a frugal, but peaceful, life in Capri.

Time passes by inexorably, and after two decades of the contemplative life, his income has dwindled down to nothing, at which point he decides

© The Author(s) 2016
S. Iñiguez de Onzoño, *Cosmopolitan Managers*,
DOI 10.1057/978-1-137-54909-9_13

to end his own life. He locks himself in his room, lights a charcoal fire that will fill the room with carbon monoxide and poison him, and lies down on the bed to die. But the next day, he is found unconscious, but alive. However, the fumes have left him brain damaged. Wilson lives on for a few years more, penniless, on the margins of the community, and sleeping in a shed provided by his former employees. In the final lines, the narrator, commenting on Wilson's situation, notes: "I think on the whole we all get what we deserve, [...] But that doesn't prevent its being rather horrible."

Maugham's assertion that "we all get what we deserve" is arguable, particularly bearing in mind the role that moral luck can play in our lives. In any event, we make decisions at important moments in our lives that influence the rest of our existence. *The Lotus Eater* provides a good example of what can go wrong when we prematurely retire to earthly paradises without sufficient funds to live comfortably. At the very least, if we were to take such a decision, it would be advisable to build a business, or to look for a job in the paradise of choice; and not simply to finance a life the duration of which we cannot guess, but also to keep us in shape physically and mentally.

This is not a view that Wilson shares: "Leisure, [...] If people only knew! It's the most priceless thing a man can have and they're such fools they don't even know it`s something to aim at. Work? They work for work's sake. They haven't got the brains to realize that the only object of work is to obtain leisure."

Do you share Wilson's opinion? Interesting enough, a recent Gallup survey shows that just 30% of employees in America feel engaged at work. Around the world, across 142 countries, the proportion of employees who feel engaged at work is only 13%.[2] In light of this, it seems likely that most people would leave their jobs tomorrow and head off to their respective paradises were their fortunes to improve dramatically, for example by winning the lottery or inheriting a large sum of money.

Wilson lost his family: it is clear that one of the main reasons that we continue to work is to sustain and improve the living conditions of our loved ones. That said, I would like to look at some of the internal reasons that motivate us to keep working, and that have to do with the job itself and our personal disposition, rather than external factors, such as raising a family.

We've all had rainy days at work. On such occasions, like Wilson, we might find ourselves dreaming of flying off to some paradisiacal destination where we could spend the rest of a tantalizing trouble-free life. What measures can we take to improve our disposition towards work, to enjoy it, and even be happy carrying out our profession? Below are a few suggestions:

- *In the first place, enjoying your work depends primarily on you* and nobody else. Your proactive approach and mood are decisive when it comes to changing things in the workplace. If you will allow me to paraphrase a renowned piece of advice: do not think what the others, your boss, and your colleagues, can do for you at work; rather, think what you can do to turn your company into a respected and preferred organization.

- *Put together a short, positive pitch about your job* and responsibilities, your achievements, and your professional objectives—something along the lines of the kind of presentation you might make at your child's school on parents' day. Try to make this presentation inspiring, and one that would earn you your listeners' praise. I am convinced after doing this a couple of times you will feel a stronger bond with your work.

- *Think about and plan out your company's development objectives* and how you would like your career to advance over the next five years, taking into account the training and education that might be required for this.

- *Set out the most important tasks for the coming few days.* Some people believe that during leisure time it is essential to disconnect completely from work. I don't agree. I think that work and leisure should flow naturally in your life. If you come up with good ideas during free time, write them down or record them.

- *Similarly, prepare your free time* so that you can properly enjoy your hobbies and leisure pursuits. Some people see free time as a blank space, or decompression chamber. This might be understandable in the aftermath of particularly stressful periods at work, but it is a good idea to plan for and diversify leisure activities.

One final piece of advice: explore the progress that has been made in positive psychology in recent years. If you think that you need outside help, talk to a coach about how they can help you focus on your career.

Our work should be a source of self-fulfillment and happiness. I believe, as this book shows, that management, when exercised professionally and ethically, can be one of the noblest professions.

Notes

1. W. S. Maugham, "The Lotus Eater," in *Collected Short Stories* (New York: Penguin, 1951).
2. http://www.nytimes.com/2014/06/01/opinion/sunday/why-you-hate-work.html.

Index

© The Author(s) 2016
S. Iñiguez de Onzoño, *Cosmopolitan Managers*,
DOI 10.1057/978-1-137-54909-9

Printing and Binding: Stürtz GmbH, Würzburg